# Handbook of
# MIDI
# Sequencing

## Dave Clackett

PC Publishing

PC Publishing
Export House
130 Vale Road
Kent TN9 1SP
UK

Tel 01732 770893
Fax 01732 770268
email pcp@cix.compulink.co.uk

First published 1996
© PC Publishing

ISBN 1 870775 38 4

**British Library Cataloguing in Publication Data**

A catalogue record for this book is available from the British Library

Printed in Great Britain by Bell and Bain Limited, Glasgow

# Preface

This book evolved over the course of many years, and many of the topics and aspects covered in these pages have been prompted by the questions customers ask from the 'Hands On' technical support team. MIDI is now an established part of today's music making, and I've felt for some time that a book needs writing that really covers the subject matter. *The Handbook of MIDI Sequencing* is intended to introduce and guide newcomers to all aspects of MIDI song programming, culminating in a complete song to program to test these new-found skills.

I recall attending one of the music trade shows in London where I mentioned my wish to write this book to a few friends – one of them happened to be Phil Chapman of PC Publishing. I believe his comment was 'Go on then'. Well here it is – I hope you enjoy it.

Dave Clackett, Hands On MIDI Software

*Dave Clackett started his musical career in 1971 with the Royal Marines Band Service at Deal in Kent. He later transferred to Portsmouth as principal flute on board HMY Britannia. Following a period as a full time professional musician engaged in concert tours with major artists throughout the country, he subsequently became an arranger for a specialist music company in London producing printed music for most of Europe's function bands. In 1989 he set up 'Hands On' MIDI Software, producing complete songs in standard MIDI file format. The company has since grown into one of England's most respected MIDI file producers, whose clients include Roland, Yamaha, CompuServe, Casio, Music Writer, IBM and Microsoft.*

# Dedication

To my wife Jan, whose continued support and encouragement have made this book a reality.

# Contents

* Chapters 5 and 6 written by Kevin Earley

# Acknowledgements

**Close Encounters of the Third Kind**
Composed by John Williams
© 1977, EMI Gold Horizon Music Corp USA. Reprinted by kind permission of CPP/Belwin Europe, Surrey, England.

**The Best**
Composed by Chapman and Knight.
© Zomba Music Publishing Ltd, EMI Music Publishing.
Used by kind permission.

Special thanks are due to Kevin Earley for his invaluable help in the writing of Chapters 5 and 6.

# 1 ❖

# *Hardware and software*

Visit almost any recording studio today and it's difficult not to be overwhelmed by the abundance of hi-tech and computer related equipment it uses. Mixing desks can now be fully automated by computers and the music itself is commonly digitally recorded direct onto hard disk. Once saved the music can be changed and edited in a variety of ways by sophisticated computer software until the final version is mastered onto compact disk or digital audio tape (DAT). The whole recording industry has undergone immense change in recent years. Powerful software can now transform the daydreams of yester-year into the commercial reality of today.

One of the biggest advances in technology has been the ability to bypass analogue tape during recording sessions and mix and master in a totally digital environment. Even in quite recent years the equipment required to perform these kinds of complex tasks was affordable only by the financially privileged or to corporate studios. Recent strides in hardware development and software technology have lowered the price of both to a more affordable level and therefore given the home studio and home enthusiast the opportunity to share in this hi-tech MIDI wonderland.

## MIDI

MIDI is an acronym for Musical Instrument Digital Interface. It enables computers and electronic instruments to exchange information between themselves via a five pin serial cable. This cable can carry considerable amounts of musical information relating to almost every facet of a musical performance. The pitch of each note, the weight (or velocity) with which it's played and its duration (length) can all be captured, changed and saved to disk. This example is just a small indication of what can be done using MIDI technology.

To some people the mention of a MIDI instrument will conjure up a picture of half a dozen keyboards linked by miles of electronic spaghetti and a keyboard player who's constantly waving his arms over his computer muttering strange MIDI incantations.

It's true to say there are thousands of MIDI keyboards but there are many other ways of transmitting and receiving MIDI information. There are MIDI guitars, saxophones, wind synths, drum kits and even accordions. Acoustic instrumentalists can now attach tiny microphones to their instruments which convert analogue pitch into digital MIDI information. I suppose it is conceivable to perform one of Mozart's Flute Concertos using a MIDI kazoo! As I explained earlier the term MIDI refers to a digital interface on a device of some kind, in reality the word MIDI has come to mean anything associated with hi-tech music making.

MIDI can recognise 128 different pitches of note starting from note 0 (C), chromatically through to note number 127 (G). To give you an idea of the range middle C is MIDI note number 60. These 128 notes give us a working range of just over 10 octaves. Remember a concert grand piano has a range of about eight octaves and most home keyboards have a range of just five. As Figure 1.1 shows, to play a piece of music using the full extremes of the keyboard is beyond the physical capabilities of man – and probably most orang-utans!

Figure 1.1 The full range of MIDI keyboard note numbers

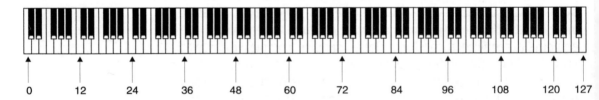

The loudness or the weight of a struck note (called velocity) has a similar range of 128 steps. A velocity level starts from 1 (very, very quiet) through to 128 (loudest).

## What is a sequencer?

A sequencer is a computer program that's used to record and manipulate MIDI data. Let's take a moment to consider what happens when we record a performance, say a piano piece. When our performer presses keys on the keyboard, felt hammers strike the piano wires and notes are produced. When we record we capture the actual timbre (tone quality) of the piano as well as the notes, their pitch, volume and duration. If those exact same series of notes were played on a MIDI keyboard and recorded into a sequencer the information would be stored very differently. A MIDI sequencer records instructions not sounds and a MIDI song is a combination of these instructions which when carried out in the right order reproduces music.

Imagine the sequencer we're using was human and we asked it to play a pre-recorded piece of music, it might say to itself, 'Hello, somebody wants me to do something, what do they want me to do – Oh I see, play a note. Right then let's see what note it is ... OK it's note 60 (middle C) and I have to play it with a velocity of 100 ... Hmm quite loud' and it is on MIDI channel 2 which is playing a bass guitar sound eh? No problem!

The note is then struck and the sequencer returns to monitoring until a new instruction needs its attention. This process is repeated time and time again until it eventually gets a message sometime later. 'Do you remember that bass guitar note number 60 with the velocity of 100 you played a while ago? Well you can turn it off now thanks'.

This simple example gives us an insight into what a sequencer does. One stunning aspect is that our sequencer can understand about 32,000 bits of information every second. When a sequenced song is played the speed of the sequencer processing each note is so fast the notes we hear seem as if they're played simultaneously. If the music were slowed right down, to about 1 beat per minute, we would hear that the music is in fact being played one event after another, in other words ... sequentially.

Another feature of a sequencer is that it allows us to edit or change the information it's just recorded. Imagine a recording session in a top flight studio. The keyboard player has just finished a phenomenal and near perfect solo over a 16 measure section, but unfortunately in the last measure a couple of sour notes crept in. In an organic studio the whole solo would have to be recorded again or (if there's enough room) the player would be 'dropped in' to correct it. Both of these methods have drawbacks. The first is that a player often cannot re-capture the exact feel and inspiration of the original solo and secondly, to be 'dropped in' requires a momentary space on the tape so that the edit is not so obvious. If this solo were played into a MIDI sequencer the offending notes could be removed or corrected. This corrected version retains the feel of the original without creating any editing glitches.

Editing features vary considerably from one sequencer to another, but the more you pay for your program the more features you'll find. Don't dismiss PD (Public Domain) sequencers as a waste of time, some offer a good basic set of features – transposing of notes (raising or lowering the pitch), increasing or decreasing speed (tempo), selecting and modifying selected notes, quantising (auto-correct) and changing the velocity of notes.

**TIP**

As we progress through the pages of this book we'll see lots of references to the upper and lower limits of some parameters and nearly all of them have a range of 128 values. This sounds quite reasonable doesn't it we start at 1 and finish at 128. Computer people – those funny men in white coats – have been arguing for years about how to count and I'm being very serious. Some boffins say we should count from 1 to 128 while others say we should count from 0 to 127 – confused? Me too! What this actually means is that whatever philosophy is adopted by a software manufacturer it will be reflected in their products. Don't be surprised if your software counts 'differently'.

## Which sequencer?

Without recommending any one manufacturer over another, consider what you require from your software. Do you need the mega power of 520 discrete MIDI channels, full digital audio hard disk recording, digital editing coupled with the ability to produce publishing quality printed sheet music – No? OK then, do you want a simple package that can only record and play MIDI data without offering any editing facilities whatsoever – No again? Probably your requirements, along with most other people, lie somewhere in the middle of these extremes. If you buy too cheap, you might end up with old and inadequate software. Too expensive and you'll be paying for cutting edge technology that you may not really need. A mid range package will probably suit you best as it won't be ridiculously expensive, should have a fair re-sale value, yet still be powerful enough to perform all the complex tasks you'll ask of it.

Check to see if your intended software has an upgrade path and make sure you register your software with the manufacturer or their representatives. When you outgrow your present version or a new version is released you'll be able to upgrade without incurring the full initial purchase cost every time.

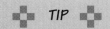

*P*ersonal budgets do enter the equation of course but if funds allow it, try and buy a machine that's about two thirds the way up its evolutionary curve. These averagely priced machines will give reasonable performance at reasonable prices. Second hand bargains are there to be had if you shop around but don't buy just on price. Remember you only ever get what you pay for so you could get stuck with a hopelessly outdated machine that's a total waste of money.

## Which computer and interface hardware do I need?

### Computer

When buying a computer it's difficult to categorically state that computer A is better than computer B. Write down a list of things you want the computer to do in order of preference ... and be realistic in making up your list, I'm sure there'll be a lot of you saying to yourselves, and to the wife that, 'I'll only use it for serious work' but apart from all that serious stuff (spreadsheets and databases etc.,) there are a lot of games out there that you may want to get around to playing sometime.

### *Mac v PC*

It's well known that some computers perform better than others depending on the task they are performing. Apple Macintosh is often regarded as el supremo when it comes to graphical applications such as desk top publishing, video editing and photographic manipulation. The PC has different strengths and these are spreadsheets and large office networks. The difference between these two major platforms has narrowed especially with the launch of the 'Powermac' range of Macintosh machines.

Figure 1.2 Which computer?

Whatever you decide to choose, try to avoid the lure of the sales patter and the curse of gear lust. Gear lust unfortunately is a common disease that strikes most men and affects their ability to rationalise the facts. Gear lust tells man that he must have the latest, fastest, most powerful bells and whistles machine that's available. This is absolutely true – not! If you need a good machine that does pretty much everything you ask of it, look through the pages of the associated computer magazines (there are enough to choose from) and check out the specification and price of the best and worst machines currently available as a production item.

### Atari ST

The Atari ST might be worth serious consideration. The ST has been around for quite a few years and has a pretty good software base. The biggest drawback with buying an ST is knowing that Atari have now stopped manufacturing them. Obtaining parts for repairs in the future might become a problem. The ST however is a powerful and cheap computer which uses the Motorola 68000 chip at its heart. Its graphical user interface (GUI) is similar to the Mac's and is built into a special ROM (read only memory). On boot up the ST is instantly ready to use, while other computers have to load their operating systems from disk. The ST is very popular in the UK and across Europe, with some excellent music software from Germany (Steinberg's *Cubase* and E-Magic's *Logic*). If you decide on the ST, ensure that the computer has at least 1 megabyte of RAM (random access memory, 1 megabyte = 1040 bytes), and that it comes with a high resolution monochrome monitor.

### Atari Falcon

The Atari Falcon, now being made by C Lab under licence, is considerably more powerful – and more expensive – than the normal ST. The Falcon is based around the faster Motorola 68030 processor and includes a custom DSP (digital signal processing) chip which enables the user to explore the wonders of direct to hard disk recording.

### Others

There are other makes of computer that we can choose from that can be used to create music, Commodore Amiga, Acorn Archimedes, Sinclair Spectrum (oops, how did that creep in?) but the choice of music software for these machines can be quite limited. Unless there is a real need to use these machines it may be wise to pass them by.

## Screen

Not to be overlooked, the choice of screen for your machine is of utmost importance. When using the computer you'll be staring into this screen for many hours. Don't underestimate the damage a bad monitor can inflict upon your eyes (you ought to see mine!). If you decide that you're going to use an Atari ST as your music computer make sure you get a monochrome monitor as part of the package (SM124 = 12 inch, SM144 = 14 inch). Not only does some software refuse to run in anything other than hi-resolution, using a medium resolution monitor or worst still a television set, will cause considerable eye strain.

Macintosh screens are excellent as a general rule but some users who are considering an old SE30 or similar may find the 8inch screen a little on the small side. New Macs do have the ability to support a second monitor so you may want to start your system with a small colour monitor and then, at a later date add a larger screen.

PC users should use a monitor with at least S-VGA resolution. Some monitors use a dot pitch code to determine the resolution of the monitor. Try and get a monitor with a dot pitch resolution of 0.28 or less. The lower the number the clearer and better the screen will be.

## Mouse – point, click, double click and drag

A mouse is a device used for selecting and changing values and has either one, two or three buttons. Mac users have one, Atari ST users have two and PC users have three (although the middle button is seldom used). Moving the mouse on a flat and firm surface moves the pointer around the screen. Pressing the left button

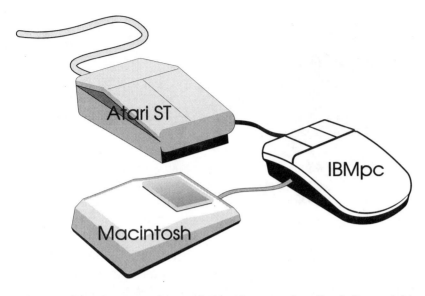

Fig 1.3 Three breeds of rodent

selects a function or value and then by pressing the left or right button we can increase or decrease it. Left is normally down and right is up although this can be reversed.

If you select an object that has an OK or confirm option, double clicking on the mouse will select and confirm in one operation. A double click is performed when the button is clicked twice in rapid succession.

Dragging items around the screen is an excellent way of editing. If you want to move something, first place the mouse pointer over the item, click and hold down the button. Once 'held' you can move the object(s) around the screen. To indicate that you'll be moving something the pointer may change into a little hand (or a similar type of icon) which holds the item. Releasing the button drops it into place.

## Disk housekeeping

SAVE, SAVE, SAVE!!! So much valuable work has been permanently lost due to system crashes. It's a fact that computers crash for what seems no apparent reason and any data held in the computer's memory when that happens will be lost forever. Get into the habit of performing a save after every major edit.

Keep duplicate copies of song data (or any other type of data for that matter) just in case you have the misfortune of experiencing disk corruption problems.

Back-up the master program disk and run your system on these back-ups. Virtually every software licence allows the user to make one back-up copy of the original disk for archiving purposes.

Fig 1.4 Back up or die!

Does your sequencer have an auto-backup function? If so, use it! The time between each of the saves can be quite important, a lot of editing can be done in 10-15 minutes, so set the auto-backup to realistic amounts.

Pay that little bit extra for good quality disks and it'll be worth it in the long term. Although it's getting better now, the quality of the media inside very cheap disks used to be very poor.

After you've made all your necessary copies and wish to keep your backed up data safe, keep your disks free from dusty environments, strong magnetic fields, flexing, bending and large thermo nuclear explosions.

## Viruses

Figure 1.5 Keep your computer virus-free!

A virus is a small, often undetectable, sometimes malicious computer program whose only reason for existence is to proliferate and clone itself onto as many computers and disks as possible. Some viruses are quite harmless although it may be annoying to see messages of some kind, even humorous ones, randomly displayed on the screen. More virulent strains are designed to destroy and corrupt as much data as they can – some even have the ability to format a hard disk! Unfortunately for the un-protected system it's impossible to tell which virus is which until it's too late and it's in the computer.

Viruses are spread by contact. This type of contact takes place when a suspect floppy disk is inserted into drive A or when an infected program is unwittingly downloaded from the Internet or other bulletin board systems. Once the virus is in your machine it will attempt to copy itself onto every floppy disk it sees. We all know that prevention is better than cure, so here's a simple 4 step guide to keeping your computer virus free.

1  Avoid swapping disks, especially if you're unsure of their origin.
2  Write protect your disks. This will prevent a virus from writing itself onto the disk. A disk is write protected when the slider (in the lower left hand corner of the disk) is pulled back, allowing you to see through the hole.
3  Get a good virus detector (killer) program. This program lives in your computer all the time. As soon as a foreign disk is read by the floppy drive it will immediately scan the disk for all known viruses and report accordingly. Most anti-virus programs can destroy a virus if one is found.
4  Make sure you keep updating your virus killer program. New viruses are being written every day!

Figure 1.6 The big bite! And it hurts.

## MIDI interface

If you're considering buying an Atari ST remember this computer includes a 16 MIDI channel interface as standard. Macintosh and PC computers – and Amiga and Archimedes for that matter – don't. An interface is a device that connects a computer to the outside world. Interfaces for Macintosh can access both the printer and the modem ports simultaneously which enables 32 MIDI channel record/playback capability.

PC users can connect their MIDI interface to either the serial (modem) or parallel (printer) ports or by installing an interface card inside the machine. In an attempt to reduce the added cost of having to purchase a MIDI interface for each computer some manufacturers are now producing modules which have a PC/Mac interface built into them as standard (Yamaha MU50/80, Roland SC7)

## Soundcards

PC owners who wish to play games on their machine might want to consider using a soundcard which combines music synthesis with a MIDI interface. The established 'industry standard' soundcard favoured by games manufacturers is the (Creative Labs) Sound Blaster. Choosing a decent soundcard is a nightmare because every manufacturer says that their card is the best, the cheapest ... etc. A soundcard, by its nature has to perform very different tasks depending what you intend to use it for. The card can be filled with sampled sounds which can be used for creating speech and sound effects in games software. The quality of samples, and the amount of samples that you can load depends upon the memory of the card.

There are normally four memory configurations in a soundcard, 256K, 520K, 1Meg, and 2Meg. The more memory the card can access the more expensive it will be, but having that extra memory can mean there will be a significant increase in sample quality. The second thing it has to do is emulate a MIDI sound module. Most soundcards can support only GM, although there are daughter boards available from Roland and Yamaha which can transform a Sound Blaster card into a GS or XG device.

It often seems that soundcard manufacturers just concentrate on producing good sample (WAV) playback features (possibly because of the percentage of multimedia/game users to music enthusiasts) and accept indifferent music synthesis. For a good all-round sound-card, with good compatibility to most games I would not hesitate to recommend the Sound Blaster AWE32.

## Which sound source shall I get?

Before General MIDI was ratified, each instrument manufacturer had complete control over how their equipment responded to incoming MIDI data. The reality was that if MIDI data, recorded for one particular instrument/manufacturer were played back on some-thing else, the results were often quite awful. Every device had its own patch/tone map, which listed all the available instruments and allocated program change numbers for each. Sending program commands to incompatible devices resulted in the wrong instru-ments being selected (trumpets became flutes etc.). Even if the tone maps did correspond, there was no guarantee that they would play in the same octave. The worst offenders by far were the drum and percussion mapping. A note which produced a snare drum sound on one module might produce a triangle on another.

Figure 1.7 General MIDI logo

The General MIDI protocol dictates that if a manufacturer places the GM logo on a piece of equipment, that device is guaranteed to behave in a certain way and have certain standardised features.

1 One GM feature is the amount of notes available for us to use. The Polyphony of GM equipment is a minimum of 28 voices. Although 28 voices doesn't seem a great deal, excellent results can be obtained if we program carefully.
2 GM allows us access to 128 different instruments although we can only play a maximum of 16 at any one time. All instruments are grouped together into their musical types: pianos, organs, brass etc. Each instrument is allocated a unique (program change) number which, if transmitted from a sequencer to the synthesiser, will select the correct instrument e.g. program change 33 = acoustic/wood bass, program change 57 = trumpet.
3 Drum and percussion instruments total 46. These instruments include snare drums, kick drums, cymbals and a wide variety of

percussion instruments (congas, bongos, cabasa etc.). GM drums use only MIDI channel 10 for playback. Each drum and percussion instrument is assigned its own note number – kick drum 1 = note 36 (C1).

4 GM (and indeed all MIDI) is based around the 16 channels used to transmit and receive data. Each channel will play one instrument.

To understand this principle more clearly, think of a television set and the number of channels it can receive. The picture (sound in our case) starts life being produced by a TV studio (sequencer). It's then transmitted across the air-waves and down the antennae cable (MIDI lead). Once inside the television set (synthesiser) the data is decoded and the channel we want to watch is displayed on screen (played).

Each channel might be showing something different, a game show on one, a drama on another and possibly the big film on the third. MIDI channels work in a similar way but in our case our channels might contain, drums, bass guitar and piano.

The GM specification dictates that the minimum polyphony should be 28 voices (16 for instruments and eight for percussion). Be aware that 'voices' do not mean 'notes'. Unfortunately the exact definition of 'voices' was never agreed upon when GM was first ratified. Some sounds, normally the big lush ones, use a combination of two voices (oscillators) to produce a single note. If these big sounds are used all the time it's well worth remembering our polyphony will be cut in half.

## How general is General?

General MIDI was initially regarded as the commercial answer to everyone's prayers. MIDI song file producers would be able to mass market product because their songs would sound exactly the same on any piece of equipment no matter who made it as long as it bears the GM logo, right? – Wrong! When GM was introduced there was no agreement made by the instrument manufacturers on a way to calculate the volume of an instrument. Although the actual GM sounds would correspond correctly some instruments would be played too quietly while others would be played too loudly.

Figure 1.8 Roland (GS) General Standard logo

Soon after the launch of GM, Roland introduced its GS range of modules (SC55, DS330, SD35). The letters 'GS' don't actually stand for anything 'officially' but in the early days most MIDI programmers referred to GS as 'General Standard' or 'Gold Standard'. In 1995 Yamaha introduced its range of 'XG' devices (MU50,

Figure 1.9 Yamaha (XG) Extended General MIDI logo

MU80). Both GS and XG can be thought of as a superset to General MIDI. The most obvious area for improvement was the ability to use different types of drum kits (GM only uses one). Apart from the standard kit, GS has a further eight kits to chose from room, power, electronic, TR808, jazz, brush, orchestra and sound effects. XG has two more than its GS rival, a standard Kit 2, and a second sound effect part.

To overcome the limitation of 128 GM sounds both Roland and Yamaha have adopted a similar approach to expanding the range. For every one of the 128 (principal) sounds there could be a theoretical 128 variations of it which if fully implemented, would give us 16,384 sounds to play with!

## Instrument options

### Keyboards

Do you need a basic keyboard or one that has auto accompaniment facilities and an on-board sequencer/disk drive? If you intend to play at home for your own entertainment you may feel the auto accompaniment feature is important but you don't need the added bonus (and cost) of having an on-board sequencer and disk drive. Many manufacturers offer keyboards with and without these features. If you're a 'working' musician you may not want to take all your computer equipment around with you to venues (see Chapter 13) and therefore an in-built sequencer/disk drive would be an distinct advantage.

### Modules

Modules are often rack mountable so transporting them is a lot easier and safer than keyboards. A sound module is a device that contains sounds but has no keyboard.

Driving a module will require an external device such as a sequencer or MIDI instrument. If you already own a MIDI instrument, even one that's mono-timbral (single-voice) like the Yamaha DX7 or possess a master keyboard (one that contains no sounds at all) consider using modules.

## Getting well connected

MIDI cables are designed to send and receive information in one direction only, so two cables are required in a normal set-up. From the computer interface there will be two sockets, MIDI IN and MIDI OUT. Figure 1.10 shows a basic set-up of computer and keyboard.

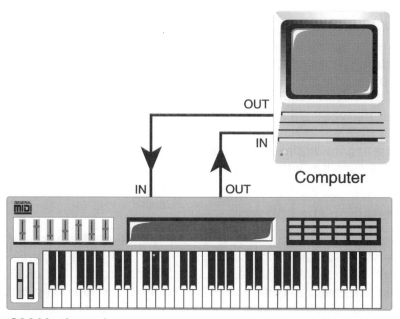

Figure 1.10 The keyboard
sends its information OUT
down the cable and INto the
computer and the computer
sends OUT its information
INto the keyboard.

**GM Keyboard**

Figure 1.11 is a combination of master keyboard, module and
computer. The keyboard still sends its data to the computer as normal, if it didn't we couldn't record could we? The computer does
its thing and sends its information back to the keyboard as normal.
Can you see the third cable running from a socket called MIDI
THRU on the keyboard to the IN of the module? This transmits the
incoming signal THRU to other devices.

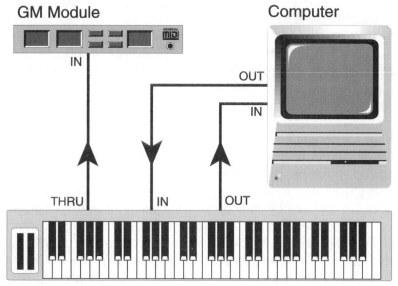

Figure 1.11 The function of a
MIDI THRU socket is to re-
transmit the Incoming signal
THRU to other devices

**Master Keyboard**

### Cables

Although a MIDI cable looks like an ordinary 5 pin DIN connector, the type used to connect up a hi-fi, the wiring inside them is quite different. Use authentic MIDI cables as much as you can especially if you're working in a critical (studio) environment.

When you're connecting up your system leave enough slack so that the cables are not straining, and tuck any loose wires away so you can't trip over them. Avoid using really long MIDI cables as it increases the likelihood of producing data errors. Lengths of up to and around the 3 metre mark should work OK.

## Installing the software

We've got our computer, we've got our GM, GS or XG sound module and we've got our sequencing software. Most of the larger professional sequencing packages (Cubase, Logic, Cakewalk, Performer etc.,) require them to be 'installed' onto the computer's hard disk before they can be used properly. There may be two or three master disks in the complete package and it's normally Disk 1 that contains the installation program. When the install program is run it analyses the computer, hard drive and peripherals and then automatically configures the computer's system to accept the software and copies it onto the hard drive.

From experience the most potentially troublesome install procedures are to be found on the PC. I understand with Windows `95 it's called Plug and Pray! The installation process often changes the AUTOEXEC.BAT and CONFIG.SYS files, which are an integral part of the computer's initialisation (boot-up) process. If these files are drastically altered the computer could fail to perform correctly and thus interfere with any peripherals (CD ROM, tape back-up, soundcard etc.) that may already be hung off the system. If such a problem does occur, suppress that irresistible urge to give the computer a good kicking, and then systematically check each IRQ and Interrupt setting in turn.

### What's a dongle?

The pirating of commercial software is a very big problem so some companies combat it by encrypting protection routines into their programs. These routines can be activated under 100% software control or as a combination of software and hardware. One protection method uses a 'dongle' hardware system. This dongle is inserted into the printer port and, as it is transparent to all other devices, it shouldn't interfere with any other programs. However if an attempt is made to run the sequencer software without it being present, an alert message will appear telling you the dongle is not present and then the software will crash. There's no maintenance required for dongles but I prefer to remove mine every couple of months or so and, using a cotton bud, remove any build up on the contacts. NEVER – NEVER – NEVER remove a dongle from the computer when it's switched on!

## Key disk protection

Another common protection technique involves using a key disk. The original program can be copied onto a hard drive or backed upon onto floppies, but when the program is run it will ask for the original (master) disk to be inserted into the floppy drive. Key disks use a non standard formatting routine which cannot be read and/or copied by the computer's normal operating system. When the program runs it first reads the key disk in a very special way, if it gets the right information back it will work, if it doesn't it'll crash.

Finally there is another, although not so common way of protecting software. This type of protection removes the need for any additional hardware (dongles) and spares the poor old floppy drive from turning itself inside out trying to read these quirky formats. During the initial installation process the install program will write special files into certain places on the hard disk drive in such a way that they are invisible to the user. This is a fairly good system but if you decide to defragment your hard drive at any time remember to un-install your software first.

When the software is installed and working correctly, you're ready to explore the realm of the musical 'Techie'. (Definition of Techie – Person with good working knowledge of hi-tech music and computer related equipment, often combined with a pompous and supercilious attitude to those that don't.) Most professions have their own jargon and there is no difference in the MIDI industry. We'll cover most of the words and phrases as we go through each chapter but if you get a bit confused at any time check the glossary at the end of the book.

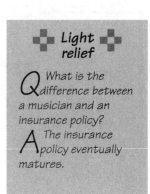

**Light relief**

*Q What is the difference between a musician and an insurance policy?*

*A The insurance policy eventually matures.*

# 2

# *Sequencer basics*

Figure 2.1 shows the main screen of a hypothetical MIDI sequencer. (A) is the transport section. The middle cluster of buttons clearly mimics the functions of a tape recorder which we can use to move us around the song, rewind, pause, play, etc. (B) displays a typical arrange page window.

(C) refers to track information. Let's examine track 4 (the highlighted track). This is called acoustic piano which is using the instrument called by selecting program change number 1 (piano 1).

Figure 2.1 Main screen of a typical sequencer

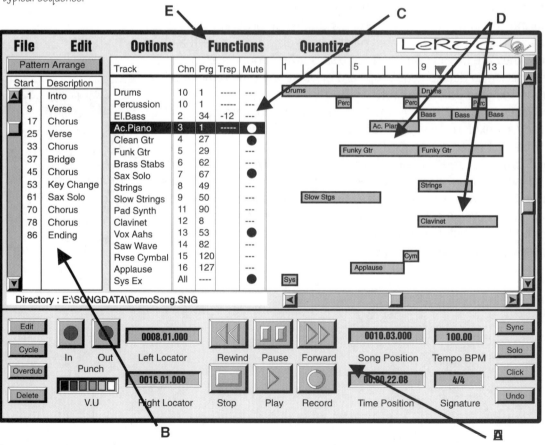

It is using MIDI channel 3 for recording and playback but because we intend to play this part, the track is currently muted.

(D) Is a graphical representation of where MIDI data has been recorded, and we can see from the part chunks that our Piano has recorded something between measures 6 to 9.

Finally (E) will be the drop down menus that contain further editing pages and facilities (Figure 2.2).

**INFORMATION**

*Some sequencers build music in tiny sections, verse, chorus, bridge etc. and when all these musical blocks are complete they can be arranged into combinations of our choice which we can build into a finished song.*

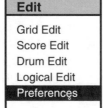

| File | Edit | Options |
|------|------|---------|
| New | Grid Edit | Multi-Record |
| **Load Song** | Score Edit | MIDI Filter |
| Save Song | Drum Edit | Synchronization |
| Load MIDI File | Logical Edit | **MIDI Setup** |
| Save MIDI File | **Preferences** | Define Click |
| Load Part | | Count-In |
| Save Part | | Fit to Frame |
| Quit | | |

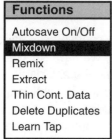

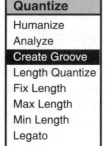

| Functions | Quantize |
|-----------|----------|
| Autosave On/Off | Humanize |
| **Mixdown** | Analyze |
| Remix | **Create Groove** |
| Extract | Length Quantize |
| Thin Cont. Data | Fix Length |
| Delete Duplicates | Max Length |
| Learn Tap | Min Length |
| | Legato |

Figure 2.2 The options one would expect to find inside each of the drop–down menus

## Measure/beat/ticks – TPQN

We often need to know the exact position of the events we've selected or played. There is a widely recognised way of describing this position using a combination of three units of measurement: measures, beats and ticks (sometimes called pulses).

1 Measure (bar). This tells us within which measure our event takes place.
2 Beat (no surprises here) refers to the beat in which our event takes place.
3 Ticks. Each beat can be thinly sliced into hundreds of tiny sub-divisions. The phrase 'ticks per quarter note' or TPQN refers to these sub-divisions. Computer based sequencers often have a TPQN resolution in the hundreds. We'll use a TPQN setting of 384 in all our examples.

Why such an awkward number like 384? The answer lies in the way it can be subdivided.

Look at the table below.

| 384 one quarter note | | |
|---|---|---|
| 192 eighth note | 128 eighth note triplet | 288 dotted eighth note |
| 96 sixteenth note | 64 sixteenth note triplet | 144 dotted sixteenth note |
| 48 thirty-second note | 32 thirty-second triplet | 72 dotted thirty-second note |
| 24 sixty-fourth note | 16 sixty-fourth triplet | 36 dotted sixty-fourth note |

If we had a note that was at position 006.02.192 it would refer to an event in measure 6 which is 192 ticks further on from beat 2. In fact 192 is exactly half way between beats 2 and 3. It should now become clear that, the more TPQNs a sequencer has, the more precise (and real) the music will sound. Other time bases exist (24, 30, 48, 60, 96, 120, 192, 240, 384, 480), although anything lower than 96 TPQN should be avoided.

## Buttons

The lower part of the sequencer screen contains several buttons. The delete button will delete any event(s) we have selected. Just in case we didn't really mean to delete or modify any data. The undo button will revert all selected data to its original condition, but only if pressed immediately after making an edit. If we undo an 'undo' command (redo) we're instructing the computer to revert back to our original data.

**Delete**

**Undo**

When recording, the overdub box offers two options: 'overdub' and 'replace'. When overdub is selected, any data recorded would be overdubbed (merged) with the existing data on the track. If this option were set to 'replace', any existing data would be lost as the new material would record over the top of all previous recordings.

**Overdub**

The sync button tells the sequencer to source its system (computer) timing from either (a) internal or from (b) MIDI/external. Normally this is set to internal so when we press the play icon the sequencer will use its in-built system clock and start to play. External synchronisation is used when we require another piece of equipment to drive the sequencer. This is a common recording technique and is covered further in Chapter 13.

**Sync**

Imagine we are composing a drum track. With cycle (loop) mode active the track loops between two points – normally set in the left and right locator positions. The first time through a kick drum might be recorded, the next time it might be the snare. This process is repeated over until the whole drum part is created.

**Cycle**

Selecting the edit button will cause an edit page to appear. These pages are used to manipulate the data depending on the type of editor requested. Common edit pages include drum, score, list /grid and piano roll.

> Edit

When editing it may be desirable from time to time for us to listen to just one track on its own. One way to do this would be to click on the mute option for every other track individually, but this is a cumbersome procedure. A better way is to select the desired track and click the 'solo' icon. This will automatically mute all other channels. After editing, selecting the solo button a second time will return all tracks back to their normal (active) mode.

> Solo

The click or metronome count can be switched on or off using this button. The parameters for the click can be altered by selecting the 'define click' option under the options menu. If we wanted to change the click setting in any way it's best to choose a percussive sound – i.e. stick across (rim shot) on MIDI Channel 10. Set the first click of each measure to have a higher velocity than the others, about 110 for the first beat and 70 for all the others.

> Click

### Tempo / time signatures

The speed and the time signature of a sequencer are often controlled by a dedicated tempo track. Different tempos and time signatures are entered at specific points. Tempos can range from 005 up to 500.00 beats per minute (BPM), but commonly accepted ones fall between 30 and 250 BPM.

> **100.00**
> Tempo
>
> **4/4**
> Time signature

### Time position

Indicates the position of the sequencer using hours, minutes, seconds and frames. This is used when synchronising to tape or video. During normal use this marker and the time position pointer (see below) will update in real time.

> **00.00.22.08**
> Time position

### Song position

Indication of the present position within a song in measures, beats and ticks.

### Locators

Normally two (left and right) locator positions are used for recording and editing purposes. In our sequencer main screen we can see the left locator is at measure 0008.01.000 and the right is set to 0016.01.000. If we select record mode we will be punched in and punched out at these points.

> **0010.03.000**
> Song position

**0008.01.000**

Left locator

**0016.01.000**

Right locator

| Pattern Arrange | |
|---|---|
| Start | Description |
| 1 | Intro |
| 9 | Verse |
| 17 | Chorus |
| 25 | Verse |
| 33 | Chorus |
| 37 | Bridge |
| 45 | Chorus |
| 53 | Key Change |
| 61 | Sax Solo |
| 70 | Chorus |
| 78 | Chorus |
| 86 | Ending |

Figure 2.3 Patterns can be named, copied and swapped to save extensive editing

Quite often the locators are used to set a range or working area for editing. Suppose we had a part that stretched from measure 1 to measure 32. If a range was set using these locators, when we increased the velocity of notes, only those within the capture points would be affected. Lastly if we needed to leap around the song editing different sections, locators offer a method of jumping to specific measures without having to wait for the fast forward button to scroll through mountains of irrelevant data.

## Pattern arrange

Unless the whole song is recorded in one take (highly unlikely and not recommended), a song will comprise many separate chunks of musical data. These chunks can be grouped together into patterns and labelled (verse, chorus, bridge, etc.) (Figure 2.3). This facility enables us to swap patterns around, e.g. the sax solo with the bridge, without having to resort to complex and time consuming editing.

## Templates

When a sequencer program first loads, it often includes a template (default) song which contains user preferences (Figure 2.4). Apart from MIDI port assignments and track set-up codes, the template song can contain information about auto-save parameters, quantise defaults, drum mapping and tempo settings.

As our example shows it's sometimes a good idea to have a structure track. This track doesn't contain any MIDI events but can be used for easy referencing for the song (er ... where did that middle 8 start?). Each part is named according to the song structure (this is one of the first things I actually do, before I start working) and it's handy for those programmers who prefer to work straight from audio tape not printed music.

Part templates contain embedded parameters that affect the way the instrument responds, including panning, volume and reverb values. For a comprehensive explanation of the contents of an average part template, refer to Chapter 12.

To perform any type of useful work, tools make the job a lot easier – try removing the spark plugs from your car without tools and you'll see what I mean. We'll be designing and making our own set of tools, explained in later chapters, that'll help us in our quest to program good song files. These tools can be saved as part of our template song and re-used over and over again when needed.

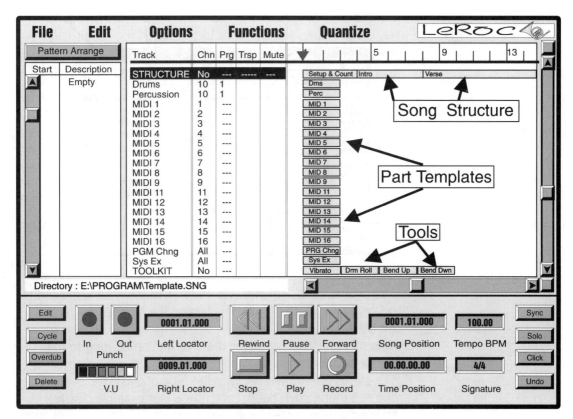

Figure 2.4 Typical default song

## Edit pages

Once we've recorded some music we'll probably want to change it a little using the edit pages. The layout and content of these pages vary from one sequencer to another. In Figure 2.5 we can see a grid system is used, while Figure 2.6 adopts more of a pianola type of display.

A The figures in this column refer to the exact position of the entered event in measures (bars), beats and ticks (TPQN)

B The figures in this column refer to the length of the note.

Figure 2.5 Grid/list edit page

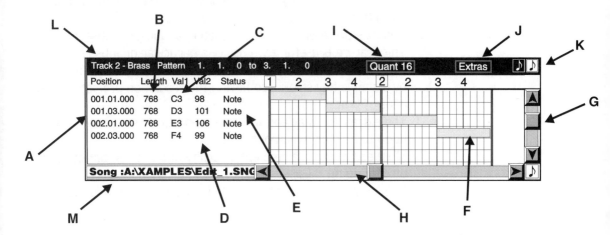

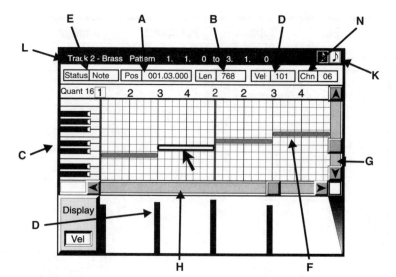

Figure 2.6 Piano roll editor

C   The figures in this column (Val 1) refer to the note name and the octave in which it's played. The higher the number the higher the pitch.

D   This column (Val 2) contains the information relating to the velocity (loudness) of the notes.

E   The status column will tell us what type of event has been entered (note, pitch bend, controller). Our example clearly shows that four notes have been entered.

F   These rectangles are the graphical representations of notes. The length of the rectangle, which stretches from left to right, indicates its length (in context) against the other notes. Using this method programmers can instantly see where notes begin and end.

G   If there is a substantial amount of data it will probably disappear down off the bottom of the screen. Using the vertical scroll bar we can scroll though our data until the events we wish to view re-appear in the edit window.

H   Used in a similar way to the vertical scroll bar, the horizontal scroll bar can position the data by measures.

I   Quantise preferences can be stored in a 'quick quantise' box. This feature is useful if we use one particular quantise setting most of the time. Some quantise commands can be performed by a simple key stroke, so having the resolution pre-set can save a lot of time.

J   The extras box may contain little 'goodies' or macros we can call upon to help us tweak our data.

K   Most editors have a step entry facility and this can be activated by clicking on these symbols.

L   Tells us which number track is being examined, in this case it's

track 2. The name of the track is clearly visible (brass) and the
length of the part.

M This is the file name we are going to give this particular song.
Notice the full file path.

N (Piano edit) – MIDI channel playback indicator.

## Velocity

The volume or weight of a note is referred to as its velocity. There
are 128 different levels of velocity available ranging from the lowest (1) to the highest (128). A velocity of 10 for example would
produce a very quiet note and a velocity of 116 would produce a
very loud one. The way a velocity sensitive keyboard deciphers how
hard a note is struck is really quite simple. There are sensors under
each key which measure the amount of time it takes to travel from
top to bottom. The harder a key is struck the faster the key will
move, which is interpreted as having a high velocity level. With
more gentle playing the keys take just that little bit longer to be
depressed and therefore the notes sounded are often quieter and
have a corresponding (lower) velocity level. Now we've covered
velocity we must never refer to the weight of a note as its volume
ever again, volume is a different thing altogether.

## Step time or step input

Step-time, sometimes called step-input, is a method of entering
notes into the sequencer without having to play them. Figure 2.7
shows a typical step input grid.

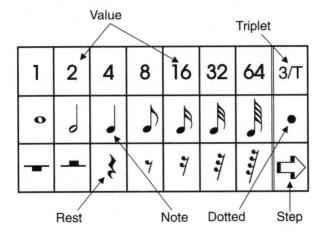

Figure 2.7 The various values for notes and rests (and their numerical equivalents) are shown along the top row. To the right is an options column which allows us to change any note or rest into a triplet or add a dot to its length. Clicking of the arrow (step) would advance us to the next position.

Look at the examples in Figures 2.8 (a) and (b): These two measures should be easily recognised as the opening theme from *Close Encounters of the Third Kind* © 1977 EMI Gold Horizon Music Corp USA. Reprinted by kind permission of CPP/Belwin Europe, Surrey, England.

*Figure 2.8 (a) Opening theme to Close Encounters of the Third Kind.*

*Figure 2.8 (b) List edit version of (a)*

| Track 1 - Synth   Pattern | 1. | 1. | 0 to | 3. | 1. | 0 | Quant 8 | | Extras | | |
|---|---|---|---|---|---|---|---|---|---|---|---|
| Position | Length | Val1 | Val2 | Status | 1 | 2 | 3 | 4 | 2 | 2 | 3 | 4 |
| 001.01.000 | 384 | D4 | 64 | Note | | | | | | | | |
| 001.02.000 | 384 | E4 | 64 | Note | | | | | | | | |
| 001.03.000 | 384 | C4 | 64 | Note | | | | | | | | |
| 001.04.000 | 384 | C3 | 64 | Note | | | | | | | | |
| 002.01.000 | 1536 | G3 | 64 | Note | | | | | | | | |

Song : Step_Ex.SNG

If we wanted to enter these two measures using a step input method, it would go something like this:

**001.01.000**

*Start position*

1 Move to the Start position – let's say 001.01.000
2 Select the length of the first note by clicking on the quarter note symbol from the palette
3 Insert the first note at the correct pitch (D4) onto the grid/stave.
4 Move onto the next position by selecting the step arrow. (The amount the sequencer will advance is determined by the note value selected).
5 Repeat steps 2, 3 and 4 for each of the next three quarter notes. E4, C4 and C3.
6 Select a whole note symbol and insert this as a 'G3' at position 002.01.000

Step input is a very reliable method of getting raw data into the sequencer but it can be a very slow and tedious process to generate anything more than just a few measures (however using keyboard shortcuts, see next section, will speed up the process considerably).

Be aware that all the notes entered will probably have the same velocity (usually 64) and be of a perfect length. Both velocity and length will need a further tweak later on to make them sound more realistic. See Chapter 11.

**Keyboard shortcuts**

We discussed earlier how to use the mouse to point, select and modify data. The mouse is a very versatile implement, but dragging it constantly around the screen to perform the smallest of edits and simple functions can become rather tedious.

Most sequencers duplicate mouse commands with various keystrokes. Minor edits require only a single key (Q for Quantise – Enter for Play – M for Mute ... get the picture?) but major edits often require a command key. Generally Mac programs favour the Apple key, PC the Alt key and Atari the Control key, but as every sequencer is different, check to confirm this (and don't be surprised if it's not!).

Using a combination of mouse and keyboard shortcuts will improve the time it takes to perform editing functions and therefore improve our performance significantly. Endeavour to learn keyboard shortcuts, the effort will be repaid tenfold!

If you often use a series of functions (i.e. open drum edit, fix drum lengths to 16 ticks and then close drum edit) there may be a way of combining them into one single command. These combinations are called macros and once defined they can be saved as part of the template song.

## Song formats

When we've finished a session with our sequencer save all the work in its proprietary format, whether it's a SONG, ARRANGEMENT, WORK or whatever (the same can be said for all our frequent backups). The reason for saving songs in a proprietary format is because a sequencer will often remember certain user settings, (I.e., muting assignments, transpositions and velocity alterations) and save them along with the normal data as an integral part of the song. As all manufacturers use a different file structure problems will occur if we attempt to load our sequencer specific song into a different package. For instance, If the song, MY_SONG.ALL was originally saved from Steinberg's Cubase and then we attempted to load it into Passport's Mastertracks Pro, the destination software would reject it.

## Disk formats

Errors compound further if our song needs to be transferred between different makes of computer. If a disk, formatted on a Commodore Amiga for instance was put into an Apple Macintosh

## INFORMATION

*Just to make things difficult, although an Atari ST can read a PC disk, a PC cannot read an Atari disk (unless it's a newer Atari which can format disks with DOS compatibility).*

disk drive, the Mac would ignore all the Amiga information and a dialogue box would appear saying that the disk is not recognised and would we like to continue with a normal Macintosh disk format – NO!!!

The differences between a computer's operating system vary considerably but a disk formatted as 720k DOS (PC) is now generally accepted as being compatible with most computer systems. Apart from being readable by a PC (naturally), the same disk can be read without any trouble on the Atari ST/TT and Falcon, as well as most other dedicated hardware MIDI file players and keyboards.

If a Mac is running System 7 or later, DOS disks can be read using Apple File Exchange. Software from third party software companies also performs a similar function (Access PC – DOS Mounter, etc.).

Owners of the Commodore Amiga can use software such as Dos-2-Dos or Cross Dos to read MS-DOS disks.

## Standard MIDI files (SMFs)

To overcome the inherent incompatibility between different sequencer packages a common file structure was introduced. The Standard MIDI file has three different versions: types 0, 1 and 2. Starting with the latter, type 2 MIDI files are saved in a pattern based format but this particular format never really caught on and is not fully supported.

### Type 1 MIDI files

Type 1 MIDI files use multiple tracks. Each type 1 SMF can have hundreds of tracks but this could be considered as being slightly excessive and totally impracticable. Having so many tracks does have some advantages though, if you want to keep every drum and percussion instrument on its own separate track for instance. This method of working would account for a few dozen tracks all by

Figure 2.9 Type 1 MIDI file has data on different tracks

itself. Most average sequencers have adopted a file/track limit of 64, which is enough for most users.

If we examine commercial type 1 SMFs we can see that each track contains the data for just one MIDI channel and that the complete file totals no more than 16 different channels.

## Type 0 MIDI files

A type 0 SMF has all the data (including tempo and time signature information) mixed down onto a single track. This type of MIDI file is smaller and more efficient than a type 1 file, and is preferred by most hardware MIDI file players and keyboard sequencers. If the tracks from our type 1 MIDI file (above) were saved as a type 0 SMF, they would look something like Figure 2.10.

Figure 2.10 Type 0 MIDI file has all the data on one track

Having all the data on a single track may be more efficient to process by the sequencer, but as everything is merged into one data track it's a real pain if we need to do any editing. To help with this editing process, most keyboard sequencers, when they load a type 0, extract the data for MIDI channel 1 and put it on track 1, data for MIDI channel 2 is put on track 2 and so on.

There are some hardware players, Roland Sound Brush (SB55), Roland SD35 (combined sound source and file player) and Viscount RD70, which can read special type 1 SMFs. These 'special' MIDI files are just ordinary type 1's limited to 16 data tracks and one tempo track. Computer sequencers can use a re-mix command which explodes the data onto separate tracks (like a hardware sequencer does) and names the tracks by MIDI channel: i.e. MIDI1, MIDI2, MIDI3, MIDI4, etc.

To ensure maximum compatibility use type 0 SMFs saved onto 720K DOS formatted disks.

**Light relief**

*Q What do you call a musician without a girlfriend?*

*A Homeless*

# 3

# *Reading music*

This book isn't designed to re-invent the wheel (as in teaching people to read music), but a quick refresher on reading music may be of help. Chapter 16 contains a MIDI score, and while we have tried to avoid favouring traditional music notation over other visual methods, it would've been impracticable to display it any other way. If at any time you intend programming from printed sheet music you'll have to understand the rudiments of music to stand any chance, so for all non readers – come on, it's time to roll up those shirt sleeves and read on.

Traditional music is written on a grid of five lines and four spaces which is called a stave or staff. Each line and each space of a stave represents a different note and there are two different types of staves commonly used in commercial printed sheet music.

The top (treble) stave is used by the right hand (Figure 3.1). The lower stave is the bass stave and is mainly used for the left hand (Figure 3.2). The type of stave is identified by a clef symbol which is placed at the start of each.

Figure 3.1 The treble stave is used by the right hand

Figure 3.2 The bass stave is mainly used for the left hand

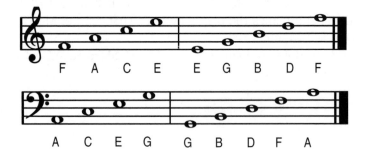

As an 'aide de memoir' try the following:

Treble Clef - Space   'FACE' for space
Treble Clef - Lines   Every Good Boy Deserves Fruit
Bass Clef - Spaces   All Cows Eat Grass
Bass Clef - Lines   G***, B***, D***, F***, A***
(I'm not doing all the work – you think of this one – and nothing rude!)

## Measures (or bars)

The stave is divided into manageable sections called measures (bars) using a system of vertical lines. The size of a measure is determined by a time signature, sometimes called a time meter, which is placed at the beginning of the first stave (after the clef). The top number denotes how many beats there are to each measure and the lower figure tells us what value those beats should be.

A time signature of 4/4 means four beats in the measure, and they're all quarter notes

## Note relationships

Lengths of notes are based around a subdivision of one larger note, the whole note. Examine the charts below.

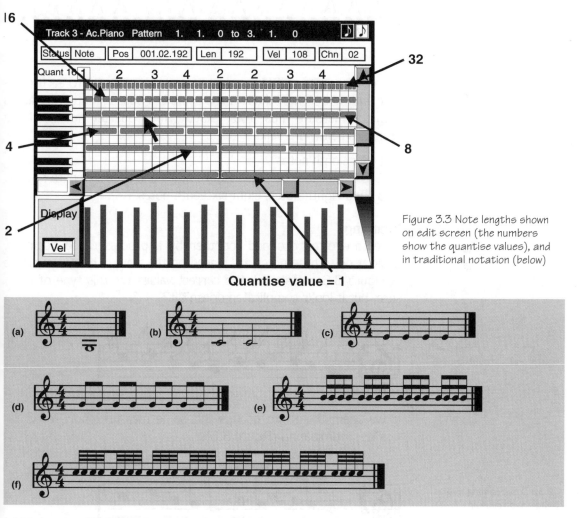

Figure 3.3 Note lengths shown on edit screen (the numbers show the quantise values), and in traditional notation (below)

(a) Whole note = 1536 (semi-breve) quantise value = 1
(b) Half note = 768 (minim) quantise value = 2
(c) Quarter note = 384 (crotchet) quantise value = 4
(d) Eighth note = 192 (quaver) quantise value = 8
(e) Sixteenth note = 96 (semiquaver) quantise value = 16
(f) Thirty second note = 48 (demi-semiquaver)  quantise value = 32

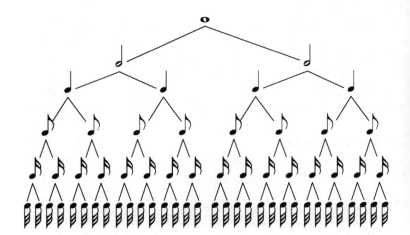

Figure 3.4 Complete note relation chart

A time signature of 3/4 means there are three beats to each measure and that each of those three beats is a quarter note. Any notes within a measure must total exactly three quarter notes, all the examples below are valid.

1 Six eighth notes
2 One quarter note, two eighth notes and four sixteenth notes
3 Two eighth notes, eight sixteenth notes.

### Beaming
Notes are often grouped together by a process called beaming. Look at how these notes are placed on the stave. The 4/4 measure in Figure 3.5 contains all the correct values for this type of measure, but it looks complicated doesn't it?

Figure 3.5 4/4 measure with eighth and sixteenth notes

If we beam them into groups this same measure now looks far less less intimidating (Figure 3.6).

Figure 3.6 Beaming makes things a lot clearer

## Dotted notes and ties

The lengths of all the notes we have previously discussed can be altered in two ways. One way is to add a dot to the note (Figure 3.7).

A dot placed immediately to the right of a note has the effect of lengthening that note by half its original length again. A quarter note (384 ticks), with a dot, would now have a total length of three eighth notes (1/4 + 1/8 = 3/8 = 576 ticks). A dotted half note will now have the length of three quarter notes.

Figure 3.7 A dot increases a note length by half as much again

Notes can be linked together using a tie (a violinist would use a bow tie – sorry bad joke!) Any note can be attached to its neighbour which is indicated on the music by using a tie symbol. A tie has the added benefit that notes of any length can be added together. The second note is not 'played'.

Figure 3.8 Tied notes

## Triplets

Triplets can be defined as being 'The playing of three notes in the same time period that two notes of the same value would normally take'.

Figure 3.9 Triplet notes – three in the time of two

# Scales

A scale is a series of eight notes whose names are based around the first 7 letters of the alphabet. A, B, C, D, E, F and G. When the 'G' is reached the scale rolls over to the A once more and the whole process is repeated over, although it should be noted the notes are an octave higher.

If we look at a keyboard we can see white notes and black notes. The white notes are considered naturals and the black ones, sharps or flats. If we start with a C and move upwards, going from one available note to another (white to black as appropriate), there will be a total of 12 steps called semitones before we reach the C one octave higher.

Figure 3.10 Octaves of C

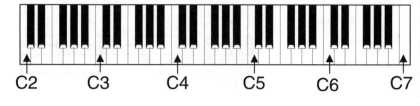

C2      C3      C4      C5      C6      C7

Scales can start on any note but we'll concentrate first on the major scale. Any scale can be constructed by applying a simple set of rules. These rules refer to the musical distance between the notes. If we select a note and move in either direction to the next available note, whether it's black or white, this is called a semi-tone. If we choose the same note but this time we skip the next available note and choose the note two places away, this would be a tone.

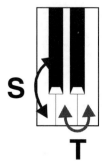

Figure 3.11 Semitone (S) and tone (T) note relationship

## Major scales
A major scale uses the following gaps (intervals) between notes: tone, tone, semi-tone, tone, tone, tone, semi-tone.

Figure 3.12 Complete major scale of C as played on a keyboard.

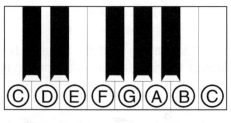

Figure 3.13 The scale of C major displayed in traditional music notation.

## Minor scales
A minor scale is constructed slightly differently and uses the following (intervals) : tone, semi-tone, tone, tone, semi-tone, tone plus semi-tone, semi-tone.

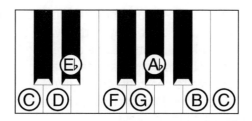

Figure 3.14 Complete minor scale of C as played on a keyboard.

Figure 3.15 The scale of C minor displayed in traditional music notation.

This version of the minor scale is known as the harmonic minor. Just to make things difficult there is another version of the minor scale called the melodic minor, but for our purposes an in depth discussion of the differences between harmonic and melodic minor scales is irrelevant.

## Sharps and flats

A sharp (#) raises a note by one semi-tone and a flat (*b*) lowers it by one semi-tone. Each note can have three variations, flat, natural or sharp. i.e; G*b*, G or G#.

Figure 3.16 A flat (*b*) lowers a note by one semi-tone and a sharp (#) raises it by one semi-tone

If we look at our keyboard once more we can see there's only one black note between the G and the A. Does this mean that a G that is sharp (G#) is the same as an A that is flat (A*b*). Yep! If this is the case, is G*b* the same as F#? Absolutely!

What about those white notes that have no black keys between them? You know, those between the B and C keys and the E and F keys. If this rule is valid it must be true to say that C*b* is the same as B natural and B# is the same as C natural – go to the top of the class!

## Key signature

Notice in our scale of G (Figure 3.17), the F is sharp. In the 'key' of G all F's are sharp.

Figure 3.17 In the 'key' of G all F's are sharp

It wouldn't be too difficult to place a sharp (#) symbol before each F to remind us to play it that way, but it's simpler to use what is called a key signature. The corresponding sharps or flats are placed at the beginning of the stave, after the clef, just before the time signature to constantly remind us.

The following chart shows the key signatures of some common major and minor keys.

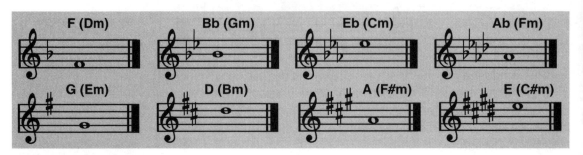

If we need to alter a note temporarily, we use what is termed an accidental. To do this we use the natural (♮) symbol. If we're playing in a flat key (say Bb major) and the natural symbol was placed before the 'E' we would disregard the key signature and play an E natural – up a semi-tone. If we're in a sharp key (say D major) and it was placed before the 'C' we would play a C natural – down a semi-tone.

### Repeats

If we're playing a piece of music and one particular passage has to be repeated, we can indicate these sections by using repeat markings. Repeat markings are placed at the start and end of a repeated section. The figure displays three measures. At the start of measure one we see the 'start of repeat' marking. Measure two not only contains the 'return to repeat' marking but the small box situated above the stave (the one with the 1 in it) tells us this is the first time measure. Measure three has a similar box and the figure 2 tells us this is the second time measure.

During the first time through the repeated passage the performer would play all the notes included in the first time measure. When the passage is repeated the first time measure(s) are omitted and the player jumps to the second time measure(s).

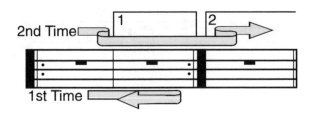

## Volume

To indicate the volume of a passage, special markings are placed under the music to instruct the player. These range from ppp (you can hardly hear anything) to fff.

## Marks of expression

Sometimes called 'hairpins' these markings can be placed under a series of notes to indicate exactly when the music should start to get louder or softer. The length of the hairpin represents the length of time to be taken to produce the effect.

## Accents/Staccato/8ve

The playing of notes can be affected in other ways.

*Accentuation* Accents can be placed above or below a note depending on the position of its tail. Accents indicate that a note must be played with added stress.

*Staccato* Staccato is a way of modifying the length of a note without resorting to complex musical notation. A dot placed above or below a note means its length should be cut roughly in half.

*8ve* To avoid the need for using ledger lines, complete passages of notes can be played up or down an octave from their written pitch by inserting an octave (Ottava) marking. '8ve' instructs the performer to play notes an octave HIGHER than their written pitch, '8ve bassa' requires the notes to be performed an octave LOWER. To indicate when the notes should return to being playe d in their written pitch, the 'loco' instruction is used.

# Guitar notation

Music for guitar can also be notated, yep – even thrash metal! The most obvious way uses traditional musical notation as described above, but three other methods are commonly employed.

## Fret diagrams

Commercial music often includes fret diagrams. The six vertical lines represent the six strings found on a rhythm guitar (E,A,D,G,B,E). The left line refers to the low E (note 40) and the right vertical line is the high E (note 64). The horizontal lines indicate the frets on the neck of the guitar and the small black dots tell us where to place our fingers.

Notice in example (i) there's an arc over the D, G and B strings. This tells us to barre those particular strings which we do by placing our index finger across the strings and exerting enough downward pressure on all the strings at once to produce the correct

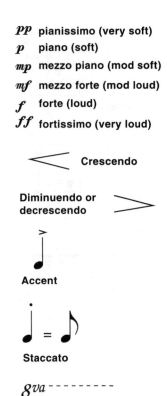

***pp*** pianissimo (very soft)

*p* piano (soft)

*mp* mezzo piano (mod soft)

*mf* mezzo forte (mod loud)

*f* forte (loud)

*ff* fortissimo (very loud)

Crescendo

Diminuendo or decrescendo

Accent

Staccato

*8va* - - - - - - - - -

*loco*

*8va bassa* - - - - -

(i) Barre mark position

(ii) o means open string

(iii) x says don't play this string

(iv) 3 indicates third fret

notes. In example (ii) we can see a small circle above the A string. This circle indicates that the A string should be played open.

Example (iii) has a small x situated over the top E string. This symbol instructs us to omit (not play) that particular string.

There will be times when playing in and around 1st position all the time will hinder technique and make some chord changes virtually impossible. To overcome this problem the hand must be positioned further up the neck and the amount we must move it is indicated by a number which tells us where we are starting the grid from. In our example (iv) we're starting from the third fret.

**Tablature**

Tab incorporates a graphical element for finger positioning but retains some of the traditional methods for indicating rhythm.

Two types of tablature are used, one for six string guitars which uses a six line stave and the other for bass guitars (which uses a four line stave). Starting from the bottom, each line of a tab stave represents a different guitar string. The numbers refer to the fret we should use. From our tab example we can see that to produce the first note (G) we should press our finger on the third fret on the first (E) string. Likewise our G major chord on beat two should be played by using the third fret on the B string (to produce the D), the fourth fret on the G string, (to produce the B) and the fifth fret on the D string (to produce the G).

Figure 3.20 Example of traditional music notation

Figure 3.21 Same example written in tablature

**Chord charts**

Chord charts are an easy but rough way of indicating to the player the chords and rhythms to use. These parts are often used by experienced gigging players as there's no indication of finger placement or chord inversions.

Figure 3.22 Chord chart with rhythm indicators

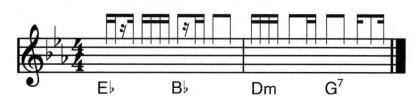

# 4

## Chords

I'm presuming most of our programming will be done from a MIDI keyboard. This chapter isn't designed to teach keyboard technique as such, but rather how to construct chords and how they should be voiced. For the correct voicing for other instruments see later chapters.

## Chords

Chords are groups of notes (often sounded together) which form the basis of a musical structure. There has to be a minimum of three notes to a chord because anything less than three would prove to be too ambiguous to label. After reading this chapter come back to this section and ask yourself how many chords could contain the notes C and E – and you'll see what I mean.

A chord is constructed from a single note called the root. From the root other notes are added in ascending order using a series of harmonic rules which determines the distance between them.

Modern music is often written in a form which includes chord symbols, and in some cases there is a fret diagram for guitarists to follow. The grouping of the chord is displayed using letter names and numbers which, when interpreted correctly, will identify the notes required to produce the correct harmonic structure. The letter names used are based upon a scale: A, B, C, D, E, F and G (so you'll never see a chord that doesn't use any one of these fundamental letter names), but be aware that any of these letter names may be flat or sharp, i.e., C#, Bb, F# etc.

It's worth remembering that the naming of chords does not include passing notes. A passing note (as the name implies) is a note that's just passing through a measure and it's totally unconnected with the underlying chord.

## Major chords

A major chord consists of three notes, the tonic, a major third and a perfect fifth. If we count the tonic (starting note) as one, a major third is the note three degrees of the scale (five semitones) away, and the perfect fifth is five degrees (eight semitones) away. If we now substitute notes instead of numbers a major chord is produced.

A chord can start on any note and always follows the same rules (root note, major third and perfect fifth for a major chord). Figure 4.1 shows a small selection of major chords.

Figure 4.1 F major
D major
Eb major
G major
F# major
Ab major

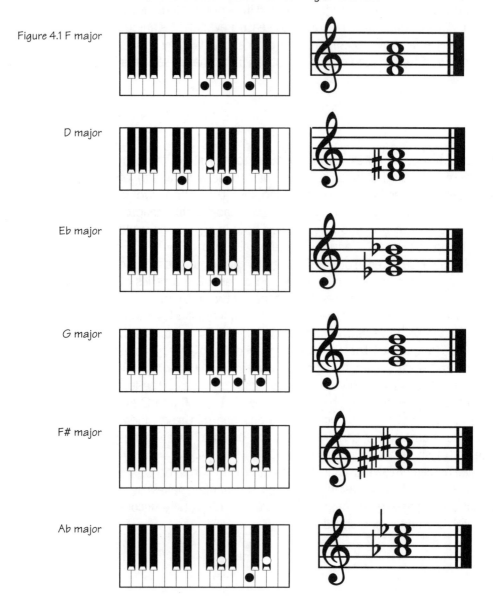

# Minor chords

A minor chord also consists of three notes, the tonic, a *minor* third and a perfect fifth. If we count up from the tonic (as we did before) the distances will be three degrees (four semitones) for the minor third (one less than the major) and five degrees (eight semitones) (again) for the perfect fifth. A minor chord has a prefix of a lower case 'm' placed immediately to the right of the chord name. If we use the same chord names as before but create minor versions we'll be able to see the obvious differences between the different types of thirds.

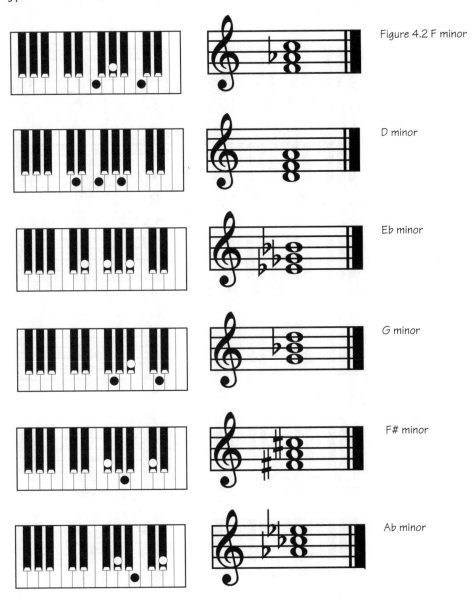

Figure 4.2 F minor

D minor

Eb minor

G minor

F# minor

Ab minor

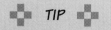 
## Seventh chords

Here are a few more types of chord that we can use. Major and minor chords can be enhanced by adding other notes to them. By far the most common is the addition of the seventh.

If we look at the scale of C major the seventh note up from the tonic is a B natural. If the note is added to our major chord, i.e. C, E, G, B, this is called a major seventh and written as Cmaj7, other examples include Emaj7, Amaj7, Abmaj7, etc.

If the seventh note were lowered by a semitone (to Bb) it would lose its major status and become a dominant seventh, i.e. C7, E7, A7, Ab7.

Figure 4.3 C7

D7

Fmaj7

Ebmaj7

Am7

Bm7

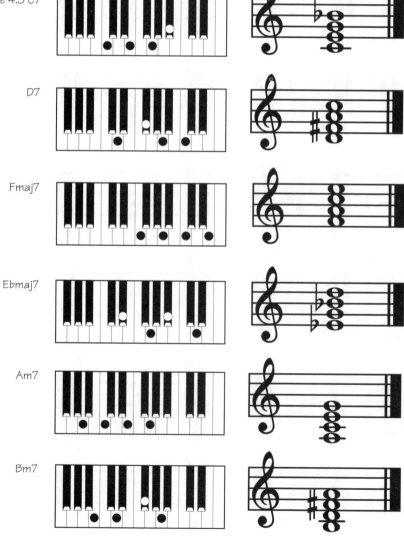

If we take our example of C once again, notice the seventh note in a chord of C7 – C, E, G, B*b*.

Let's examine a few more seventh chords to get really familiar with the concept. What notes do we use in the chord of D7? We know a seventh chord is built upon a major triad so we already know our first three notes will be D, F# and A. The seventh degree in the scale of D major is C#. But as our chord is just a dominant D7 (not a major seventh), the C# has to be lowered by a semi-tone to a C natural and added to our other notes. Our chord of D7 therefore contains the notes D, F#, A and C natural.

## Compound chords

Compound chords are the basic triad chords to which other notes, such as the 9th, 11th and sometimes the 13th degrees of the scale, have been added.

Figure 4.4 shows a selection of compound chords.

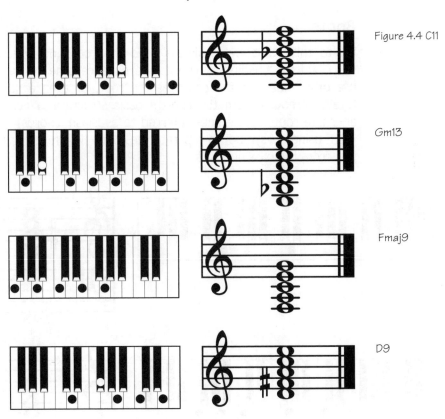

Figure 4.4 C11

Gm13

Fmaj9

D9

Figure 4.5 Chord of C7
b5/#9/11 (phew!!)

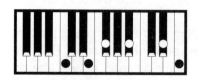

When using compound chords, slight modifications can be made to them by using a flat (*b*) and/or sharp (#) symbols to alter certain notes (Figure 4.5).

When constructing compound chords it's common practice to add every extension if possible. A ninth chord would automatically include the seventh, an eleventh chord would include the seventh and the ninth and a thirteenth chord would include the seventh, ninth *and* eleventh. If we see the chord symbol C11 we know that the 11th degree of the scale is the note F. (C = 8, D = 9, E = 10 and F = 11). Our chord of C11, including every note would comprise of C, E, G, B*b*, D and F.

## Roots

Up to this point we've always used the root note when we've described the building of chords. To enhance tone colour we can use other notes of the chord as the root, or even a note that's totally removed from the chord's basic structure. When we use alternate roots (sometimes referred to as 'slash' chords) we write them using a / symbol to separate the chord (D7 in our first example) from the bass note (F#).

Figure 4.6
D7/F#

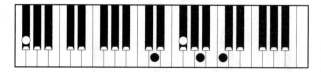

A9/E

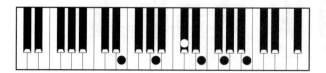

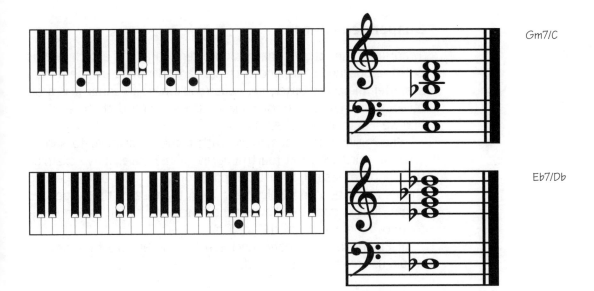

Gm7/C

Eb7/Db

## Sixths

There are a few chord types that still require our scrutiny. Let's start with a favourite jazz chord, the sixth. A chord of C6 would comprise C, E, G and A and would be played in close voicing. This means the A (the sixth) would be played just a tone away from the G, a combination which adds tension to the chord.

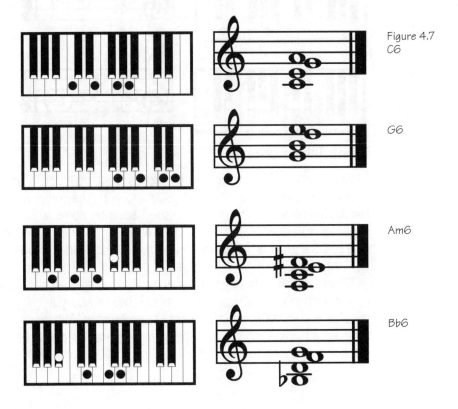

Figure 4.7
C6

G6

Am6

Bb6

## Suspended chords

There are other chords that produce tension and one such type is called 'suspended'. Suspended chords are identified by the letters sus after the chord letter, i.e. Csus (you'll have to admit it is a bit obvious isn't it). The most widely used suspended chord and the one we'll examine is the sus4.

When using suspended fourths it's common practice to substitute the third with the fourth degree of the scale. If we examine the chord of Csus4 it will comprise of C, F and G. Suspended chords cry out to be resolved and with the case of the suspended fourth, this is done by allowing the fourth (F) to fall back a semitone (or tone) to the third E (or Eb).

In Figure 4.8, the notes enclosed in brackets are the ones we would use to resolve the chord.

Figure 4.8 Csus4

Gm (sus4)

Eb7sus4

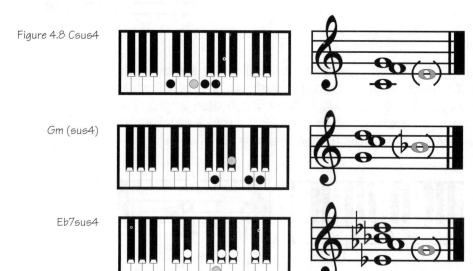

## Diminished chords

Diminished chords are four note chords built up upon a series of minor thirds (three semi-tones). Starting with the tonic, the minor third, diminished fifth and diminished seventh notes are all added together to build up the full chord. A chord of Cdim comprises of C, Eb, Gb and Bbb (A). C#dim has C#, E, G and Bb and Ddim uses, D, F, Ab and Cb (B).

There are only three patterns of notes that exist in the make up of diminished chords. Study the chords below and you'll find every note of a chromatic scale is there – somewhere. Whatever note is selected a diminished chord, albeit the note names might be enharmonically changed to suit (C# = Db, Gb = F# etc.,) can be made.

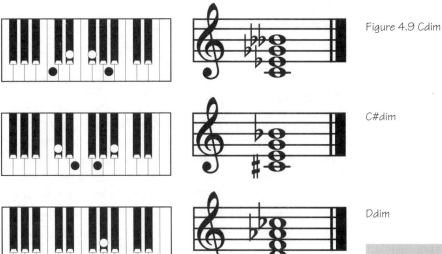

Figure 4.9 Cdim

C#dim

Ddim

A diminished chord of F# would consist of F#, A, C and Eb (an inversion of Cdim. Likewise the diminished chord of G (the same as C#dim) would use the notes – G, Bb, Db and Fb. Notice that the note names are enharmonically changed to produce the right letter names.

## Augmented chords

Augmented chords are normal major triads which have the fifth degree raised a semitone. In the chord of C augmented the notes would be C, E and G#. Some augmented chords are written using the + symbol to indicate the raised fifth, i.e. C+, E+7, Bb+ etc.

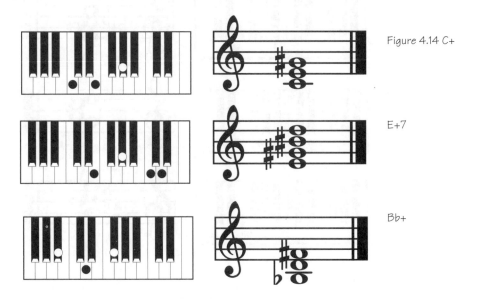

Figure 4.14 C+

E+7

Bb+

Some arrangers and composers prefer to use the − symbol to indicate a flattened note. A chord written as Gm7−5 is another way of writing Gm7b5 and C7−9 would be C7 b9.

## Chord inversions

If we play chords in root position all the time (apart from the alternate rooted chords), our technique will be become severely hampered and the music we produce will sound rather lumpy and disjointed. There's no reason why notes can't be carefully swapped around so that our fingers don't have to leap all over the keyboard. Chords produced by swapping around of notes into different positions are called inversions.

In the next example, we'll use a selection of chord examples but this time we'll use inversions to produce smoother progressions.

Figure 4.10 C major

Gm7

Ab7

D7sus

E6

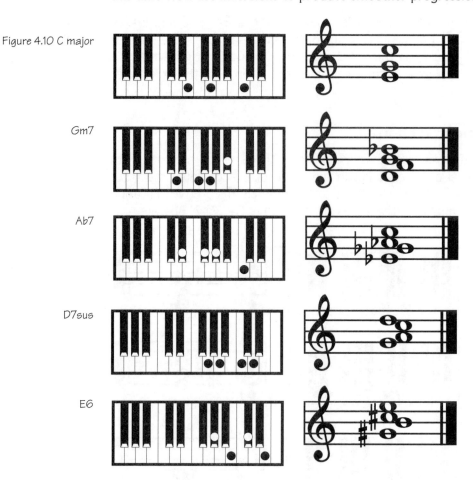

## Odds and ends

Hopefully you're getting the idea how chords can be written and how they are best interpreted. You'll be pleased to know we're nearing the end of this harmonic torture but before we finish there are still the odd one or two chords we need to look at.

(i) The first, Cadd9, refers to a chord which comprises of C, E, G and D. The D is played an octave and a tone above the tonic C. This chord allows us the flexibility of adding the ninth without having to add the seventh degree.

(ii) Bm7*b*5. This chord is constructed using B, D, F and A. Firstly notice that the F# (normally found in Bm) is lowered a semitone by the *b*5 instruction. This chord is nearly the same as Bdim but notice that the seventh degree we've used is an A natural and not the A*b* that would be found in Bdim.

(iii) G(no 3rd). This is a straightforward instruction telling us our G chord should be played without the third – no B, i.e. G, D and G.

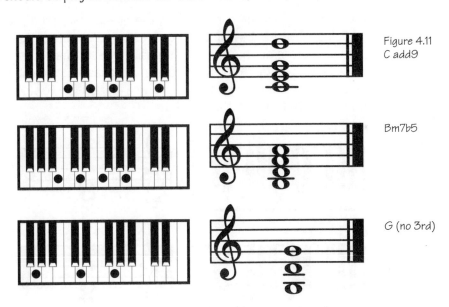

Figure 4.11
C add9

Bm7b5

G (no 3rd)

## Polyphony

At this point it's worth remembering that GM equipment is limited to a maximum of 28 voices. Imagine if our piano continually uses 6 note chords and uses the damper pedal as well, it'll cut deeply into the number of available notes. With careful selection we can compromise slightly on a full voicing but still obtain good results without wasting valuable polyphony. Most chords can be played using just three or four notes. But which notes do we leave out?

Consider a chord of C7 (C, E, G, B♭). The most important note in this chord is the seventh, followed by the third (as this tells us if the chord is major or minor), next comes the fifth and finally the tonic. As the root of the chord is probably being played by the bass guitar or bass synth our obvious three note chord will be B♭, E and G.

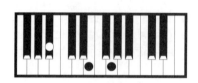

*Figure 4.12 Cut down version of C7*

So far so good I hope, but what if the chord is Cmaj7/9/11? The available notes we can choose from are C, E, G, B, D, F. With a compound chord like this use a four note chord, G, B, D and F. Labouring the third (E) is not such a good idea as in this instance we'll produce a note cluster of D, E and F which may sound rather dissonant. Any omitted notes could now be distributed to other chord playing instruments to fill in the blanks. We'll still produce a complete chord but we'll be spreading the load within the rhythm section. Before all the puritanical musicologist's (thank heavens for a spell checker) reach for their pens in indignation, remember these voicings are mere suggestions and if a particular voicing sounds good then to hell with them and use it!

*Figure 4.13 Cmaj7/9/11 reduced to manageable proportions*

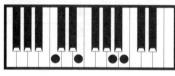

*Dm6/9*

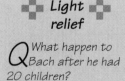
## Voicing

All of our previous examples have been presented using whole notes to aid clarity. Although this is good way of explaining how chords are structured, if the chords in a song were always played theoretically complete, and only as whole notes, our music would be very difficult to play, cut huge swathes into our polyphony, and sound awful.

# 5

## Guitar programming

### Listen first

When trying to imitate any real instrument by sequencing with MIDI equipment, it'll always help if we understand the ways in which the actual instrument plays notes and pitch bends, how volume is controlled, and how the tone of the instrument can be changed by the player. This is particularly true of the guitar, both acoustic and electric due to the large number of ways to both play and control each note.

It's always a good idea, in fact it's rather a must, that before we attempt to sequence guitar based music, we should go and see (er … I mean hear) good players who specialise in particular styles to get a good idea how all those creaking and squealing noises are made!

The human ear is an incredible piece of engineering, capable of detecting the slightest changes in a note or chord, so unless our sequenced music follows the correct methods of producing, bending, and vibratoing notes, the ear is not deceived, and it sounds 'unreal' in some way. Even when the listener is not a trained musician they won't be fooled, even with the best sampled sounds in the world.

I personally believe it always helps to know the 'nitty gritty' of how a particular instrument produces its sound so that obvious mistakes in style are avoided. As with most MIDI sequencing, we aren't so much trying to copy the notes being played, as this should be easy for anyone with a good 'ear' and reasonable patience, but we're trying to create the realistic 'impression' of that instrument, including all the tricks and frills of the real thing, which all combine to convince the ear that we are hearing a real guitar. In order to do this we must first know what we're actually hearing, then use the best method to recreate that sound.

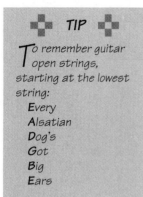

**TIP**

*To remember guitar open strings, starting at the lowest string:*

Every
Alsatian
Dog's
Got
Big
Ears

## The basics

A guitar usually has 6 strings which are tuned E, A, D, G, B, and E when moving from the thickest string (lowest open note) to the thinnest (highest open note). The lowest note on a guitar in standard tuning is an E1 with a MIDI note number of 40, and the highest practical note on a two-octave neck is E5 with a MIDI note number 88, spanning a range of four octaves of fretted notes. It is possible however, for a downward pitch bend to take a guitar note down another octave below E1, and harmonics can be used which produce notes higher than E5.

The strings stretch from the body of the guitar over the bridge, up along the neck, passing above the frets. At the other end they pass over the nut to the machine heads where the strings are tensioned to tune them to the correct pitch.

The guitar is a transposing instrument. If we see a written note (say middle C) on a printed sheet of music the actual note produced will sound an octave lower. This means all the written examples we've used in this chapter should be immediately transposed down an octave to ensure they sound correct.

When scoring for guitars the six string guitar uses the treble stave and the bass guitar uses the bass stave.

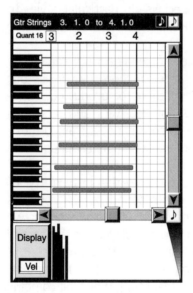

Fig 5.1 Piano roll edit screen of guitar open string notes. Note different start times for each string (see strumming section later in this chapter)

Fig 5.2 Guitar open notes, as written in traditional music notation

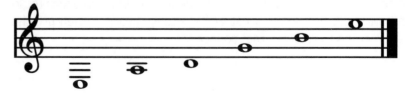

A note is chosen by touching or 'fretting' a string against the metal frets which are placed at intervals along the neck to give the correct intervals in an 'even tempered' scale.

A note is normally played by twanging or 'picking' the string with the non-fretting hand, either with fingers or by using a pick (plectrum).

## Chords

Unless we've got hands like an ape (well actually ...), there are only certain chord shapes the guitarist can use owing to the relative pitches of the strings. Because of this, most full guitar chords (i.e. using all six strings) will span about two octaves of a piano keyboard. We must bear this in mind when we're searching for chord inversions – a guitarist's chord will often look impossibly wide on a keyboard, and vice-versa.

### INFORMATION

*P*ianos are tuned to notes which aren't in perfect pitch for one particular key, but instead they're set up under a compromise arrangement whereby a chord will sound acceptable in any key – the so-called 'Even Tempered Scale'. The guitar is also tuned to this scale.

Figure 5.3 Guitar chord of A major

## Reggae

Depending on the style of music we're programming, not all guitar chords will use all six strings. In reggae style music often only the three highest pitched strings are used in an upward stroke, keeping the chord to a high-pitched short twang. On upward stoke chords remember the highest note will be played first, although to reproduce the right feel there shouldn't be any noticeable gaps between any of the notes. Also in reggae, chords are held or fretted so that the strings barely touch the frets, the dampening effect of the fingertips causing them to sound as a chunk with hardly any discernible pitch.

To reproduce this sound authentically we can use two different techniques. The first uses only very short notes depending on the speed of the song – try experimenting with note lengths between 16 and 32 ticks. The second method uses a more complicated technique.

1 The note lengths of the chopped chord are left just as they were played.
2 Use the re-map feature on the sequencer to re-map the damper pedal (controller 64) so that it produces expression events (controller 11).

3 Set a second track to the same MIDI channel as the guitar notes and record the expression markings. As soon as the chord is played lift the foot off the damper pedal. This produces an expression value of 0 (min). Holding the pedal down will send an expression value of 127 (max) enabling the next series of notes to sound.

4 Mix the note track and expression tracks together.

The reason I like this particular technique is that it dampens the note without sending a note off command. If I happen to adjust any of the sound's performance parameters (attack, decay, sustain or release) I can increase the expression value '0' off from the floor and give it a new value which produces a different (better) result.

Figure 5.4 *Reggae chop*

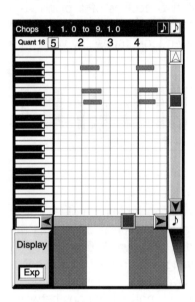

## Rock

Heavy rock guitarists like Bert Weedon (joke!) produce their distinctive sound using power chords. Power chords are usually played on a down stroke using the three lowest strings, as 'root, fifth and octave' (lowest note sounding first). Notice that the third degree of the scale is deliberately missing. Why? Power chords by their nature can sit happily underneath a major, minor or seventh chord without causing any harmonic problems.

### Tip

If the chord at the end of a phrase (measure 7) is played higher up the neck than the chord which starts the next (new) phrase, re-play and accent the original chord on the fourth beat and then fall down onto the new chord of the next phrase.

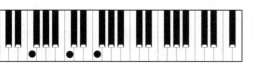 

Figure 5.5 Power chord of F

This can be done in two ways, either by using the whammy bar (pitch bend fall) or secondly by sliding the fingers down the fret board (note fall). If we decide to use a note-fall then use notes chromatically as each fret represents a semi-tone. Whatever technique is employed remember to decrease the volume (velocity) for all of the smaller (secondary) notes we've used in creating the fall-off effect.

## Tip

To play a song and restrict ourselves to just playing a single sustained power chord per measure throughout the entire song will sound very amateurish and not very realistic. One way to liven up the part is to play a couple of 'chopped' chords just before a new phrase begins.

The chord starts as normal but on the second half of beat four (xxx/04/192) play two sixteenth notes at position 192 and 288 respectively. As mentioned earlier, play these chords chopped, that is without any noticeable pitch or duration as we're only using them to produce an effect. For the really adventurous use the same technique at beat two (xxx/02/192 and xxx/02/288). Notice that we are still working in conjunction with the natural accents of the song, but don't get silly and over-use this particular technique – less is more!

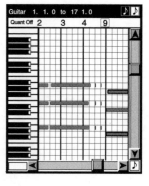

Figure 5.6 Two sixteenth notes on the second half of beat four will liven up your guitar part. traditional notation (left and piano roll (above)

## Strumming

Creating realistic guitar strums is one of the most difficult effects to reproduce well. First let's analyse the way a strum is produced. A strum is created by moving our fingernails or plectrum up and down across the strings. The number of strings we use depends on the style of music we're creating. As a 'rule of thumb' the full six strings are only used in folk music, earlier folk-pop music of the 60s, and country and western.

❖ **TIP** ❖

*W*hen alternating between a down-strum and an up-strum the down is always slightly more powerful, and therefore louder, than the up. Adjust the velocity characteristics to reflect the difference between each type.

There can be only two directions for strumming, 'up' and 'down'. Most players use a downstroke on the natural strong(er) beats in the measure – for beats 1 and 3, and an upstroke for the weaker beats (2 and 4). For rhythms using eighth notes, each beat is played with a down stroke and each half-beat is played as an upstroke. This relationship is very important because it will determine the order in which the notes are played. When a chord is played with a downstroke it's the lowest note we'll be hearing first and then, as the plectrum passes across each string, the following notes are played in an ascending order of pitch. The reverse is true for upward strums. This strumming effect produces a characteristic timing gap between the notes in a chord; when strummed slowly, a definite arpeggio effect can be heard.

The amount of gap between each of the strings is critical in creating a realistic strumming effect. For slow strumming (as heard in folk music or ballads), a gap of about a 64th note will give acceptable results. Don't be fooled into thinking that by creating a step-entered part whereby every note has an exact gap of a 64th note it will solve the problem, it won't! If you listen *really* closely you'll notice the first (lowest) string is slightly emphasised and is held just a millisecond longer than the others.

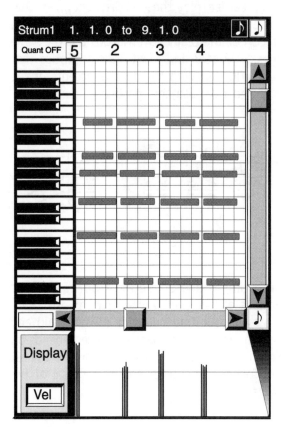

Figure 5.7 Strummed E chord – beat 1 down, beat 2 up, beat 3 down, beat 4 up

Reduce the tempo of the sequencer to something manageable and record a five measure phrase consisting of down and up strumming. Placing your hands in the correct position over the keyboard and rocking them up and down accordingly will produce the strum. Start playing on the first beat of measure two. This means that the first measure is left empty, however if you examine the notes very closely you'll see that the first actual note is played a fraction before the start of the beat. If you recorded just a four measure phrase there is a strong possibility that any pre-emptive notes would've been missed or automatically hard quantised onto the beat to get them inside the measure. If you use this pattern and copy it elsewhere in the song remember your notes actually start to play from measure two.

Re-record similar phrases but this time use different chord inversions. Likewise, increase the speed of the sequencer and repeat the whole process. Save these phrases as discrete MIDI files or as sequencer parts so that they can be pasted into other songs when required.

### Tip – create parts in both major and minor keys

These parts can be transposed up and down to change the chord but take care not to transpose them down too far and produce a bass note lower than a D. Although the lowest open string is an E, sometimes a string or couple of strings are deliberately detuned to create a special effect – especially true for creating those special chords which use open strings.

If you're using just one guitar and you hear notes dropping out due to polyphony problems, you have rather a problem don't you? Another 'trick' is to drop different notes in the strumming pattern. If you think about the chord of E once again. When the first chord is played you could probably ignore the low E. Why? Well the bass guitar or bass synth will probably be playing the root of the chord anyway – the E, your E would become superfluous.

To be honest, if polyphony drop out is very bad, you may need to drop a couple of notes on the first beat of each measure. It works best to limit such drastic note cutting to just the first beat because this is when most of the other instruments will start playing. Keyboards will be playing something, even it's just establishing the new chord, there will be bass and drums playing and perhaps other instruments floating over the rhythm section. Whatever the line up of the song, if there's a problem with polyphony you're obviously working the unit quite hard so there must be quite a few instruments playing to cause the problem in the first place.

When an organic guitar player strums away you can often notice that some notes in the chord don't sound as loud as others they've played. It's this relationship we're using to our advantage and the dropping of some notes will go some way to completing the illusion.

### Six note strum

Using a full six note strum can sound quite effective, but there may come a time when using all six strings bites into our polyphony too much and notes start to drop out elsewhere. This happens quite commonly if you're using two guitars which are strumming away throughout the song. If this happens reduce the notes played by each to a maximum of five, four is better. Imagine you are playing a chord of E major (E, B, E, G#, B and E). If you omit the second E in one part (and let the second guitar play it) and in the second guitar part omit the second B (and let the first guitar play it) you may be able to fool the ear into thinking that both guitars are playing every note in every chord.

### Twin guitar strumming

Figure 5.8 is a complete six string chord of E major.

Figure 5.8 Complete strum voicing

If you needed to play this strumming pattern by two types of guitars but kept experiencing severe drop out, one answer would be to get the two guitar parts to play cut down versions, see Figures 5.9 – 5.12.

Such severe cannibalising of notes in this way has to be undertaken carefully so as not to cut away too many notes, losing the overall effect. I would regard this example to be an extreme solution to this kind of problem.

Unless the guitar has a very dominant strumming pattern this technique can be quite effective. The tonic and the fifth are the most obvious notes to drop from the chord. You can drop the third from time to time but be careful, you don't want to do it too often because it's a very important note in the make up of a chord.

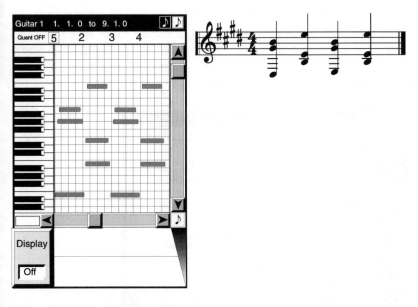

Figure 5.9 and 5.10 Guitar 1

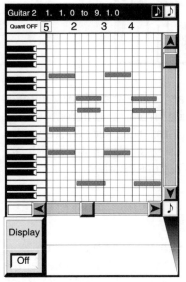

Figure 5.11 and 5.12  Guitar 2

## Finger picking

This is a style which can drive a non-guitarist to tears when trying to reproduce it through MIDI, and for several reasons.

Firstly, the picking hand is used in a 'claw' shape, and the thumb and fingers may pick in different rhythms and with different patterns of soft and heavy strokes. Secondly, a note played on any string can continue to sound on until manually damped or until a different note is played on that same string, and it's this 'ringing on' of notes which takes a lot of thought to reproduce convincingly.

Seen in the piano roll editor (Figure 5.13) this method looks quite complex, and it should always be remembered that some notes will be played on the same string, so the previous note should always cut off just before the new one starts.

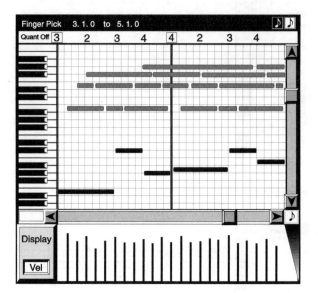

Figure 5.13 Finger picking with bass melody. Finger picking leaves notes ringing on until they're retriggered, but the changing bass line (shown in black) is actually using two different strings when played on a real guitar.

As a very general rule, if notes are more than five semitones apart they're likely to be produced from a different string, although there are some exceptions to this rule, such as suspended chords, where different strings are used to play notes which are closely pitched so that they 'ring' against one another.

## Jazz comping or vamping

It's also possible to play a low note with the thumb and then 'pop' several strings together with the fingers to sound their notes at the same time. This is a favourite technique of jazz guitarists when comping or vamping. This technique gives the guitarist time to find the bass note before selecting a chord to play over it. It also gives a more rhythmic feel to help the song chug along.

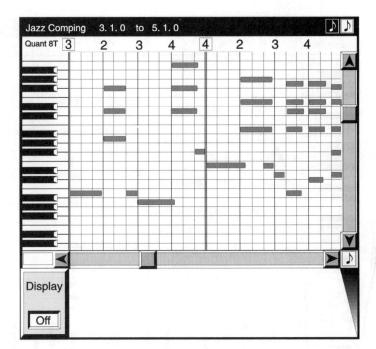

Figure 5.14 Jazz comping with bass rhythm. The low notes should usually sound first, followed by the high chord with all its notes together. Alternatively, the whole chord along with its bass notes is popped together.

## Flamenco

Flamenco is a style almost always used when playing 'Spanish' style acoustic guitars with nylon strings. Apart from picking and fretting notes only with the fingers, the most distinctive part of the flamenco style is the chord playing where fingers on the picking hand are 'un-curled' across the strings, one after the other, sounding the chord as a drawn out rattle.

Look at the well known flamenco guitar riff in Figure 5.15. Since all four fingers of the picking hand are drawn across the strings, each one will sound three short notes before being allowed to ring on, and it's this which gives the 'rattle' sound. To reproduce this on a sequencer, we must place several short notes of the appropriate length before each note in our chord to simulate the sound of the 'finger rattle', then sound the chord itself and allow it to ring on as normal.

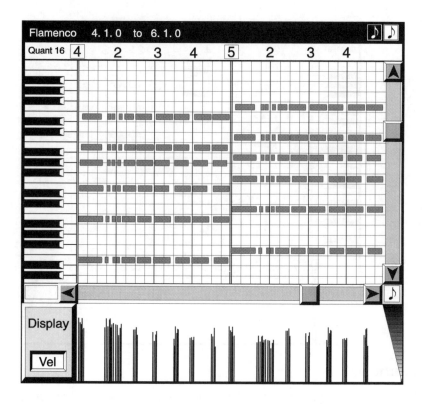

Figure 5.15 Flamenco style finger rattle

## Damping or 'stubbing'

Damping the strings by resting the heel of the picking hand on the strings at the guitar's bridge will produce notes which sustain much less than usual and which have a definite muffled sound. A good example of this technique is the guitar intro to *Every Breath You Take* by The Police, where a mixture of stubbed notes and a few normal ones create that particular rhythmic feel.

## Using a guitar pick

A pick will produce notes which are bright, even in volume, and have a high harmonic content. This style is favoured by rock musicians who like speed and clarity. The advantage for us is that a pick will only play groups of notes at any one time (as opposed to the multi rhythms of finger style) so it's easier to mentally separate what's happening.

For imitating notes played with a pick use a standard guitar sound with a normal attack. Pay attention to the way the notes die away after being struck as the character of the decay can also affect the realism of the finished result. However there are a whole bag of 'tricks' used by the guitarist which makes it even more difficult to decide what is actually happening on the record.

# Guitar tricks

### Hammer-ons

Guitarists have many different ways of producing notes with a different tonality or sustain character. The first is called a hammer-on, where the first note is fretted and picked in the usual way, but the second or third is produced by snapping a finger of the left hand (if you're a right handed guitarist) onto the fretboard to both twang the string and choose the note at the same time.

The sound of a 'hammered on' note is different in that it won't be quite as bright or as loud as a picked note, but will follow it with no timing gap. This results in the first note appearing to change instantly into the second. It's possible to hammer on several notes in a row, but usually only on a string which is already vibrating (It is possible to snap a finger on to the frets to start a note from scratch, but it is rarely used).

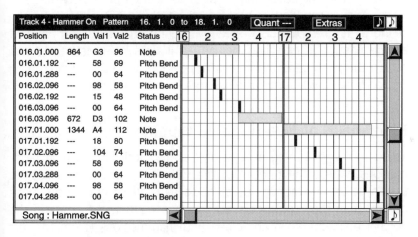

Figure 5.16 Hammer-on using pitch bend to re-pitch the notes without retriggering the attack.

When simulating the sound of hammered-on notes, I've found the following method works the best:

Play the first note as normal, making sure it's long enough to continue sounding while other hammered-on notes are produced, and then use pitch bend events, placed exactly where you want the new note(s) to sound. This method works because it avoids re-triggering the attack of the note which could spoil the effect you're trying to create. Again, this method is for getting the sound correct, if you're scoring from our MIDI data you'll probably have to do another version. If you had used conventional notes instead of pitch bend commands the same passage would look, and sound very different (Figure 5.17).

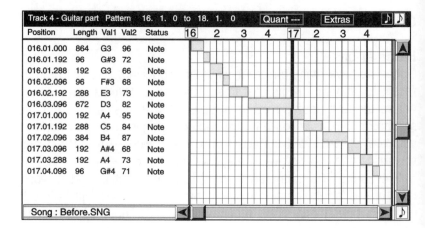

| Track 4 - Guitar part | Pattern | | | 16. 1. 0 | to | 18. 1. 0 | Quant --- | Extras | | |
|---|---|---|---|---|---|---|---|---|---|---|
| Position | Length | Val1 | Val2 | Status | | | | | | |
| 016.01.000 | 864 | G3 | 96 | Note | | | | | | |
| 016.01.192 | 96 | G#3 | 72 | Note | | | | | | |
| 016.01.288 | 192 | G3 | 66 | Note | | | | | | |
| 016.02.096 | 96 | F#3 | 68 | Note | | | | | | |
| 016.02.192 | 288 | E3 | 73 | Note | | | | | | |
| 016.03.096 | 672 | D3 | 82 | Note | | | | | | |
| 017.01.000 | 192 | A4 | 95 | Note | | | | | | |
| 017.01.192 | 288 | C5 | 84 | Note | | | | | | |
| 017.02.096 | 384 | B4 | 87 | Note | | | | | | |
| 017.03.096 | 192 | A#4 | 68 | Note | | | | | | |
| 017.03.288 | 192 | A4 | 73 | Note | | | | | | |
| 017.04.096 | 96 | G#4 | 71 | Note | | | | | | |

Song : Before.SNG

Figure 5.17 Using notes instead of pitch bends gives a very different effect

## Pull-offs

Having hammered on a note, it's then possible to sound the original low note (the one still being fretted) by using a pull-off, where the finger (which previously hammered on the note) now flicks the string as it's removed, so making it sound again. Pull-offs almost always happen after a hammer-on, so it's a simple method to just return the pitch bend to the centre position or to a new pitch with one command, while the original note is still sounding.

## Right-hand or two-fingered tapping

This is not a plumbing expression but a logical extension of hammer-ons, where the fingers of the right hand are tapped against the frets, usually higher up the neck, to produce high notes more quickly than they could be reached when fretting the notes in the normal manner. When combined with hammer-ons (from the left hand), it's possible to play a series of notes with blinding speed.

As with hammer-ons, use pitch bend events to sound notes without retriggering the attack of a note for an authentic sound, but remember that when notes jump to a new string you'll have to play a note in the normal way before using pitch bend to carry on. As with hammer-ons, use your list or grid editor to place exact pitch bend commands to get exactly the right note.

### Sweep picking 72    73

Sweep picking is a recent technique developed by rock guitarists to give more speed (surprise surprise) to a series of notes which can't easily be played using hammer-ons. This involves dragging the pick across the strings from low to high and back again while simultaneously fretting the actual notes required from each string and unfretting them when they're no longer required, but still keeping the fingers touching the strings to stop them sounding by accident! Tricky !! Sweep picking will play very distinct notes very rapidly, with each note sounding cleanly, so use ordinary note events for this type of fast playing.

## Harmonics

Harmonics can be created on a guitar by strategically placing a finger of the left hand so it just touches the string at a harmonic point. When the string is picked it will resonate at the appropriate pitch in a bell-like tone.

Since the sound of a harmonic note is very different from a normal one, you may have to try different methods to get things to sound right. GM, GS and XG devices have a guitar harmonic sound included (program change 32) but as with many 'effect' type sounds which can be made by a guitar it may be worth considering the use of a second track for another sound (try a totally different type of instrument and play it well above its normal range) to reproduce the bell like quality of a harmonic note.

## Violining

When playing hard rock the amp is often set so that it distorts even under the most gentle caresses to maintain the distortion effect at all times. In this case the guitar itself would have to be turned right down at its on-board controls in order to achieve a clean sound. Some players use these on board volume controls or sometimes a foot volume pedal to achieve another 'effect' called violining, named because it emulates the sound of a violin when it starts a note from almost no volume and swells it to full volume. To reproduce an effect like this you should use expression commands (controller 11).

For best results use the controller drawing window to 'draw' expression data from just before the note starts (where expression should be set to 0) smoothly up to full expression (127). The effect of removing the attack portion from a distorted guitar does indeed produce a sound very like that of a violin (but don't tell Yehudi).

## INFORMATION

*For pitch bend to note relationships refer to Appendix E)*

# Pitch bend

## Normal pitch bend

I read quite recently in a book on sequencing that the guitar can only bend notes upwards when performing pitch bending or vibrato. This is wrong on both counts! There are two distinct methods of altering the pitch of notes. The first is to push the fretted string sideways increasing its tension, bending the note upwards.

The second method is created by using the so called tremolo bar (also called variously a wang bar, whammy bar, trem, etc.) This is an assembly which carries the bridge on a special pivot connected to springs inside the guitar body. This mechanism counteracts the pull of the strings, making it possible to use a long arm attached to the tremolo to pull the strings up or down in pitch.

The difference when pitch bending with a tremolo is that notes may be smoothly bent by several semi-tones up or down. If we hear a note being bent up several tones and then vibrato'd, it will almost definitely have been done using the tremolo bar. There's just isn't enough strength in human fingers, or enough room across a guitar neck, to bend up much more than two whole tones.

I use pitch bend set to one of two possible ranges; a full left or right push on the pitch wheel gives me either two semi-tones or 12. With a bend range set to two, it's easy to play some passages in real-time, giving a natural feel to the timing of the bends and their position. However for serious guitar work, especially for rock style playing, I always use a range of 12 and use a 'cut and paste' technique to place pitch bends manually. This may sound like hard work, but most guitar pitch bends are impossible to play with any degree of accuracy, so I cheat!

**Controller list for setting pitch bend ratio to 12 semi-tones**

| Val1 | Val2 | Status |
|---|---|---|
| 101 | 0 | RPN MSB |
| 100 | 0 | RPN LSB |
| 6 | 12 | data entry |
| 101 | 127 | RPN MSB |
| 100 | 127 | RPN LSB |

Figure 5.18 Correct, the note is bent back to its correct pitch.

Figure 5.19 Wrong, although this example produces the same effect, we've been forced to use an extra two pitch bend events to get the same result.

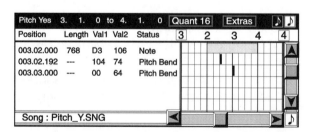

This may seem complicated at first, but if we look at this method using the list or grid editors (Figure 5.18) we can see that it is a very simple and cost-effective way to use pitch bend data.

## Pitch bend method 2

I feel it's good practice when bending notes to place a note at the correct destination pitch and then bend from *off* pitch back to *on* pitch (Figure 5.19). In other words, we are taking the following distinct steps:

1 Place a pitch bend event just before the start of the note in question, which will bend the note to the pitch we wish to start bending from.
2 Now place a note of the correct final pitch at the point in time where the bend is to begin.
3 Insert a series of pitch bend events to gradually bend the note back up to its correct pitch.

This method has the added advantage that it always leaves the pitch bend setting at its centre position after a series of note bends. This greatly minimises the chance of notes being inserted or played wrongly due to the pitch bend being accidentally left off centre, it also enables us to construct a score from the sequence because all the notes are displayed in their correct pitch. In using this method we're applying pitch bend, playing the correct note, and then allowing the pitch wheel to centre, so the MIDI note number will be correct. Use this method wherever possible unless the results sound so 'wrong' to the ear that it doesn't work.

## Pitch bend method 3

As I've previously mentioned, pitch bend can be used for several techniques. When imitating fast passages of hammer-ons, pull-offs and two-handed tapping, pitch bend allows us to make a note 'jump' from one pitch to another in semi-tone (or other) steps to avoid the attack sound caused by retriggering a note. Assuming we're using a pitch bend scale of 12 semi-tones, we can play a series of notes which 1 is normal, 2 and 3 are hammer-ons/finger tapped and 4 and 5 are pull-offs (Figure 5.20).

> **TIP**
>
> *Method 3 is great for doing soundalike guitar heroics, but it has some disadvantages. Firstly, if our sequencer sends a 'reset all controllers' message when we press the stop button, the note will revert back to its correct pitch, making it awkward to check the data in small sections. To overcome this problem we must always run through the complete section to hear the pitch bends work in relation to each other.*

| Guitar | 3. | 1. | 0 to 4. | 1. | 0 | Quant --- | Extras | ♪ ♪ |
|--------|----|----|---------|----|----|-----------|--------|-----|
| Position | Length | Val1 | Val2 | Status | 3 | 2 | 3 | 4 | 4 |
| 003.01.000 | 1487 | G3 | 110 | Note | | | | | |
| 003.01.096 | --- | 18 | 80 | Pitch Bend | | | | | |
| 003.01.192 | --- | 105 | 106 | Pitch Bend | | | | | |
| 003.01.288 | --- | 18 | 80 | Pitch Bend | | | | | |
| 003.02.000 | --- | 0 | 64 | Pitch Bend | | | | | |
| Song : Heroics.SNG | | | | | | | | | |

Figure 5.20 pitch bend guitar heroics. Four of these five notes are made using pitch bend

### Pitch bend method 4

Another trick a guitarist can perform is bending the pitch of one note while keeping others the same. On a keyboard this can be difficult or impossible to actually play (unless it's specially set up to do it that way) because when we move the pitch wheel we'll generally be changing the pitch of all the notes we're playing. Since we can't always choose which note to bend from among the several we're playing, we must find another way to imitate this sound.

The only way to get the correct result is to use at least two MIDI channels for our one guitar part, one for the main chord or rhythm playing part, and the another for the ornaments or other notes which need special treatment such as pitch bending while other notes remain normal.

Using this method, chords or pairs of notes must be split between the two tracks in order to apply different effects to each. Usually two tracks will be enough, but it's possible (in country and western music) to bend one note up, another down, while the pitch of the third note remains unchanged. If you don't believe me, there's an old guitarist who lives near me who'll be happy to teach you how. For a few beers, that is!

## Vibrato

Vibrato on a guitar can be achieved in a variety of ways, by moving the fretting finger(s) sideways to create gentle pitch movement up from the correct pitch of a note, and back down to it. Wobbling the finger gently back and forth across the string in this way can produce a fast vibrato effect, but with the pitch changing only up from, and back to, the note in question.

With a tremolo bar, gentle wobbling of the bar will create pitch movement which goes either up or down from the correct pitch creating a sine wave type pattern. Tapping the bar will produce vibrato which moves only down in pitch, pulling the bar will result in an up only vibrato. Vibrato can adopt a more 'classical' approach (mainly used on nylon strung guitars due to the lower tensions involved). The fretting finger actually pushes against the fretboard and 'pulls and pushes' the note in the direction of the string's length in almost the same way as a violinist, giving an effect similar to tremolo vibrato.

Although it's possible to play some things using modulation vibrato, if a piece of music has very expressive guitar playing it's often full of very different vibrato styles which change from measure to measure. In this situation it's often quicker to use gentle pitch bend events to produce vibrato of exactly the type and style

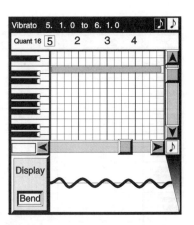

Figure 5.21 Using pitch bend data to produce a realistic vibrato effect.

we need from moment to moment. This can be produced manually with the pitch wheel, or drawn in with the mouse using the sequencer's graphical editing window.

## Guitar wah-wah effect

Using wah-wah guitar parts can gobble up lots of valuable polyphony. A similar effect can be produced using just a single note. Create a measure which contains very short 16th notes (semiquavers) – with a length of between 10 and 20 ticks (about 64th triplets).

When the filter is opened and closed we hear the effect it produces but not actually the notes themselves. If we apply a gentle sweeping pan effect (controller 10) and sink it down into the mix the effect can be quite effective.

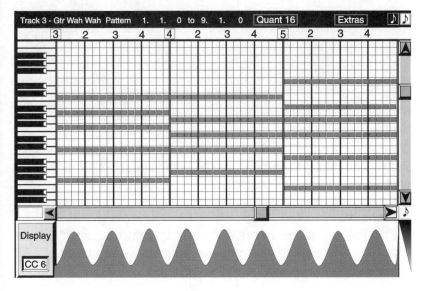

Figure 5.22 Wah-wah effect using full (complete) chords.

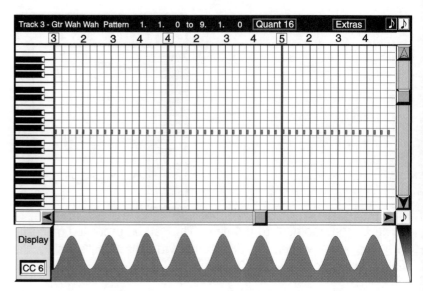

Figure 5.23- Wah Wah effect using a single note.

Best results are obtained if you use the root or fifth of the underlying chord. I have used the same principle and used just one note for the complete duration of a song! The reason this technique works is that these very short notes don't really produce a definite pitch as such.

### Roland GS

There are other methods of creating a wah-wah effect. One technique uses the resonance parameter (32) and can be used quite effectively with Roland GS devices.

| Val1 | Val2 | Status |
|------|------|--------|
| 99 | 01 (01H) | Non registered parameter number MSB |
| 98 | 32 (20H) | Non registered parameter number LSB |
| 6 | xx (mmH) | mm=14 to 114 (64 is the default) |

Data entry (controller 6) has a value of xx. It's this value that should be undulated to produce the wah-wah effect. Notice we've omitted the locking off controllers.

### Yamaha XG

XG devices are more versatile in their implementation of control codes, therefore creating a wah-wah effect in XG can be done a lot more easily using ordinary controller events.

| XG Controllers | Functions |
| --- | --- |
| Controller 71 | Resonance |
| Controller 72 | Release |
| Controller 73 | Attack |
| Controller 74 | Cut-off frequency |

XG devices sometimes sound better if we undulate the cut-off frequency (Cntrl 74) to produce the wah-wah effect instead of the resonance. The tone of the voice we're using could benefit from a slight increase in its resonance level before the wah-wah proper gets underway.

| Val1 | Val2 | Status |
| --- | --- | --- |
| 71 | 100 | Resonance |
| 74 | xx | Cut-off frequency |

## MIDI guitar controllers

Several people have told me that they assumed I would use a MIDI guitar controller to sequence up my guitar based music, and they've been quite surprised to learn that I don't. There are several reasons why.

I've tried most of the current controllers, and found that the amount of spurious information generated by them makes more work than it actually saves. Often large amounts of pitch bend information are created, and in general the tracking speed of most controllers still lags way behind any seriously fast playing. While this type of controller can be used to enter chords fairly quickly, I can work those out in my head just as fast and input them using a normal keyboard. As for complicated passages I find that by the time I've edited out the spurious data, corrected all the pitch bends, and sorted out all the general tracking problems, I'm still left with far more data than I would have created by actually editing-in the data in the first place.

Don't get me wrong, as a performance device, the MIDI guitar is setting many players free from traditional sounds in a wonderful way. However, I consider it an integral part of 'professional sequencing' that all data should be as compact as possible. This approach will both maximise the number of songs that can be loaded into a hardware sequencer in a live situation, and the reduction of continuous controller information will also minimise the chances of producing MIDI choking.

## Keep things tidy

The two enemies of good sequencing are limited polyphony and untidiness. In general it's good practice to keep all data as tidy as possible for several reasons. Notes which are left hanging on for too long will overlap with the next ones, stealing valuable polyphony, sometimes to the extent that the song just won't work until we go through and tidy things up. This is especially true when sequencing up guitar parts, as the guitar uses a fairly large amount of data to produce good results. Since we often work in sections (which can be copied to other parts of the song), fixing and tidying up our data as we go along will actually save time. Also remember that we may have to come back to a song later and re-edit it, so I give myself the best chance of remembering exactly what I did the first time around by keeping things as uniform as possible. Find a system which works for you and stick to it whenever possible.

## Choosing and selecting a sound

Use your ears – never mind the name!

### Classical or nylon string guitar (program change 25)

Most of the notes played by a nylon strung acoustic are played 'straight', with few of the tricks associated with the electric, so bear this in mind when sequencing. Be sparing with any audio effects such as chorus and reverb, but a good dose of reverb can help if there isn't much else happening in the song at that point.

### Steel strung acoustic (program change 26)

You can use more chorus on a steel string acoustic and get away with it because most of its sound is at the top end of the spectrum, so it doesn't become 'muddy' when chorus is applied. Avoid drowning it in reverb if strumming, or it'll become a wash of noise, but you can apply a fairly high of reverb effect if playing a solo or a ballad.

Steel strung acoustics are one of the most 'creaky' types of guitar due to the string tension and type of strings. If this sound were coupled with fret noise (program change 121) on another track this will create more realism. Remember the squeak always happens just before a new note or chord is played.

## 12-string acoustic

The most important part of the character of a 12 string guitar comes from the natural chorusing which happens as a result of the six pairs of strings being slightly (and quite deliberately) out of tune with each other.

With GS and XG devices a 12 string exists as a variation of the steel string guitar – program change 26).

## 'Clean' electric guitars (program change 28)

By 'clean' we usually mean 'not distorted', so we'll often find this type of sound in country and western, rockabilly, jazz or big band etc., or hear it heavily chorused when used as a rhythm instrument in funk, reggae, or general pop music. When we move on to electric guitars we must concentrate more on the actual sound we're trying to reproduce, so the choice of program or sound is less clear. The clean guitar (program change 28) can be used in many situations. Generally I would assume a sprinkling of chorus on a clean guitar will work under most circumstances.

## Distorted guitar – blues, rock, fusion, thrash metal, punk, grunge etc.

The obvious choices for distorted guitar sounds are program change 30 – 'Overdrive Gt' and program change 31 – 'Distorted Gt'. The Overdrive guitar is best used for bluesy playing, or for softer melodic work, while the distorted guitar is better for heavy rock where the extra brightness helps to keep the notes well defined.

One noticeable thing about real life distorted guitar is that it's usually being played loud, even if it's set back into the mix, and this has an effect on the tone and response of the strings. Most synthesised guitar sounds don't have enough energy in the bass range, so usually a bit of extra 'bottom' on the graphic equaliser or tone controls will help.

## Pedal steel

It's often rumoured that this strange breed of guitar was invented by overweight country and western guitarists who preferred to play sitting down in order to avoid heart attacks (but hey, that may just be a nasty rumour started by fat bassists!) However there are some major changes in the way notes are played which affect the tone and sustain of the instrument, giving it its very individual sound.

The pedal steel is like a guitar which has been placed flat on a table and is played sitting in a chair. A metal 'slide' is placed over

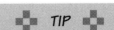

*TIP*

*To create the illusion of a 12-string guitar with non-GM equipment, you can use a similar method as when creating natural chorusing. Just copy the notes to a new track (which uses the same sound), and detune this track slightly. The copy track should be transposed up an octave (12 semitones), as the thin strings from each pair on a 12 string are tuned this way. Hey presto – instant 12-string, and now for my next trick ...*

the second or third finger of the non-plucking hand, and this is used to fret notes at different positions on the wide neck while the plucking hand both picks and damps combinations of notes. The unique difference with a pedal steel is that foot pedals are used to press combinations of dampers up under the strings, quickly forming different chords – a bit like driving a foreign car on our roads, but with the gearstick on the wrong side – no wonder they pull such faces!

The strings of a pedal steel are usually extra heavy gauge and are stretched much tighter than those on an ordinary guitar. This tension produces notes which have a long ringing sustain and a bell-like tone with very clear inter-note discernibility.

When sequencing to imitate the pedal steel, remember that it sounds very similar to slide guitar, and often several tracks/channels must be used because the combinations of slide and pedals make it possible to have notes bending both up and down in pitch.

Choose a guitar patch with a smooth round sound, possibly a bluesy distorted one. Pedal steels can be used with the full range of guitar effects like chorus, delay and distortion, but don't go overboard or it'll spoil the clarity of tone.

Pitch bend is usually best set to one full octave for the pedal steel, since players use the full range possible to glide gently between chords and through melodies. A gentle use of echo or delay will also enhance the realism as this is often used to accentuate the glide effect between notes.

In country ballads it's common practice to use a pedal on the floor to 'swell' the volume of the instrument on certain notes or chords. This is the same effect as 'violining' on a normal guitar but it's used a lot more on the pedal steel. Use expression events (controller 11) to perform this function.

## Feedback

No matter what equipment you're using there are ways of producing a guitar feedback sound. Firstly you must know exactly where you want your feedback to appear, then (using a spare track – possibly the same one used for twin note pitch bends as described earlier) you can place a high pitched note in position. Now use expression events (controller 11) to fade this note up underneath the chord or note (which is supposed to be 'feeding back') until it reaches the right level. If necessary, cross fade the original chord or notes down in level as the feedback note rises.

### Fall-offs or glissandos

Just as with brass instruments, a guitar can perform a fall-off by sliding the fingers down the neck. This has the effect of sounding each note or note in the chord, one semitone at a time, as the fingers slide. To achieve this effect simply copy the note or notes, and lower their pitch by one semitone at a time. You must keep repeating this until you've dropped the pitch by five or six semitones. Each time the notes drop in pitch you must reduce the velocity as the energy in the strings decreases.

## Guitar chord voicings

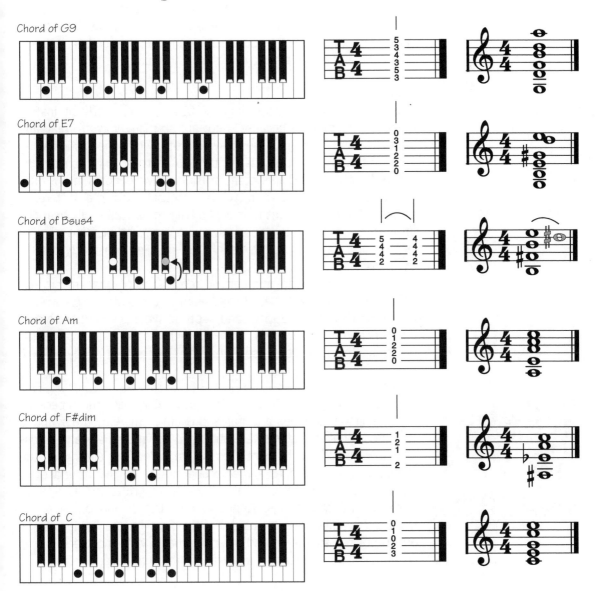

## Other instruments in the guitar family

### Ukulele

The ukulele is essentially a small four-stringed guitar, except that it can be tuned in several different ways, depending on which country it is being used in! Since there are only four notes to a ukulele chord it should be a simple method to listen and hear the notes in use. The sustain of each note will not be particularly long, as the shorter length of nylon/catgut string doesn't store energy as well as a longer guitar string.

As the GM tone set doesn't have a ukulele sound as such, try using the nylon guitar (program change 25) and adjust the decay so it is shorter than normal. The ukulele is primarily a rhythmic chord accompaniment instrument (anyone remember George Formby?) and rarely plays a solo single note passage.

### Sitar

The Indian sitar (program change 105) is a very difficult instrument to impersonate because there are so many ways to play and alter the notes. The sitar uses a system of open drone strings along with fretted notes, but there are two factors which should be noted. Firstly, the Indian system of tuning divides notes into a finer resolution than we use in western music, and the difference between them is so slight that only a trained ear can really hear the difference. Secondly, the notes always seem to be bending in pitch as they are played, so pitch bend must be used constantly to give the correct effect.

In recent years the number of recordings of sitar music has greatly increased, and they always seem to use quite a high level of reverb on them to give space and depth to what is essentially a solo instrument, since the sitar is often only accompanied by tuned drums and singing. Don't use high levels of chorus, it rarely works!

### Banjo

The banjo (program change 106) is a peculiar instrument because it falls halfway between a guitar and drum in the way the sound is amplified. While the strings are stretched down the neck and across a hollow-bodied shell, there's no sound hole. The energy of the strings is transferred to a membrane similar to that found on a snare drum or tom-tom, and it's this which vibrates the air around it to amplify the strings. Although the strings ring on much as those on a guitar, the membrane only picks up the louder attack portion of the sound, and so the banjo has a very short decay, and an unmistakable 'twangy' sound all of its own. Used in trad jazz

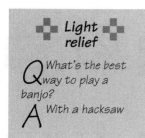

**Light relief**

*Q What's the best way to play a banjo?*

*A With a hacksaw*

and country and western music, the banjo is often found playing a rhythmic role, where it's busily 'chugging' along in the background, but when it does take the main role it often plays mixed triplets and sixteenth notes with a finger picking style where the melody is played over a picked background. If authenticity is required, try not to use reverb or chorus with this instrument as it'll often sound out of place.

The banjo rarely bends notes, although it sometimes happens, but more usually the favourite technique is to slide notes a semi-tone either side of the correct pitch by moving the finger from one fret to another, or to treat them as grace notes which are only sounded momentarily until they slur to the correct pitch. This is best done by using a single pitch bend command to jump a semi-tone to the new pitch without re-triggering the attack of the sound.

## And finally ...

The guitar (and its various cousins) is a fiddly instrument to play well, and there are so many ways to play the same note that the tone is constantly changing, even when notes follow closely. It's possible to change the tone of a note just by moving the pick to a different position along the string!

With this in mind, when sequencing to imitate the sound of a guitar, always try to listen out for what is happening on record (or what you would like to hear, if you are writing from scratch) and do your best to reproduce the 'feel' and style of the playing. Attention to detail is particularly necessary when emulating the guitar, but the results are worth it.

**Light relief**

Q *What's the range of a sitar?*

A *About twenty yards if you've got a good arm*

# 6

## Bass guitars and upright basses

### Bass basics

The bass guitar is essentially the same as the normal guitar except that it usually has only four strings (sometimes five, rarely six) which are tuned an octave lower than the four lowest guitar strings (E, A, D and G). The five-string bass usually has its extra string at the bottom, tuned to the B below E, giving it an earth rumbling bottom end. Sometimes we'll come across a six-string bass which is exactly like a guitar, but an octave lower in pitch.

Although there is no pre-defined lower limit for bass guitars, if we intend to score the part remember most bass players only use a four string bass – unless we know for certain that our bass player has access to a five or six string bass it may be prudent to play safe.

Figure 6.1 Four string bass guitar open notes

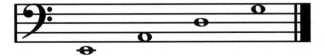

One major difference between the bass and other instruments is that reverb is hardly ever used (reverb doesn't agree very well with low rumbling sounds) The obvious exception is for any solo work it may be doing. Basses are almost always chorused however, because this has the effect of fattening and adding interest to the sound.

All the playing methods in the guitar chapter apply equally to the bass, apart from the tremolo bar, which is hardly ever used on a bass. There are, however, some styles of playing which are used only on a bass.

### Upright acoustic bass (program change 33)

The acoustic upright bass is a different instrument entirely, which developed from the orchestral contra (string) bass. The strings are often tuned differently from the bass guitar, and then again, sometimes not! As with the fretless bass guitar the upright bass can glide notes up and down in pitch. The glides don't usually sustain very long since more energy is lost to the body of the instrument, but they're used a lot in laid back, sleazy jazz styles to such an extent that over half the notes played may move as soon as they are played.

Slapping the strings against the fingerboard produces a dull slap which is used in trad jazz, rockabilly and other styles as a rhythmic 'helping-hand' to the percussion section. Often there will be one note followed by a couple of slaps in a 'boom, ta-ta, boom, ta-ta' sound. Keep this in mind when listening for style tips.

## Rock bass guitar (program change 34 and 35)

In general there are two methods of playing rock bass, either using a plectrum (pick) or fingers. As with the normal guitar, a pick will give a brighter sound with sharper attack, so choose the correct sound (program change 34 for fingered bass, and program change 35 for a picked bass).

One particular characteristic of the rock bass guitar is that it's often played as a drone where notes almost roll into each other. To actually play this on a keyboard may be more difficult than it sounds, especially if we want to emphasise certain notes, but most sequencers have a way around this called 'force legato', or sometimes just 'legato'. This function means that we can record notes in a much more staccato (normal) way, allowing us to concentrate on the velocity emphasis (where some notes are played harder than others) and rhythmic feel. The note lengths can be fixed later by setting a suitable non-overlap amount for the legato function, and applying it to the selected notes or parts.

> ### INFORMATION
>
> *The reason why we almost always use a small gap between notes (sometimes stated as a negative overlap) is so that only one note at a time is used to play the bass line. This saves polyphony. For a bigger sound, use plenty of chorus, but as before, try to avoid reverb unless it's absolutely necessary*

## Fretless bass guitar (program change 36)

Fretless basses are different from the norm because, as the name suggests, they have no frets to press the strings against when choosing a note. This gives two changes to the sound. Firstly the fretless bass sounds smoother and slightly more dull than normal because the fingers touch the strings against the neck, gently damping the sound, and secondly, because the fingers are free to slide up and down the neck, it's possible to 'glide' between notes in a very particular way. The sound of this gliding is the main characteristic of the fretless bass, and to reproduce it authentically we must use several types of pitch bend.

## Slap bass guitar (program change 37 and 38)

On a perfectly normal bass guitar, if the thumb is used to literally 'slap' or 'hit' the strings against the frets, a note will sound which has a distinct click at the start which helps to define the start of the note rhythmically and give it more emphasis. This method is usually used for the lower strings, while the complementary method for the high strings is to tug the string away from the neck and release it so that it springs back against the frets giving a short sharp twanged note.

By using these two methods together, a very fast rhythm can be maintained, along with more rhythm to push the song along. To copy this style using GM equipment, the main thing is to use one of the correct slap bass sounds. Always remember to keep the high notes short and fairly loud and a good dose of chorus effect will usually help things along nicely.

Figure 6.2 Slap bass using pitch bend

| Position | Length | Val1 | Val2 | Status |
|----------|--------|------|------|--------|
| 005.01.004 | 194 | G1 | 101 | Note |
| 005.01.190 | 92 | G1 | 95 | Note |
| 005.01.291 | 98 | G1 | 86 | Note |
| 005.03.195 | 281 | G1 | 92 | Note |
| 005.04.093 | 28 | G2 | 123 | Note |
| 005.04.186 | 35 | F2 | 119 | Note |
| 006.01.098 | 569 | G1 | 116 | Note |
| 006.02.357 | --- | 45 | 55 | Pitch Bend |
| 006.02.369 | --- | 93 | 57 | Pitch Bend |
| 006.02.375 | --- | 12 | 59 | Pitch Bend |
| 006.02.382 | --- | 56 | 62 | Pitch Bend |
| 006.03.004 | --- | 00 | 64 | Pitch Bend |
| 006.03.012 | 190 | C2 | 98 | Note |
| 006.03.285 | 25 | G2 | 125 | Note |
| 006.04.101 | 91 | F2 | 121 | Note |

Track 3 - Slap Bass   Pattern   1.   1.   0 to 9   1.   0        Quant 16    Extras

Song : BassSlap.SNG

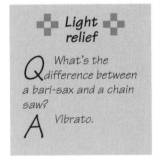

## Dance bass sounds (program changes 39 and 40)

For special bass sounds such as techno, rave, rap, acid, house etc., the choice is almost unlimited. Although there are two synth basses in the General MIDI sound set (program changes 39 and 40), it's possible to use almost any sound which gives the right feel. When looking for alternatives, try synth brass, electric piano, acoustic guitars, in fact almost any low sound with the right harmonic content.

# Drum programming

Most sequence programs have designated screens (called edit pages) which are specially designed to manipulate drum and percussion data. Drum and percussion information is normally displayed in the drum edit page.

For those musicians who prefer it, we've included conventional drum notation as well. Here's a quick run down of the notes used in case you're not familiar with them.

*Conventional drum notation*

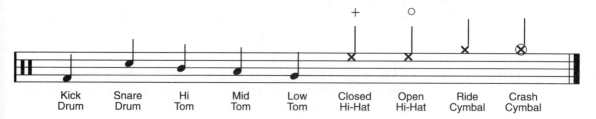

| Kick<br>Drum | Snare<br>Drum | Hi<br>Tom | Mid<br>Tom | Low<br>Tom | Closed<br>Hi-Hat | Open<br>Hi-Hat | Ride<br>Cymbal | Crash<br>Cymbal |

## Drum edit page

Figure 7.1 shows a typical example of the type of drum editor that can be found in a sequencer package.

### Instrument number (A)

Every drum, cymbal and percussion instrument can be triggered by a different note on a MIDI instrument. Each note can be referred to in two different ways. The first is to use the note name and then a number which depicts the octave that it's playing in, i.e. – C3, A#1, F#2. The second way uses note numbers.

Remember that MIDI has a note range of 128 notes – slightly more than 10 octaves. General MIDI drums utilise note numbers 35 to 81 as has one standard drum set.

Roland's GS system has a slightly larger note range (27-87) and the option of using nine different types of drum sets – Standard (1), Room (9), Power (17), Electronic (25), TR-808 (26), Jazz (33), Brush (41), Orchestra (49) and Sound Effects (57).

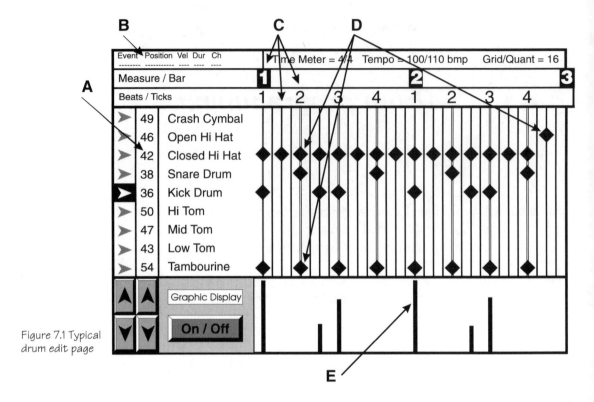

Figure 7.1 Typical
drum edit page

Yamaha XG devices have a similar specification although they do
have an extra two drum sets to choose from. When note numbers
are now substituted for instruments, note 35, for instance, would
refer to the Acoustic Kick drum, note 40 is Electric Snare, and 69
becomes the Cabasa. For a complete GM drum allocation table see
Appendix B.

### Select event bar (B)

In any edit page of a sequencer there's a considerable amount of
information available for us to digest. Sometimes the sheer weight
of this information is too much for us to comprehend at any one
time. In an effort to avoid 'information overload' some sequence
packages require the user to specifically ask for full details by
selecting or highlighting the desired event. All the information
about that event is then displayed. First to be displayed is the type
of event (note on, pitch bend, aftertouch etc.), next comes the
exact position in measures, beats and ticks, and then note velocity,
duration and finally the MIDI channel.

It's worth mentioning at this point that General MIDI dictates
that drums and percussion will use only MIDI Channel 10 for playback. Using Roland GS and Yamaha XG equipment it's possible

(using SysEx commands) to dedicate an otherwise normal channel into playing a second drum part. This would enable us for example, to use a Power kit on channel 10 and a Brush kit on channel 11.

### Measure, beat and ticks (C)

The first two lines refer to the measure (or bar) and the precise position of the instruments within it. Reading from left to right on the upper line, the white numbers 1, 2 and 3 in the black boxes refer to the current measure/bar.

Located below this is the beats/ticks line in which the numbers 1,2,3 and 4 refer to whole beats. The vertical lines between them divide each beat into four equal parts of one sixteenth note (96 ticks) each.

### Note heads (D)

Each diamond depicts the note on position of an instrument. If the apex of the diamond falls exactly on a vertical line the note would be considered to be perfectly on the beat or sub-beat. If the diamond was slightly to the left it would indicate that the note was played early and if located to the right, it was late. When we refer to the positioning of notes or events the standard protocol is to use measures, beats and ticks, therefore our second kick drum event would play at position 1/2/192

### Velocity grid (E)

This is a graphical representation of the velocity used for each note. The higher up the vertical line the louder the note will play. Velocity response between models can vary considerably. A velocity level of 64 on one machine might produce quite a loud note but the same note played on another device might sound rather weak. Study the velocity characteristics of your equipment and modify the velocity values in our examples to produce better results.

There are many things that require careful consideration when programming drums and percussion tracks. All programmers should realise that the word drums is plural and refers to a combination of different percussive instruments. At first this may seem an odd thing to mention but some people think of drums as one single unit and not as the several instruments they really are.

## Tempo

While it may seem an ideal situation for songwriters and programmers to use a sequencer to create rhythm parts which are perfectly in time, the actual musical result of having such rigidity produces

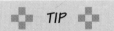

**TIP**

*If every instrument is
studied prior to
programming, the task
of creating realistic
drum parts won't seem
so intimidating as we
first thought.
Remember that a basic
drum kit comprises
nine instruments - kick
drum, snare drum, hi
hats (open and
closed), crash cymbals
and three toms (some
drummers like to
include the cowbell).
Before we start
examining each of
these instruments in
turn perhaps we should
first recognise the
importance of tempo
and rhythm.*

songs which are rather sterile and mechanical. No matter what any real drummer might say about his ability to play exactly in time throughout a song, the truth is that humans can't play that precisely. Every beat in every measure has tiny differences in tempo. These may be too small to hear individually but they can be seen quite easily in the edit pages of a sequencer.

Suppose a drummer in a band has a tendency to play the kick drum marginally late, the hi-hats slightly early, and has the annoying habit of slowing down a fraction in the middle of verses (what are you doing working with such a bozo?). If that same drummer used a MIDI drum kit these habits could be analysed and corrected accordingly. Let's take an example eight measure phrase played in 4/4 time with a sequencer tempo of 120 beats per minute. If we measured the true tempo of each measure it might be:

| Measure/bar | 1 | 2 | 3 | 4 | 5 | 6 | 7 | 8 |
|---|---|---|---|---|---|---|---|---|
| Tempo | 119 | 122 | 120 | 119 | 118 | 121 | 119 | 122 |

These tempos would still give an average result of 120BPM but we can clearly see that only measure 3 was played at exactly 120BPM. Closer examination of this perfect measure might reveal that each of the four beats in it were played with tempos 121, 117, 123 and 119 respectively.

So you see that these subtle, but constant changes in tempo go towards creating a live feel to our music. Quantising removes most, if not all, of these tiny imperfections so it should be used very carefully (see Quantising – Chapter 10).

In an effort to make songs feel alive we can change the tempo at certain sections in the song. One example of this could be:

| | |
|---|---|
| Intro | 122 |
| Verse | 120 |
| Chorus | 123 |
| Verse | 120 |
| Chorus | 123 |
| Bridge | 118 |
| Chorus | 123 |
| Chorus | 123 |
| Outro | 100  > (rall) |

Every song is unique (we hope) so tempos will vary from song to song. We might find that a song will sound better if the speed of the verses and the chorus are reversed, with verses played slightly faster than choruses. Try experimenting with different tempos but listen carefully to what feels right, as more often than not the song itself will dictate the best tempo.

**Project 1**

Put the sequencer into play mode with the audio metronome active. Play a normal audio recording of any artist and attempt to synchronise the beep of the sequencer to the music. Fine tune the speed so that after the introduction of the song we're able to set the sequencer off in time.

Examine how long it takes for the synchronisation to deteriorate. Try with different styles of music and notice that some styles stay synchronised longer than others.

**Project 2**

Put the sequencer in record mode and record two minutes of music, at 120BPM at 4/4, using the kick drum (C1 – 35) and snare drum (D1 – 37). Play the kick drum on beats 1 and 3 and play the snare on beats 2 and 4. After 30 seconds of recording disable the metronome click but still continue to record. After the recording has finished examine how much drifting took place. At a speed of 120BPM there should be exactly two notes played every second.

## Rhythm

What is rhythm? It's impossible to quantify exactly what rhythm is in clinical terms but we can soon tell when something has it or not. We do know that rhythm is made up of notes and accents working together and that all structured music has accents, both natural and artificial.

As it's probably the most common time signature (meter) used in modern music, let's start by examining music written in 4/4. The strongest beat is the first beat of each measure, next is the third beat with a medium strength and beats 2 and 4 are the weakest and are played with equal stress.

If we subdivide each beat further into eighth notes, a similar relationship also exists. The first of the pair is always stronger than

*INFORMATION*

*Some sequencer packages allow tempo changes to be entered via a tap tempo technique. This method requires the programmer to tap as close to the beat as possible using a MIDI instrument. The sequencer listens to this human tempo and creates tempo events to match. The faster the key is struck the faster the tempo becomes. This way of entering values is quite fast but erratic playing can produce disastrous results! Another relatively simple way of entering multiple tempos is by using the mouse as a tempo slider, using the mouse in a similar way to the sliders on a mixing desk. Pushing up increases the tempo and pulling down will reduce it.*

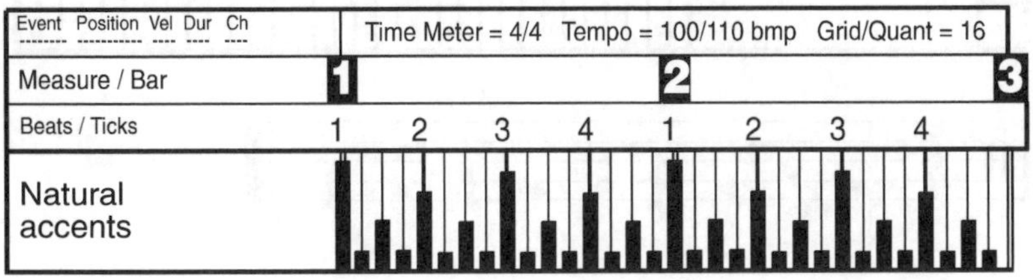


Figure 7.2 Natural accents in 4/4 time

the second. All these variations in natural accents undulate the music and start to create rhythm.

Accents (both natural and artificial) can be used to give excitement and character to our drum tracks, but if artificial accents are used too frequently they'll make the track sound cluttered. On the other hand to play safe all the time makes the track sound bland and boring.

We'll now explore some of these tricks and tips as we examine each instrument in turn.

## Kick drum

Often wrongly referred to as the bass drum, (even in the GM spec!). A bass drum is considerably larger and found in the percussion section of an orchestra.

If we understand how an organic drummer plays the kick drum this'll enable us to program more realistic parts. Imagine a drummer is playing the kick drum on beats 1 and 3 (in a 4/4 measure). To play each note they would press down hard on the kick drum pedal which throws the beater forward against the skin. Most drummers would leave the pedal depressed until it's time to play the next note. When that happens the foot is lifted off the pedal, the spring pulls the beater away from the skin and the process is repeated over.

Figure 7.3 could be thought of as one of the most basic of all kick drum patterns because it only plays on the first and third beats of each measure. Although this is a rather simple pattern it can be used to very good effect depending upon the style of music. It's particularly well suited to fast up-tempo numbers from country rock to swing.

At the marked tempo of 100-120 if additional kicks were introduced on the off beats from time to time (Figure 7.5), either mid

Figure 7.3 Basic kick drum pattern which plays on the first and third beats of each measure

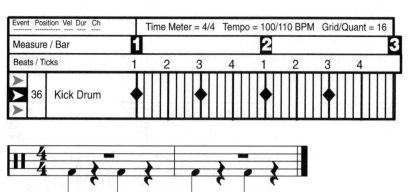

phrase or at the end of a phrase, it can enhance the song. But if the tempo starts to creep above 140 these embellishments can sometimes (but not always) get in the way. As with most up-tempo music try and keep the drums quite simple giving space to the other instruments. When working with a slow and lightly orchestrated ballad try using kick drum 2 (B0 – 35) which has less of an attack than kick drum 1.

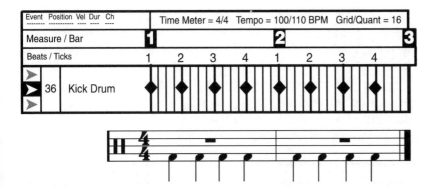

Figure 7.4 Four beats per measure provides the music with a solid pulse

The pattern in Figure 7.4 can be incorporated into light ballads and can also be used as a basis for moderate tempo disco, dance and rave rhythms. The loud and constant thump of the kick drum provides a solid pulse, ideal for these styles. As this type of music is generally heavily compressed our kick drum velocities should be fairly high and pretty even.

Figure 7.5 is a good solid pattern that can be used in a wide variety of styles and speeds. As this rhythm is very versatile, particular attention should be placed on creating the correct type of velocity characteristics.

When we examined natural accents we discussed how drummers produce notes, but, now that more notes are being introduced, the technique would begin to change. Figure 7.5 shows the kick drum not only plays on beats 1 and 3 (as Figure 7.3) but on the second

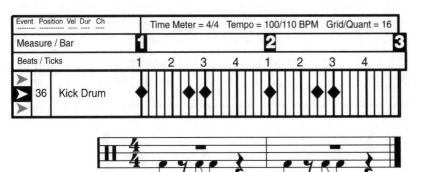

Figure 7.5 The kick drum plays on beats 1 and 3 and on the second half of the second beat and on the second half of the fourth beat

half of the second beat and on the second half of the fourth beat. When a drummer plays these kinds of rhythms, unless told otherwise, he will subconsciously aim for the dominant beat. When playing eighth notes (at 1/2/192 and 1/4/192) the pedal is used, like a diver using a springboard, to launch themselves onto the beat. This technique has a double effect of producing a strong dominant beat and a weaker off beat.

Most of us have experienced this springboard effect in our everyday lives. Think of the two syllables that we produce when we sneeze: *Ah* and *Choo* and which one is the stronger. Like most people the *Choo* is the most dominant, and as we sneeze we seem to concentrate on that syllable above the *Ah*.

Figure 7.6 could be considered a variation of Figure 7.5. Perhaps not as versatile, but it can still be used in a wide variety of situations. The double kicks on the first beat, as well the off beats, give an interesting undulation to the music.

Figure 7.6 The double kicks on the first beat and the off beats give an undulation to the music

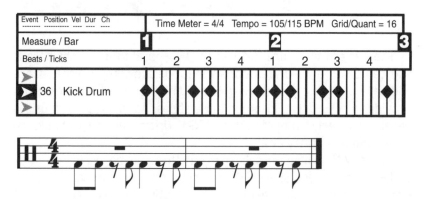

We now know that if we have an off beat leading onto a natural accented note the off beat is weak. Similarly the first of the two notes falls on the strong beat of the measure and the next eighth note falls on the weak off-beat between beats 1 and 2. As before

Figure 7.7 A funkier kick drum rhythm

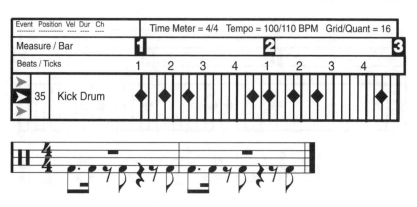

with our sneezing analogy we can also use a similar phrase – *Push Off!* (to be honest another phrase immediately sprang to mind but decency forbids its use). The *Push* would be the stronger and the *Off* the weaker.

Figure 7.7 is our most complex kick drum rhythm so far which could be incorporated into most ballads, funk or soul music. Notice that the only natural accent used here is on the first beat of each measure. The velocities of the first three notes in this particular rhythm are often played strong, weak, medium. If you don't understand this relationship refer back to the paragraph on rhythm.

## Snare drum

The snare often plays just on beats 2 and 4 (the weaker beats in a normal 4/4 measure) which acts as a kind of counter-balance to the kick drum (normally on beats 1 and 3), see Figure 7.8.

When listening to snare drum parts have you ever noticed the different tones used? The whole character of a song can change considerably if we substitute a crisp and bright snare with one that's deep and gated.

**INFORMATION**

*Snare drum 1 = note 38 (D1)*
*Snare drum 2 = note 40 (E1)*

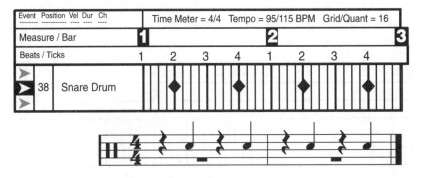

Figure 7.8 Snare drum playing on beats 2 and four

Figure 7.9 and Figure 7.10 shows us variations on our basic 2 and 4 beat pattern. Notice in Figure 7.9 there's a snare playing at position 1/2/288 (the sixteenth note just before beat 3).

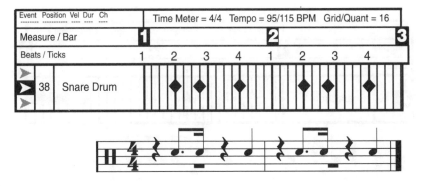

Figure 7.9 A variation on our basic 2 and 4 beat pattern

Figure 7.10 This pattern and that of Figure 7.9 are commonly found in dance music

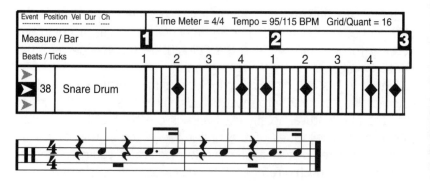

Another similar effect is created when the snare plays a sixteenth note on 1/4/288 (just before the first beat of the next measure) as in Figure 7.10. Both these snare patterns (patterns in Figures 7.9 and 7.10) are commonly found in dance and house type music.

### Snare drum fills

The snare, because of its distinctive sound, is ideal for fills and embellishments. As Figures 7.11 and 7.12 show, the fills normally occur at the end of a phrase. Notice with both fills they start around the third beat in measure 2, continue through the fourth beat and then finish, often with a crash cymbal, on the first beat of the new phrase.

Figure 7.11 A useful fill for the end of a phrase

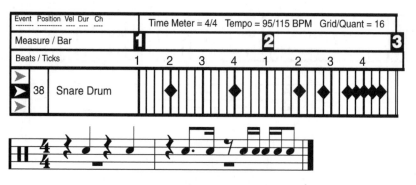

Figure 7.12 And another

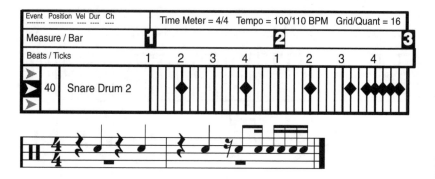

Most fills build to a climax on the first beat of the next measure but you may wonder how we can do this if the snare is already playing at a quite a substantial volume (velocity). Listen carefully and you'll notice that drummers hit the first note quite hard, rapidly drop in volume and then crescendo back to their normal level.

## Tom toms

We'll introduce the toms as this point because they're often used along with the snare to play fills. Figure 7.13 illustrates a full kit and tambourine part playing a fill at the end of a phase (measure 8) and into the beginning of a new one (measure 9). Pay particular attention to:

1 The hi-hats have stopped when our fill is underway, although there are times when they continue through (played as a foot hats) – after all drummers only have two arms don't they?
2 The crash cymbal plays on the first beat of the new phrase.
3 The toms are played in descending pitch order.

> **INFORMATION**
>
> *High tom 1 = note 50 (D2)*
> *High tom 2 = note 48 (C2)*
> *Mid tom 1 = note 47 (B1)*
> *Mid tom 2 = note 45 (A1)*
> *Low tom 1 = note 43 (G1)*
> *Low tom 2 = note 41 (F1)*

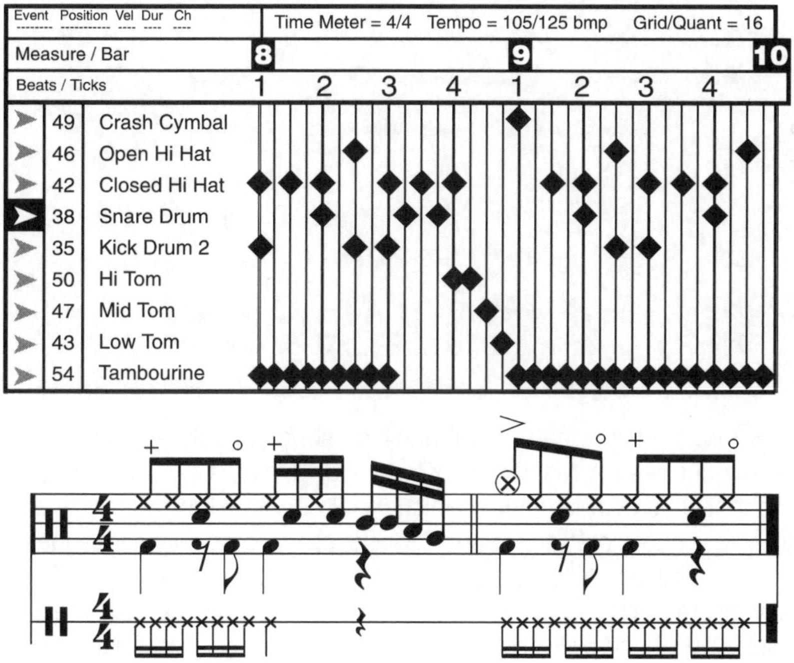


Figure 7.13 Tom tom fill at end of measure eight

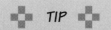 
## The roll

To program an authentic roll is probably one of the hardest disciplines to master. There are two common traps that unwary programmers often fall into. The first is using too many notes to perform the roll. Although our computer can create notes to a resolution of 64th triplets and sometimes beyond, a real drummer would use far less. The effect of using too many notes produces a horrible buzzing effect, more like a bee caught in a jam-jar. The second trap is programming a roll with flat (even) velocities which produces a horrid noise, more like a machine gun.

Both these errors can be avoided if we think of how an organic drummer produces a roll. There is physical limit to the number of notes a human can produce in any given amount of time. The number we'll have to play depends upon whether the roll is to be tight (fast) or loose (slow). The table gives a few suggestions to the spacing of notes, and therefore the number of notes, for a given selection of speeds. The lower values produce loose rolls the higher values produce tight rolls.

| | { — BPM — } | | |
|---|---|---|---|
| Ticks apart | Loose | Tight | Resolution |
| 16 | 75 to | 90 | 64th triplets |
| 24 | 90 to | 110 | 64th |
| 32 | 140 to | 170 | 32nd triplets |
| 36 | 160 to | 190 | 64th dotted |
| 48 | 180 to | 220 | 32nd |
| 72 | over | 250 | 32nd dotted |

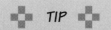 
If we wanted to create a roll and our song speed was about 120, we would need a resolution between 64th notes (which would be too fast) and 32nd triplets (which would be too slow). If we're able to create notes that are about 28 ticks apart, that may prove ideal.

Now let's examine velocities. Every person has a dominant arm. Any drummer who tries to play a roll as evenly as possible will notice one hand will always come out stronger (therefore louder) than the other.

Figure 7.14 illustrates this point and it can be seen quite clearly that every other note has a slightly reduced velocity. When programming, start with a difference of about 10 ticks and increase

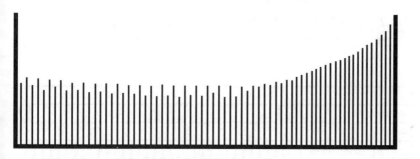

Figure 7.14 The result of one arm being stronger than the other

and decrease the values by steps of 2 listening carefully to the results. Too wide a gap makes the roll sound lumpy, too flat and we're back to our AK47!

### Variations on a roll

Figure 7.15 shows a crescendo roll. Notice the velocity differences are quite visible on the flat part of the roll and that the roll tightens up as it reaches its peak.

**TIP**

*Remember, these techniques work equally well for cymbal and tom rolls*

Figure 7.15 A crescendo roll

Hi-hats generally play the most complex and intricate patterns, frequently alternating between and mixing eighth and sixteenth notes. Our first example (Figure 7.16) is a simple but versatile hi-hat pattern of closed eighth notes.

## Hi-hats

Hi-hats generally play the most complex and intricate patterns, frequently alternating between and mixing eighth and sixteenth notes. Our first example (Figure 7.16) is a simple but versatile hi-hat pattern of closed eighth notes.

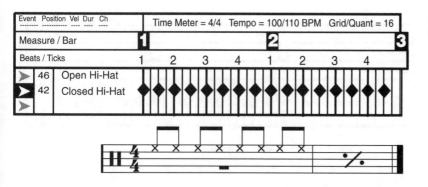

Figure 7.16 Closed hi-hat playing straight eighth notes

In Figure 7.17 we've introduced sixteenth notes into our pattern. Notice this particular pattern comprises two identical measures and beats 1 and 2 are the same as beats 3 and 4. The rhythm of one eighth note then two sixteenth notes followed by two eighth notes is repeated over. If we introduce too much variation into our drum patterns they will start to sound disjointed.

Figure 7.18 shows a typical 70's 'disco' pattern. Try alternating between the closed hi-hat and the pedal hi-hat. A drummer would stick to closed hi-hats (as written) but the tonal quality of the pedal hi-hat produces a slight (but effective) change in overall timbre.

Figure 7.17 Previous pattern with added sixteenth notes

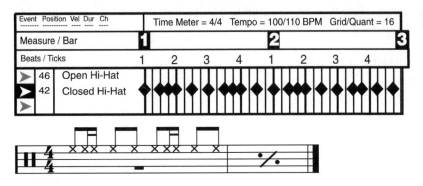

Figure 7.18 Typical 70's 'disco' pattern sixteenth notes

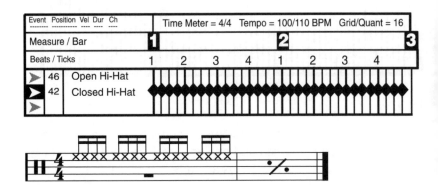

Figure 7.19 Based on Figure 7.16 but every fourth note is played open. The o above the note means open hi hat, and the + means close it again

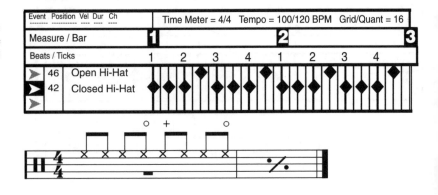

Figure 7.19 introduces an open hi-hat to create a more interest-ing and complex pattern. This pattern is based around our original Figure 7.16 pattern but notice every 4th note is played open.

Figure 7.20 shows a pattern that alternates between an open and a closed hi-hat. To hear the effect this combination produces say the word *teaser* or *pea-soup* over and over.

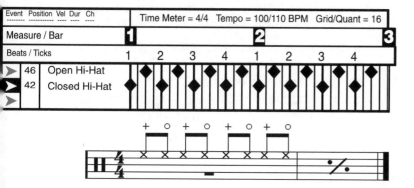

Figure 7.20 Alternating between open and closed hi=hats

Figure 7.21 is a different combination of open and closed hi-hats. Note that beats 1 and 3 are identical which we hope will pro-duce a solid foundation (as Figure 7.17) and beats 2 and 4 are giving the variety to produce an interesting and useable pattern.

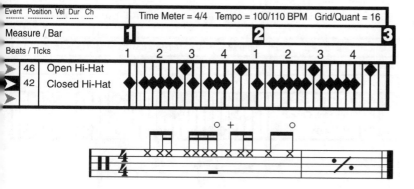

Figure 7.21 Another open and closed hi-hat pattern

# Tambourine

Probably the most versatile percussion instrument is the tam-bourine. The tambourine works well in a variety of styles. It's loose human feel in folk music differs considerably to modern dance/rave and house music where (like the hi-hats) it's played with similar (even) velocities. When programming 'human' tambourine the velocity peaks and troughs are quite extreme.

Visualise playing the tambourine in straight sixteenths, the first note (of each group of four) would be loud as this is when the tambourine first strikes the palm of the hand. The hand pulls back (note 2) which produces a quieter note and then bounces forward (note 3), this time without striking the palm. This produces a slightly louder note, and then finally the tambourine is pulled back once more for note 4 (as 2). This whole process is repeated over again for each group of 4. Velocity values for each note in a group of four might resemble 105, 38, 84 and 43.

Experiment with these suggestions for tambourine patterns:

1 If the hi-hats are playing eighth notes play sixteenth notes on tambourine (or vice versa)
2 Double the snare drum on beats 2 and 4
3 Use the tambourine to replace the hi-hats or the snare.
4 If used in ballads play only the 4th beat of each measure.

## Conga drums

Conga drums can be used to add interesting tone colour and weight to drum parts. Although conga drums are considered as being primarily a Latin percussion instrument, their versatility enables them to be used extensively in a wide variety of styles.

Conga patterns (Figures 7.22 and 7.23) often start with the higher pitched drums and descend to the lower pitched ones.

Figure 7.22 A typical conga pattern

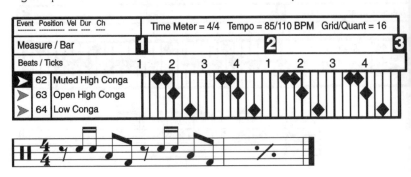

Figure 7.23 And another

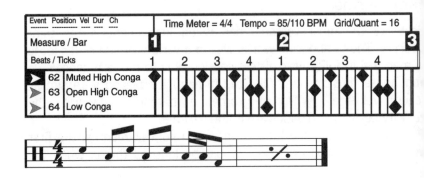

With both these patterns the substitution of other instruments should be explored. Try using bongos instead of congas or perhaps use a shaker in place of the muted high conga, cabasa for the open high conga and woodblock for the low conga.

## 12/8 time signature

All the drums and percussion examples we've examined so far have all been in a time signature (meter) of 4/4. As we know 4/4 is very popular but thankfully not all music is played that way. Shuffle, blues, R&B and swing are all styles which have a triplet (3) feel and therefore need a different meter. 12/8 is a compatible time signature as it still plays with a four in the bar feel but all the sub-divisions are triplets not duplets.

## Advanced techniques

Using just a GM or GS/XG drum kit could be considered as rather restrictive, but there are many interesting effects that can be obtained by using interesting programming techniques.

### Raising the pitch of all the drums
Insert a pitchbend command at the beginning of the track to globally raise or lower the pitch of all the drums. Ensure that the range isn't too excessive or the quality of the samples will deteriorate rapidly.

### Change the pitch of individual drums
Pitching individual instruments on GS/XG equipment can be achieved by using control codes. For an in depth discussion of RPNs (registered parameter numbers) and N-RPNs (non registered parameter numbers) refer to Chapter 12. To experiment with changing the pitch of a drum enter these following commands into the sequencer:

| Val 1 | Val 2 |
|-------|-------|
| 99 | 24 |
| 98 | xx (xx refers to the instrument number (i.e. 54 = tambourine) |
| 6 | yy (yy refers to how many semitones to change the instrument by. Each step equal to 1 semitone - 64 is the default setting) |
| 99 | 127 |
| 98 | 127 |

### Cymbal rolls

It's difficult to produce a good cymbal roll if the samples on the instrument don't have the capability of being re-triggered. Before a cymbal can play the second note it will have to stop playing the first. This stop – start routine produces a slight hic sound every time. One way to overcome this would be to use two different crash cymbals (#49 & #57). Cymbal 1 would continue to sound when cymbal 2 is struck and vice versa. This overlapping of notes will help produce a more genuine roll.

Alternatively it should be noted that some devices allow a part to have a different assign mode setting (not to be confused with the mode setting in a MIDI implementation chart). There are basically three types of assign mode which can be modified using system exclusive commands, single, limited, and full multi.

Each assign mode refers to the way a note responds if it encounters another note of the same pitch being played while it's still sounding. The Roland GS default is single assign mode, which means that, if a note is played and then the same note is retriggered before the first has finished, it will stop playing it and play the second.

Limited assign mode allows two notes of the same pitch to be played simultaneously (a third occurrence of the same note will then stop the first) while full-multi assign mode allows multi retriggering of a note.

Using full-multi assign mode will prevent previous notes from cutting short allowing notes to roll into one another. This technique does allow for the creation of realistic cymbal rolls but it plays havoc with our polyphony.

When I use these modes I normally select full-multi assign mode just before the roll begins and as soon as the roll is underway (after 3 or 4 notes) I switch back to single assign mode and use the ringing on of the first few notes to carry me through. For a detailed examination of system exclusive commands refer to Chapter 12.

*Roland assign modes*

| | |
|---|---|
| Single assign mode ( default) | F0, 41, 10, 42, 12, 40, 10, 14, 00, 1C, F7 |
| Limited assign mode | F0, 41, 10, 42, 12, 40, 10, 14, 01, 1B, F7 |
| Full-multi assign mode | F0, 41, 10, 42, 12, 40, 10, 14, 02, 1A, F7 |

### Use a second drum part

Second drum part in GS/XG. The only way to create another drum kit in GS/XG is via system exclusive commands (refer to Chapter 12). Below are two such messages. The first will produce a kit on MIDI channel (part) 9 the second on MIDI channel (part) 11. Both messages are displayed with decimal and hex values.

*Roland GS*

| Kit on Part 9 | Hex | 41,10,42,12,40,19,15,02,16 |
|---|---|---|
| | Dec | 65,16,66,18,64,25,21, 2,16 |
| Kit on Part 11 | Hex | 41,10,42,12,40,1A,15,02,0F |
| | Dec | 65,16,66,18,64,26,21, 2,15 |

*Yamaha XG*

| Kit on Part 9 | Hex | 43, 10, 4C, 08, 08, 07, 03 |
|---|---|---|
| | Dec | 67, 16, 76, 08, 08, 07, 03 |
| Kit on Part 11 | Hex | 43, 10, 4C, 09, 0A, 07, 03 |
| | Dec | 67, 16, 76, 09, 10, 07, 03 |

## Adding snare and kick drum slapback echoes

Imagine you want to produce the effect of an echoed or double struck drum. If the source track was duplicated and delayed (played slightly later) with a reduced volume, the results are quite acceptable. At a tempo of 100BPM try delaying the drum by about 70 ticks (in a resolution of 384) and reduce its velocity by about 25 steps.

| Snare | 2. 1. 0 to 3. 1. 0 | Quant 16 | Extras | ♪ ♪ |
|---|---|---|---|---|
| Position | Length Val1 Val2 Status | 2 | 2  3  4 | 3 |
| 002.02.000 | 16  D1  78  Note | | | ▲ |
| 002.02.075 | 16  D1  38  Note | | | |
| 002.04.000 | 16  D1  89  Note | | | |
| 002.04.068 | 16  D1  43  Note | | | ▼ |
| Song : Snare.SNG | | ◄ | ► | ♪ |

*Slapback echoes*

## Double strike the snare

To create an interesting double strike sound (on the snare for instance), duplicate the track and play both of them together. The interaction of this double hit (using the same sample) can produce interesting results. If you intend using this technique you must

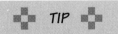

*If you experience real trouble producing a good cymbal roll you can always wimp out and use the Reverse Cymbal patch on another MIDI channel (program change 120)*

ensure that you use a separate track for the duplicate snare. Many sequencers become very upset if they see duplicate notes in the same track and any MIDI files created from this kind of data could be corrupted.

### Turning sounds off

All drum, cymbal and percussion notes are assigned into groups. The rules of this grouping dictate that no two members of it can be sounded simultaneously (see previous section on cymbal rolls). If an instrument in a group is playing a note and another instrument of the same group is also played the sound of the first instrument will be truncated and the second would sound.

If we needed to stop/choke an open hi-hat from ringing on, we could insert either a closed hi-hat or a semi closed hi-hat immediately after the open hi-hat and give it a velocity of 1. This very low velocity will stop the sound of the open hi-hat (as we want it to do), but as its velocity is so low we won't actually hear it.

No two members of the same group can be sounded simultaneously

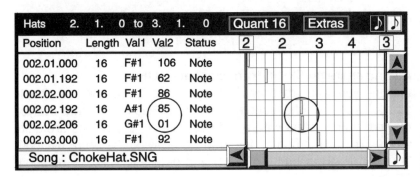

### Snare flams

When creating a snare flam remember the leading note (*acciaccatura* to all the theory junkies) should have a quieter attack (velocity) than the principal note.

## Rhythm styles

The next eleven examples are complete patterns suitable for use in a wide variety of styles. Use them as a basis to work from but experiment and change them to produce your own unique variations.

### Rock 1

Rock 1 uses a combination of examples we have described earlier. The kick drum is playing the pattern in Figure 7.5, Figure 7.8 provides the snare drum and a combination of Figures 7.16 and 7.19 the hi-hat pattern.

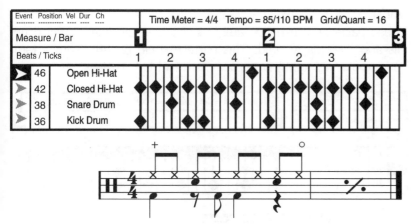

Figure 7.24 Rock 1

## Rock 2

Rock 2. This pattern could also be used as a disco rhythm. Notice the interesting syncopation around beat 3.

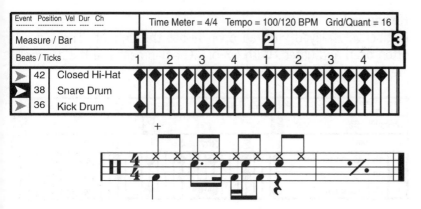

Figure 7.25 Rock 2

## Disco

A true disco beat. The (in)famous open and closed hi-pattern and kick on each beat. Make sure the open hi-hats are not too loud in the mix. This is a common programming fault and should be avoided.

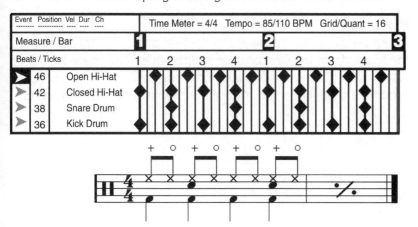

Figure 7.26 Disco beat

## House

House patterns are deliberately played machine like. Snare drum fills are particularly rigid. This pattern could benefit from a tambourine playing eighth notes against the hi-hat sixteens.

Figure 7.27 House

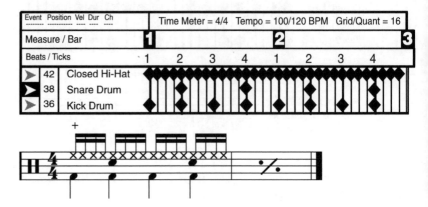

## Heavy rock

Distinctively played with an open hi-hat throughout. The snare is often deep and gated. With GS or XG equipment use the appropriate rock kit.

Figure 7.28 Heavy rock

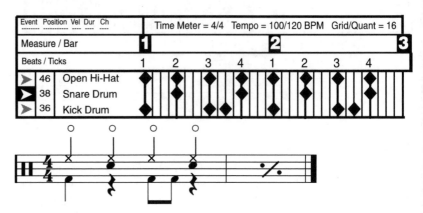

## Bluegrass

Bluegrass patterns are played quite fast and characteristically use the snare drum to play constant eighth notes. The snare should be played with heavy accents played on the second and fourth beats to produce a train like effect. Notice the simple hi-hat and kick parts.

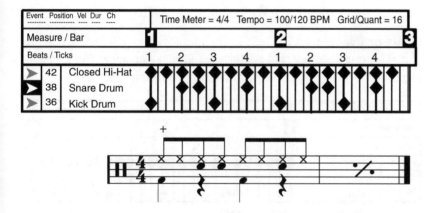

Figure 7.29 Bluegrass

## Rock 'n roll

Rock 'n roll. Typical of Chuck Berry in the 50's, this pattern gets its feel from the snare which plays double eighth notes on beat 2.

Figure 7.30 Rock 'n roll

## Jazz waltz

Although often written with a meter of 3/4 the Jazz waltz should be played in 9/8 with swing or doobie quavers. A good effect can be obtained if the snare part is replaced by a brush tap.

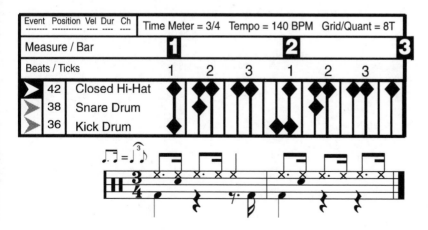

Figure 7.31 Jazz waltz

## 5/4 time

Synonymous with the 'Mission Impossible' theme or Dave Brubeck's 'Take 5'. This style does lend itself very well to the jazz idiom. To grasp the feel of 5/4 think of it as a measure of 3/4 followed by a measure of 2/4.

Figure 7.32 5/4 time

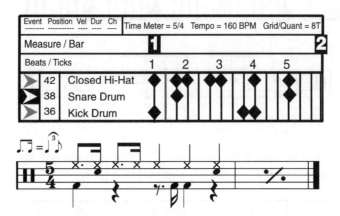

## Blues or jive

If played quite slowly this pattern could just get away for a bluesy piece. A more up-tempo version would produce a jive.

Figure 7.33 Blues or jive

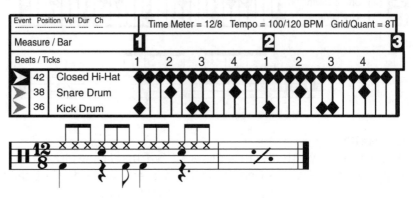

## Swing

With nearly all 12/8 patterns the triplet feel is produced by the cymbals. When programming swing style use the ride cymbal or closed hi-hat and use the rim-shot (stick across) instead of a snare drum. For accents and phrasing however, deliberately switch back to the snare to deliver that extra 'punch'.

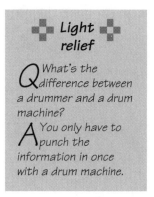

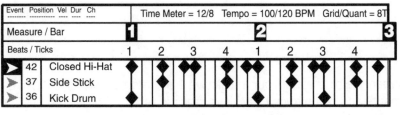

Figure 7.34 Swing

# *Wind instruments*

When we're creating our music we'll be using a variety of instruments and techniques to achieve realistic results. To get the best, a basic understanding of orchestration and a knowledge of an instrument's characteristics is essential. This chapter concentrates on examining how to program wind instruments.

## Brass

A real brass section comprises trumpets, trombones and saxophones. The timbre (tonal quality) of this sound is very bright and punchy so it should be used carefully. One of the most important considerations should be the range we intend to use it in. If it plays too low (below C in the bass stave – note number 48) its tone soon begins to break up. At the other extreme, too high (say, the G above top C – note number 91) the sound becomes thin and reedy.

Figure 8.1 Octave stab

One common technique, and particular to brass is the stab (sometimes also referred to as a punch or shot chord). A stab (Figure 8.1) should be considered as a musical exclamation mark and it sounds bright and punchy if it's played in unison octaves and played in a range which produces the brightest sound (the higher up its working range the better).

We can also play stabs as full chords (Figure 8.2) which increases tonal weight, but take care, if it's played too low for the patch it'll produce a rather muddy effect. Voicing of stabs can be of utmost importance. As we can see in Figure 8.2, the top two Cs

Figure 8.2 Full chord stab

are an octave apart and don't have the third or fifth degree of the chord between them. If we wanted to add a bit of bottom (bari sax or trombone) we could safely add the G below middle C (note number 55) and the root note C (note number 48). Notice I deliberately omitted the E (note number 52). Playing thirds in the bass register doesn't work very well. Notice Figure 8.3 uses a combination of legato and staccato notes.

Figure 8.3 The ring shows legato notes followed by staccato notes

| Track 4 - Power Brass | Pattern | 1. | 1. | 0 to 9. | 1. | 0 | Quant 16 | Extras |
|---|---|---|---|---|---|---|---|---|
| Position | Length | Val1 | Val2 | Status | | | | |
| 007.02.002 | 95 | G3 | 105 | Note | | | | |
| 007.02.103 | 92 | A3 | 92 | Note | | | | |
| 007.02.195 | 50 | C3 | 98 | Note | | | | |
| 007.02.290 | 47 | D4 | 106 | Note | | | | |
| 007.03.099 | 48 | G5 | 105 | Note | | | | |
| 007.03.104 | 52 | G4 | 94 | Note | | | | |
| 007.03.290 | 49 | G5 | 112 | Note | | | | |
| 007.03.294 | 54 | G4 | 86 | Note | | | | |
| 007.04.196 | 46 | G5 | 123 | Note | | | | |
| 007.04.197 | 54 | G4 | 98 | Note | | | | |
| 007.04.286 | 51 | G5 | 126 | Note | | | | |
| 007.07.288 | 49 | G4 | 104 | Note | | | | |

Song : BrassEx3.SNG

## Trumpets and trombones

Apart from their obvious solo work, the combined sounds of the trumpet and trombone may be better employed for ensemble and sectional work than our brass patch. If we use trumpets and trombones for playing stabs and riffs we must consider that their combined sound is slightly softer than the brass patch and should be used accordingly.

If you want to create an interesting brass combination, and if you have an available empty MIDI channel, try sitting a single brass note on top of an existing trumpet and trombone figure.

Using Figure 8.3 as an example you might let the trumpet and trombones play the four sixteenth notes on beat two as normal, but you might want to add the extra punch the brass patch will give us, on the octave G's.

## Swells

A sustained chord which crescendos (moves from quiet to loud) or diminuendos (loud to quiet) produces an interesting change in tonal colour. Changing the volume mid-way in a note's duration is achieved by using Expression (controller 11) events.

Figure 8.4(a) A crescendo using a *logarithmic* curve. If at all possible use a logarithmic curve as much as possible as this emulates more closely the natural responses of the human ear. All volume knobs on amplifiers use logarithmic pots.

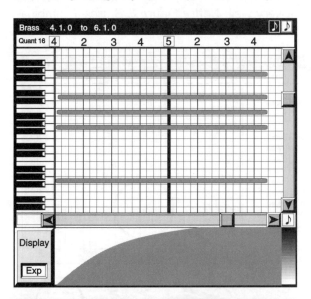

Figure 8.4(b) A diminuendo using a *linear* line

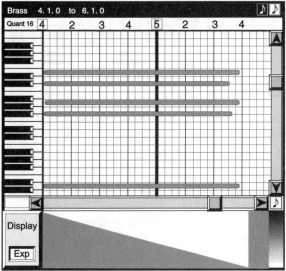

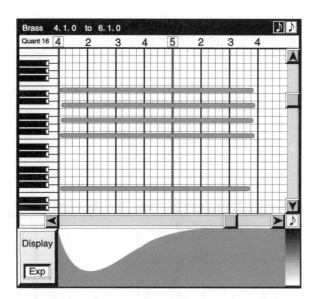

Figure 8.4(c) A *forte – piano* and *crescendo*. The chord is played initially loud (*forte*) and then it immediately drops down in volume (*piano*) and it then increases back up in volume (*crescendos*) to its optimum level.

The distance between each of the expression events will depend upon the speed of the song and the amount of smoothness you require. For slower songs (under 75 BPM) a gap of about one 64th note between each event will probably be enough to produce a smooth change. At higher speeds, say above 140 BPM, a gap of one 32nd triplet per event will probably suffice.

Notice that in Figure 8.4(a), because we intend to produce a crescendo, we must first lower our initial expression level to a point just before the notes start. This event can be inserted just a few ticks to a full 16th note before. When producing a diminuendo effect notice the final expression command which returns the part to full volume (controller 11 set to 127) comes not only after the note has stopped playing but after any natural reverb or other residual effects have died away. Failure to remember this will produce an annoying hic when the voice (instrument) returns to its maximum volume if it's still sounding.

## Vibrato

Expressive lead lines can be warmed using vibrato. When we hear a singer (a good one) hold a sustained note, the note starts clean and then, once the pitch is established, vibrato is gradually introduced. The easiest method of producing vibrato is by using the modulation command (controller 1). If we do use modulation this way we could fall foul if our song is played on a different instrument with a differing vibrato rate. Our wonderfully expressive part could end up having a vibrato so wide and fast it might resemble a goat dur-

**TIP**

Avoid using expression events with too fine a resolution for a couple of good reasons. The first is that there comes a point when some events won't make any audible difference (who can really tell the difference between an expression level of 67 and 68?). The second reason is that too much controller data hinders the effectiveness of the software and could result in MIDI choking.

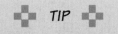
Figure 8.5(a) Modulation events to simulate vibrato

ing the height of the mating season, or it might be so slow that the note wanders painfully between flat and sharp.

With modulation events we can call upon its 128 steps to achieve our effect. A value of 0 is min and 127 is max. When we come to use modulation we don't need to ramp all 127 steps to produce vibrato. Acceptable results can be produced using just half a dozen.

Notice that we've used only four control messages to produce our vibrato effect (25,36,47,54). As we near the end of the note the next two values (32 and 15) return the note to a more stable

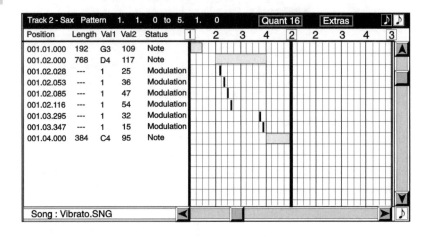

| Track 2 - Sax   Pattern   1.   1.   0 to 5.   1.   0 | | | | | Quant 16 | Extras | ♪ ♪ |

| Position | Length | Val1 | Val2 | Status |
|----------|--------|------|------|--------|
| 001.01.000 | 192 | G3 | 109 | Note |
| 001.02.000 | 768 | D4 | 117 | Note |
| 001.02.028 | --- | 1 | 25 | Modulation |
| 001.02.053 | --- | 1 | 36 | Modulation |
| 001.02.085 | --- | 1 | 47 | Modulation |
| 001.02.116 | --- | 1 | 54 | Modulation |
| 001.03.295 | --- | 1 | 32 | Modulation |
| 001.03.347 | --- | 1 | 15 | Modulation |
| 001.04.000 | 384 | C4 | 95 | Note |

Song : Vibrato.SNG

Figure 8.5(b) How vibrato is shown traditionally

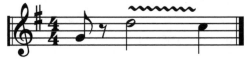

condition. The final value (left at 15) could have been set to 0 to completely remove all traces of vibrato, but I prefer to leave a minimal amount just to warm the sound slightly.

If we rely upon modulation to produce our vibrato effect we can, with GS and XG instruments, use non registered parameter numbers to configure three aspects of our modulation effect. The three parameters we can alter are vibrato rate, vibrato depth and vibrato delay. Examples and an in depth discussion of NRPNs can be found in Chapter 12.

Another way of producing vibrato is to use small amounts of pitch bend information to produce the wavering effect. Pitch bend vibrato is a lot more difficult to program, so unless there is a specific need to use this technique (which is vital to the song) try and avoid it if at all possible.

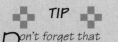

# Slurs

One textbook definition of a slur is 'a line placed over a note or series of notes to indicate they should be played smoothly'. Every time we play a new note we always get a tick, hick, clank, clonk, or whatever every time. The attack of a note is no problem for a vast majority of the time but there might be occasions when we don't want to hear it.

Let's suppose we wanted to slur down from a C to an A (as Figure 8.6 shows). The only way of producing a truly authentic slur would be to use pitch bend events. We would first extend the C to be twice its normal length and then, at the desired time point (beat 3), insert a pitch bend of the correct value which lowers the pitch exactly three semitones.

Figure 8.6(a) Traditional notation for a slur

Figure 8.6(b) Slur using pitch bend events

| Track 8 - Alto Sax  Pattern  2.  1.  0 to 6.  1.  0 | | | | Quant 16 | | Extras | |
|---|---|---|---|---|---|---|---|
| Position | Length | Val1 | Val2 | Status | | | |
| 002.01.000 | 1536 | C3 | 115 | Note | | | |
| 002.03.000 | --- | 15 | 48 | Pitch Bend | | | |
| 003.01.048 | --- | 00 | 64 | Pitch Bend | | | |

Song : PitchX-1.SNG

At the end of the note A we would insert another pitch bend command to return the altered note back to normal. (For a further explanation of pitch bend commands see Chapter 12.) The amount of pitch bend to use is critical and if we're just a few degrees out from true we'll produce notes that'll be out of tune.

Figure 8.7 is more complex but the same principle applies. Saxophones and other woodwind instruments produce particularly good results.

| Track 8 - Tenor Sax  Pattern  1.  1.  0 to 9.  1.  0 | | | | Quant 16 | | Extras | |
|---|---|---|---|---|---|---|---|
| Position | Length | Val1 | Val2 | Status | | | |
| 004.01.000 | 192 | C3 | 101 | Note | | | |
| 004.01.192 | 384 | C3 | 95 | Note | | | |
| 004.01.192 | 384 | E3 | 86 | Note | | | |
| 004.02.000 | 384 | C4 | 92 | Note | | | |
| 004.02.192 | --- | 15 | 48 | Pitch Bend | | | |
| 004.02.382 | --- | 00 | 64 | Pitch Bend | | | |
| 004.03.000 | 661 | G3 | 116 | Note | | | |
| 005.01.000 | 1152 | C4 | 103 | Note | | | |
| 005.01.096 | --- | 104 | 74 | Pitch Bend | | | |
| 005.01.192 | --- | 00 | 64 | Pitch Bend | | | |
| 005.01.288 | --- | 98 | 58 | Pitch Bend | | | |
| 005.01.381 | --- | 00 | 64 | Pitch Bend | | | |
| 005.02.000 | 746 | G3 | 98 | Note | | | |

Song : My_Song.SNG

Figure 8.7(a) More complex example of using pitch bend events to create slurs

Figure 8.7(b) Traditional
display of Figure 8.7 (a)

## Bends and glisses

We've all heard the bends and glisses that instrumental players use naturally to enhance their performance. Before we attempt to program them we must be able to determine which is which.

### Bend

A bend is a pitch sweeping effect applied to a note. The bent note can have a bend applied to it as it is initially played or as it finishes – or even midway. For blowers this is produced by the player altering their embouchure (chops) and changing the amount of lip pressure used to create the note. If a weak pressure is applied the note will start off sounding quite flat but, as the player increases the amount of pressure, the note is lifted into tune. Alternatively at the end of a note (that's being played in tune) the pressure is reduced and the note falls in pitch – a favourite for the trombone.

### Bend to ...

If you need to produce a smooth bend up to a note, use the following codes. The values under columns Tick A and Tick B refer to the tick points only so remember to insert the measure and beat numbers before them. Note: These values will work only if the pitch bend range is set to plus or minus 12 semi-tones.

Tick A is based around a resolution of 4 ticks per event which will probably suffice for bends within a tempo range of about 100 to 140 BPM. If you want to produce bends for slower songs, use column Tick B which has a smaller resolution of 3 ticks. I suggest creating two further bend templates, one with a resolution of 2 ticks and one with 5. When they're all created you can save them, as small parts, patterns or MIDI files, and import them into a track when they're needed.

Notice we're not just using pitch bend information but we're also using expression (controller 11) events to temper the attack of the note. If you listen very carefully to a bend you'll notice the note starts slighter quieter than normal and builds up in volume after a few millseconds. Figure 8.8 shows the relationship graphically between expression commands and pitch bend events.

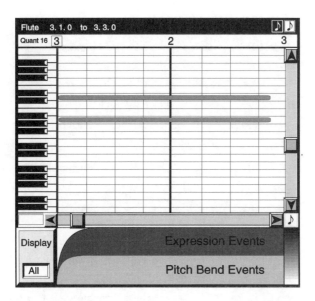

Figure 8.8 Expression and pitch bend relationship

## Bend templates

| Tick A +4 | Tick B +3 | Status | Val | Status | Val1 | Val2 |
|---|---|---|---|---|---|---|
| 000 | (000) | Control 11 | 113 | | | |
| 000 | (000) | ..................... | | Pitch bend | 00 | 57 |
| 004 | (003) | Control 11 | 114 | | | |
| 008 | (006) | ..................... | | Pitch bend | 64 | 57 |
| 012 | (009) | Control 11 | 115 | | | |
| 016 | (012) | ..................... | | Pitch bend | 00 | 58 |
| 020 | (015) | Control 11 | 116 | | | |
| 024 | (018) | ..................... | | Pitch bend | 64 | 58 |
| 028 | (021) | Control 11 | 117 | | | |
| 032 | (024) | ..................... | | Pitch bend | 00 | 59 |
| 036 | (027) | Control 11 | 118 | | | |
| 040 | (030) | ..................... | | Pitch bend | 64 | 59 |
| 044 | (033) | Control 11 | 119 | | | |
| 048 | (036) | ..................... | | Pitch bend | 00 | 60 |
| 052 | (039) | Control 11 | 120 | | | |
| 056 | (042) | ..................... | | Pitch bend | 64 | 60 |

**Bend templates (cont)**

| Tick A +4 | Tick B +3 | Status | Val | Status | Val1 | Val2 |
|---|---|---|---|---|---|---|
| 060 | (045) | Control 11 | 121 | | | |
| 064 | (048) | ............................. | | Pitch bend | 00 | 61 |
| 068 | (051) | Control 11 | 122 | | | |
| 072 | (054) | ............................. | | Pitch bend | 64 | 61 |
| 076 | (057) | Control 11 | 123 | | | |
| 080 | (060) | ............................. | | Pitch bend | 00 | 62 |
| 084 | (063) | Control 11 | 124 | | | |
| 088 | (066) | ............................. | | Pitch bend | 64 | 62 |
| 092 | (069) | Control 11 | 125 | | | |
| 096 | (072) | ............................. | | Pitch bend | 00 | 63 |
| 100 | (075) | Control 11 | 126 | | | |
| 104 | (078) | ............................. | | Pitch bend | 64 | 63 |
| 108 | (081) | Control 11 | 127 | | | |
| 112 | (081) | ............................. | | Pitch bend | 00 | 64 |

(Controller and pitch bend information is printed offset for clarity only)

**TIP**

Using bends this way can significantly enhance instrumental solos and/or lead lines, but knowing exactly where to place (paste) them makes all the difference. In any phrase or series of notes there'll be a few notes that appear so obvious for treatment they'll stand out from the rest.

Figure 8.9 is a simple two bar phrase. The two notes marked with an asterisk lend themselves to upward bends. The F at 5/1/192 marked in brackets (*) might be enhanced if you give it a tweak either using pitch bends or inserting a grace note just before it. The amount of embellishment to use depends on the speed and style of the song. To get really mushy try a bend off from the C in the first measure to the G on the first beat of the next.

Figure 8.9(a) A simple two measure phrase ready for the treatment

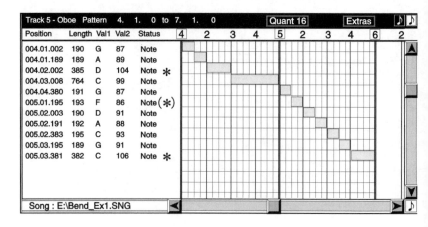

Figure 8.9(b) Traditional notation

## Bend off (er, 'bend down' doesn't sound quite right does it?)

If you look at the values listed below you'll notice the value for our expression controller falls to 62 (just below half its maximum value). The reason the expression level falls this low is to conserve realism. When a player bends off a note we hear the note starting to fall away but we never actually hear exactly when and where it finishes do we? The sound disappears into nothingness. When it's finished the last expression event is increased back up to 127 which returns the track, and all the notes following, back to normal.

The insertion of the fall has to be absolutely precise to ensure it works correctly. Depending on the sophistication of your software it may prove a little difficult to paste these codes to start exactly on tick 246 (the first event in the series), so we've introduced our anchor code system. Notice our anchor (controller 11, value 127) is at position 192 and this should be considered to be the starting point of our complete string of events. If you now paste from position x/x/192 the complete series of codes will be inserted correctly. If you can't insert these events on a 192 tick point, move the anchor to tick position 000 (on the beat) and paste from there.

**TIPS**

*As with our previous example the values in brackets are for bends with a resolution of 4 and 3 ticks respectively. Program these, repeating the process using a 2 and 5 tick spacing, and save them for future use.*

### Bend templates

| Tick A +4 | Tick B +3 | Status | Val | Status | Val1 | Val2 |
|---|---|---|---|---|---|---|
| 192 | (192) | Control 11 | 127 | | | |
| 246 | (282) | .......................... | | Pitch bend | 64 | 63 |
| 254 | (285) | .......................... | | Pitch bend | 00 | 63 |
| 262 | (288) | .......................... | | Pitch bend | 64 | 62 |
| 266 | (291) | Control 11 | 123 | | | |
| 270 | (294) | .......................... | | Pitch bend | 00 | 62 |
| 274 | (297) | Control 11 | 121 | | | |
| 278 | (300) | .......................... | | Pitch bend | 64 | 61 |
| 282 | (303) | Control 11 | 118 | | | |
| 286 | (307) | .......................... | | Pitch bend | 00 | 61 |
| 290 | (310) | Control 11 | 116 | | | |

**Bend templates (cont)**

| Tick A +4 | Tick B +3 | Status | Val | Status | Val1 | Val2 |
|---|---|---|---|---|---|---|
| 294 | (313) | ........................... | | Pitch bend | 64 | 60 |
| 298 | (316) | Control 11 | 113 | | | |
| 302 | (319) | ........................... | | Pitch bend | 00 | 60 |
| 306 | (322) | Control 11 | 111 | | | |
| 310 | (325) | ........................... | | Pitch bend | 64 | 59 |
| 314 | (328) | Control 11 | 106 | | | |
| 318 | (331) | ........................... | | Pitch bend | 00 | 59 |
| 322 | (334) | Control 11 | 102 | | | |
| 326 | (337) | ........................... | | Pitch bend | 64 | 58 |
| 330 | (340) | Control 11 | 99 | | | |
| 334 | (343) | ........................... | | Pitch bend | 00 | 58 |
| 338 | (346) | Control 11 | 91 | | | |
| 342 | (349) | ........................... | | Pitch bend | 64 | 57 |
| 346 | (352) | Control 11 | 84 | | | |
| 350 | (355) | ........................... | | Pitch bend | 00 | 57 |
| 352 | (358) | Control 11 | 77 | | | |
| 358 | (361) | ........................... | | Pitch bend | 64 | 56 |
| 362 | (364) | Control 11 | 70 | | | |
| 366 | (367) | ........................... | | Pitch bend | 00 | 56 |
| 370 | (370) | Control 11 | 62 | | | |
| | | | | *** GAP *** | | |
| 380 | (380) | ........................... | | Pitch bend | 00 | 64 |
| 380 | (380) | Control | 11 | 127 | | |

Notice the deliberate gap between 370 and 380. The last two events (pitch bend centre and expression maximum) are placed just before the start of the following beat. If these codes are used on a slow decaying instrument the length of the played note may be shortened slightly enabling the natural ambience of the sound's decay to continue the illusion. A full value length might produce that horrid hic as the note resets itself.

## Glisses

Trumpet, saxophones and most of the other woodwinds use notes instead of pitch bend information when they fall off a note.

Figure 8.10, shows us a typical note fall off. Notice that each of the smaller descending notes overlaps the preceding one by a small amount and their velocity decreases rapidly. The starting velocity of our first fall off note is considerably lower than the principal note. Remember a gliss is an effect and the secondary notes shouldn't really have any recognisable substance. Don't use too many notes otherwise it'll ruin the effect.

Figure 8.10(a) Traditional view of a note fall off

Figure 8.10(b) A note fall off

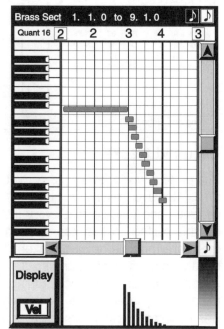

## Echo effects

Lead lines can be enhanced by applying small amounts of echo. As Figure 8.11 shows, the brass line is playing a group of four sixteenth notes (G3, D4, C4 and B3). On beats two and three in the same measure the D, C and B are repeated over.

Figure 8.11(a) Echo effects

This technique, used at the end of a riff of some kind, can sound quite effective. The echoed notes should diminuendo rapidly – as the grid clearly shows. Interesting variations can be achieved if (i) each echo (group of three) is transposed up or down an octave or (ii) each echo is placed in a different part of the audio spectrum using panning (controller 10) information.

*Figure 8.11(b) Echo effects (use of diminuendo is effective here, see reducing velocity values)*

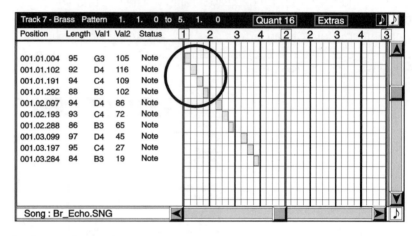

## Detuned tracks

In a perfect world, every player would play perfectly in tune all the time. However reality is quite different. Our MIDI module was designed and built so that every instrument is in perfect tune and it's this perfection that can sometimes produce a sterile sound. If there are multiple brass or saxophone tracks try inserting a pitch bend command right at the start (after the set-up codes) to shift (normally lower) the overall tuning of the track. Don't change the pitch too drastically but a mere suggestion of a different pitch (say 64, 63) can thicken the track and produce a more live sound. (Pitchbend range set to 12 semi-tones. The 64 is the fine tuning and the 63 is the coarse tuning values.)

## Grace notes (acciaccaturas)

Not all embellishments are produced by pitch bend commands, and one common exception for blowers is the grace note. A grace note is a small duration note which is crushed onto the principal note. Try saying the word *Chum* and you'll get the idea. The *Ch* is the grace note and the *um* is the principal note. Notice the *um* is the most dominant (and longer sounding) of the two, so the grace note should be played with a weaker velocity value. Try mixing combinations of sweeps, bends and grace notes to produce character and style to solo passages.

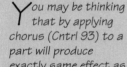

**TIP**

*You may be thinking that by applying chorus (Cntrl 93) to a part will produce exactly same effect as detuning with pitch bend, I've tried it and it doesn't!*

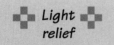

**Light relief**

*Q What's the difference between a tailor and a trombone player?*

*A The tailor tucks up the frills.*

# 9 ♥

# *Strings*

Within the GM standard, there are quite a few string sounds available for us to use. These include solo sounds – violin, viola, cello and contrabass (program changes 41 to 44) as well as ensemble sounds – tremolo strings, pizzicato strings (program changes 45 and 46), string ensemble 1 – normal attack, string ensemble 2 – slow attack, synth strings 1 and synth strings 2 (program changes 49 to 52). Each sound has its own individual characteristics.

The solo string voices sound better when they're limited to non symphonic classical music – string quartets etc., but there may be times when floating a 'solo' string sound over 'ensemble' strings will add refreshing tone colour.

## Ensemble strings

Playing pad string parts is quite different to playing piano parts – the same can be said for pad synth parts. If a note is common to adjacent chords try sustaining the note through. This technique produces a smoother performance than re-playing every note in a chord change.

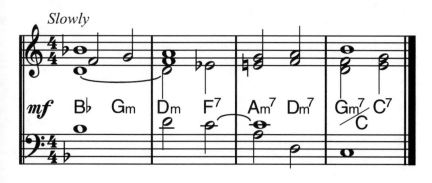

Figure 9.1 Sustained notes produce a smoother effect

## Programming tips

### Advancing/delaying tracks

String pads sound quite effective if played legato (full length) by slow attack strings or synth strings. If a slow string part sounds too late advance it (play it earlier), to make it sound as if it was played on the beat. Even if the part is hard quantised, advancing it will reduce MIDI traffic as the four notes (that initially start the part) will actually play up to xx ticks before the main song body (xx = try it and see).

This shuffling of tracks can equally apply to any type of instrument that has a slow attack transient. Even with perfect quantisation a slow sounding part could sound late. Delaying tracks can be quite dangerous and could throw the whole song into a state of unbalance, although this is exactly what we must do if we intend to echo a track (see Chapter 11).

### Bend

String players can bend notes by placing their fingers slightly lower than their normal position and then as soon as the note is bowed the fingers slide up the neck fractionally moving the note up into an 'in tune' position. See Chapter 8 for more information.

### End of phrase/notes

If there's a sustained chord at the end of a phrase or a long sustained note that fades away (or fades in for that matter), insert expression events (controller 11) to temper the start and end points. With slow attack/decay sounds remember there is often a brief residual sustain. If the expression reset command is sent too early it will produce an annoying hic – if possible leave a gap of about an eighth note (192 ticks) before re-setting.

# 10 ♥♥

# *Quantising*

One of the most sensitive areas, if not the most sensitive area, of sequenced music relates to the quantisation of the music. Does it auto correct or auto destroy? Critics of sequenced music often roll out the same tried and trusted argument that it sounds robotic, sterile and soulless. Although I hate to admit it, there are times when I'm forced to agree with them.

Musicians, especially drummers, hate to think that their time keeping is anything but rock solid. Wandering around the beat, however, is a vital ingredient in creating feel to our music but if there's too much wandering the music seems amateurish. The way to overcome any errant wandering is to use the quantise function to nudge any wayward notes back onto the beat. The first thing we must do is set a quantise value by selecting one of the numbers from the quantise options below.

| | | |
|-----|-----|-----|
| 1. | 1 | 1T |
| 2. | 2 | 2T |
| 4. | 4 | 4T |
| 8. | 8 | 8T |
| 16. | 16 | 16T |
| 32. | 32 | 32T |
| 64. | 64 | 64T |

Note: the dot . means dotted values and the T means triplets.

If we frequently write in 4/4 time, there's a good chance the notes we'll be using will be combinations of whole notes (semibreves), half notes (minims), quarter notes (crotchets), eighth notes (quavers) and possibly sixteenth notes (semiquavers). If we chose a quantise value of 8 this would push or pull notes onto the nearest eighth note. This would cause a big problem if sixteenth notes (semiquavers) are used somewhere in the song. These sixteenth notes will be moved along with all the others, resulting in two notes being moved onto the same time point.

To fully grasp how quantising works we must know the quantise increments in TPQNs (ticks per quarter note). When we're working hard on a song, knowing them instinctively will definitely increase our efficiency. Don't try to remember every single note value (you'll end up wanting to be a train spotter!), simply jot down on paper a few of the well used ones – sixteenth, eighth and quarter notes. It won't be long before they're all committed to memory.

Let's now imagine a single note has been played and its exact position is 0001.01.034. If we select a quantise value of sixteenths, we know it will pull or push any note data to the nearest sixteenth note (plus or minus 48 ticks from its centre position). In this case it would pull the note back onto position 0001.01.000 (as it falls inside our + or – 48 capture area) and give us the desired result. If that same note were at position 0001.01.052 (falling outside) it would push it onto the next available sixteenth increment – 0001.01.096.

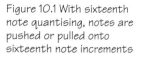
Figure 10.1 With sixteenth note quantising, notes are pushed or pulled onto sixteenth note increments

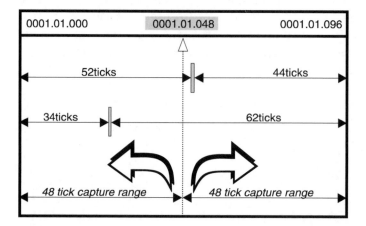

When using quantisation keep in mind that notes could be moved to the wrong destination if there are timing errors of more than 50% (see below).

Let's suppose we're programming a simple tune that comprises just five notes D, E, C, C, and G (see Figure 2.8(a)). The first four are quarter notes (crotchets) and the fifth is a whole note (semibreve). If we record this into the sequencer and then carefully look at the results in an event edit window we might see tiny imperfections in our playing. I'm sure it comes as no surprise to see that our notes are not situated exactly on the beat.

Let's suppose the positions of each of our notes are:

D4 = 0001.01.046   (error +46 off true)
E4 = 0001.02.008   (error +8 off true)
C4 = 0001.02.331   (error -53 off true)
C3 = 0001.04.029   (error +29 off true)
G3 = 0002.01.005   (error +5 off true)

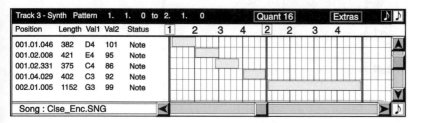

Figure 10.2 Playing imperfections result in slightly off the beat notes

If we quantised to sixteenth notes, our third note (C4) would be pushed back to 0001.02.288 while all the other notes would be moved correctly onto the beat. Remember our 50% error rule – a sixteenth note has 96 ticks (half = 48) – note C4 is out by 53 ticks which makes it over the limit for pulling it up onto a whole beat. If we change our quantise value to eighth notes all notes would be forced onto the beat, like Figure 10.3.

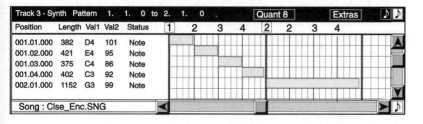

Figure 10.3 Eighth notes have 192 ticks – if we apply the 50% rule now (96 ticks), even with an error margin of 53 ticks it now falls easily inside our new capture range

What we have examined here is hard quantisation, that is, notes within our capture range will always be moved exactly onto the beat. If we do this to every track, to every note all of the time we'll run the real risk of our music becoming mechanical.

## Soft quantise

It's not a good idea to use hard quantising all the time, so in most circumstances a softer kind of quantise should be used that intelligently tries to understand what we're trying to achieve. Quite a few pro sequencers have the ability to quantise by increments. That means the sequencer shuffles note data to its destination a few ticks at a time. Having such a facility can help considerably in cor-

### INFORMATION

*There's always an exception to the rule isn't there? and there a few styles of music such as dance, rave and house that prefer to use more of a hard quantised feel.*

recting all the really badly played notes but it still retains quite a healthy amount of human 'looseness'.

Figure 10.4 Soft quantise
nudges notes a bit at a time

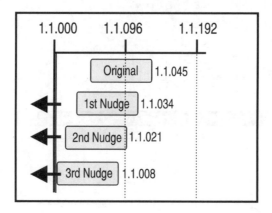

The amount of quantisation to apply is defined in the quantise window (Figure 10.5). The quantise value box is obvious but what of the other functions? The 'don't quantise' option refers to a position, in ticks, extending from a centre quantise position in which note data will be ignored. In our example its set to 12 ticks, which means any data falling within 12 ticks (plus or minus) from our centre point will be left alone and any data moving into this area (after a nudge) will also be ignored.

We have the facility, using a range feature, to apply quantisation to all notes or just to notes that fall within a particular range of pre-defined measures (bars). The amount of note quantisation we can apply can be set as a percentage, 100% would mean hard quantise. Use smaller settings 25 – 40% and gradually nudge the

Figure 10.5 The quantise
window gives you various
options

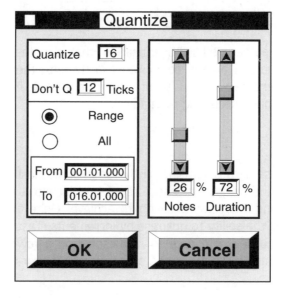

notes onto the beat, as Figure 10.4 shows. If there is not enough significant change, keep repeating the quantise at lower values rather than increasing the strength percentage factor.

Notice the duration quantise option, often included in a sequencer. This specific function is designed to adjust note lengths (sometimes called 'gate time'). A setting (of 72%, in this instance) would produce a small gap between the end of one note and the beginning of the next. In fact it would leave a gap of 27 ticks.

How did we arrive at this figure? We know that a sixteenth note is made up of 96 ticks, 72% of 96 is 69, Subtract 69 from 96 and – hey presto – we're left with 27.

**TIP**

*A word of caution to the unwary. Ensure notes don't overlap, especially if they're the same note. Problems like this happen when the note lengths are made legato before they're quantised (see Figure 10.6).*

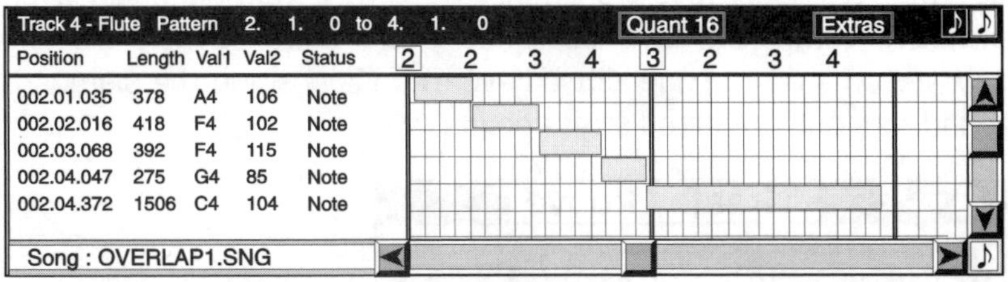

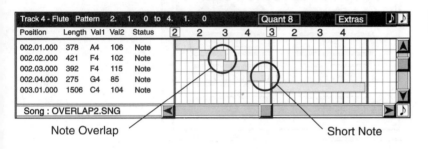

Figure 10.6 Note lengths adjusted but no quantising has been applied

In this example we've adjusted the note lengths but the notes haven't been quantised. At this stage everything seems satisfactory.

Figure 10.7 Figure 10.6 after hard (100%) quantisation

After hard (100%) quantisation (Figure 10.7), we can immediately see two errors. The first is the overlapping F4's, How can we possibly play the F4 at beat three when we are still holding the same note (F4) over from beat two?

In addition, we've now produced a short(er) note on beat four. If this example was saved as a standard MIDI file the short note (G4) will be saved correctly, as well as the slight overhang from the F4 to the G4 (as they are different notes), but those dual F4 overhangs will probably cause a problem, either severely truncating one of them or producing the good old MIDI drone. Even if it does save a MIDI file correctly we can see that at two specific points we've actually reduced our precious polyphony as well!

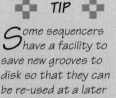

Figure 10.8 The groove window allows saving and loading of grooves

# Get into the groove

Creating an ideal groove is considerably easier if there's a dedicated groove facility. Grooves are a way of altering the time points of notes in a slightly more sophisticated way than ordinary quantising. Let's suppose we've just created a killer bass track that's just perfect, we'd ideally want to copy its style and feel to all the other tracks. If we use the source (bass) track as a template we can transfer its subtle feel to all the others so that the complete song grooves in a similar manner.

If no template exists and we need to create an original groove, use the 'create groove' function to create it, although it's a bit primitive compared to a dedicated drum editor. When creating grooves on a drum page all we have to do is position the diamonds to indicate our preferred stress points.

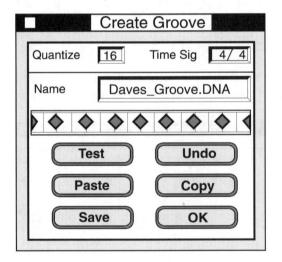

It's a feature of quantising that it only affects note data and ignores all continuous data (pitchbend, controllers). There could be hundreds of events attached to a note so perhaps it wouldn't be such a good idea to quantise them would it? Be careful that playback is not affected if the notes are moved and the controller/pitch bend data isn't. If a note is moved before a pitch bend sweep for instance, that note will have a distinctive whoop sound as it's played before the pitch bend information takes effect.

# Quantising in general

There's no hard and fast rule regarding the quantising of instruments. It's true to say however that the drums and bass should be the tightest instruments in the band. With a medium to fast song (100 – 120BPM) try setting the 'don't capture' quantise range to about 3 to 5 ticks. This breathing space will still allow a small amount of freedom and could help with MIDI traffic and choking problems (refer to Chapter 11).

The rest of the rhythm section can enjoy a wider range – say 10 to 15 ticks, but pay particular attention not to interfere with any strumming guitars. Monophonic (single note playing) instruments that float over a song (strings) and solo passages should be left alone as much as possible but brass stabs and guitar cuts can benefit from a tighter quantise.

Triplet quantisation (as we know) is based around an 8T resolution. This would place all our notes onto ticks 128 and 256 of each measure. Even though this gives us a good approximation of a triplet feel if we 'fine tune' these notes (particularly on drums), we can reproduce a pretty good lazy swing. Try subtracting about 10 ticks from all the notes that fall on these time points.

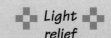

*Q* What do a guitar solo and premature ejaculation have in common?
*A* You know it's coming but there's nothing you can do about it.

# *11*

# *Sequencing tips*

It's been said so many times before that the amount of benefit we receive from something is proportional to the amount of effort we put in to it. Authors spend hundreds of man hours creating manuals designed to help us use their software correctly. Most causes of frustration in using any piece of software often come down to simple user error, although understanding those wonderful Japanese to English translated user manuals is an art form in itself. I often wonder, with the amount of English speaking people in the world, why these companies don't employ English people to write the manuals first (in English) and then translate them back into Japanese! Answers on a postcard please to Yamaha, Korg, Casio, Roland ...

A great deal can be learnt from using an intuitive hands on approach as it gives a good indication of how easy the software will be to use, or not as the case may be, but don't forget to use the manual, there may many short cuts and key stroke combinations that'll save you hours of work in the long term. If things don't seem to be working out too well ... RTFM (read the flippin' manual!).

## Tempo tricks

To produce a good human feel to your music you really need to leave it as un-quantised as much as possible. If the song you're working on is cracking along at a blistering 180+ BPM there'll probably be the occasional timing error, so if you reduce the tempo to something more manageable you should be able to substantially reduce them. When the recording take is over, you can increase the tempo back up to its original 180+ and no one will ever know the difference, Unless ...

1  If you reduce the speed of the song too much, you're likely to fall into the sequencer speed trap. Let's say you're working on a

song and you've just finished recording an improvised synth solo. It might sound pretty hot when you play it back at the (recorded) tempo or even slightly faster but when it's played back *a tempo*, the end result sounds as if you've dropped one acid tab too many! Why? Playing too fast is the most common problem. During the recording take it's easy to slip into a state of unreality and experiment with clever tricks and embellishments hoping they'll come out pretty hot 'in tempo'. Until you gain experience recording at slow tempos try and concentrate on limiting those creative juices to around sixteenth (semi-quaver) notes.

2  Pitch bend information will also be affected when the song is speeded back up. If you've set the recording tempo to be 80 BPM and the playback speed is 160 BPM, a half second bend when recording will produce a quarter second bend effect on playback. If you want a half second pitch bend on playback you must record a bend that lasts a full second. Recording a bend this slow will be torture on the ears as the pitch of the note will be dreadfully flat for quite some time. You must resist the natural temptation to resolve the pitch of the note too quickly.

3  If you're playing chords on the keyboard there'll always be a natural gap which happens when your fingers are lifted from the keyboard between changes. No matter how fast you might try, there'll always be a gap. Experiment with different amounts of gap when recording a part until the speeded up (in tempo) version sounds realistic.

## Overtype for complex passages

Suppose you have to play a series of fast complex passing chords and you really don't have the ability to play them in context at any speed, your first thought may be – step time. Well yes, step time will overcome the problem but it could take ages, especially if there are a lot of notes.

   If your sequencer can read the MIDI input from the keyboard while it's in an edit page try this:

1  Decide how many notes you'll need to play to make up each chord – let's say for example that each chord will always contain four notes – you now need to allocate a different note for each (i.e. F, A, C and E) . Don't worry if the notes you've selected are not part of any of the underlying chord, the most important thing is to keep playing these same notes.

2  At a low speed, record the rhythm you want using only these notes (Figure 11.1) As you know there'll be some dischords

**TIP**

*Use this kind of technique for other uses such as creating rapid hi-hat or tambourine patterns. It is fairly difficult to keep re-striking the same key over and over and maintain a regular and even feel. One way to get over this is to play two different notes, one with the left hand and one with the right. When the recording take is over simply change all the wrong notes so they play the correct instrument.*

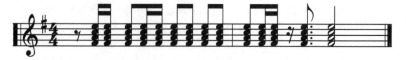

Figure 11.1 Record the rhythm with easy notes, then ...

produced it's often wise to mute all other tracks before recording.

3 When the recording is over, open up an edit window and then (starting at the beginning) play the correct notes you would've used to create the proper chords – one note at a time (Figure 11.2). Your sequencer should step through and overtype the notes you've already played and substitute the new ones.

4 You'll probably need to tweak the velocities of your new notes to make them sound authentic and it'll help if your sequencer will let you ignore (mask) all incoming velocity information as you overtype.

Figure 11.2 ... open up an edit window and substitute the right notes

## Volume/expression/velocity ... confused?

Controller 7 is the main volume command (which controls volume), controller 11 is the expression command (which also controls volume in some way) and note velocity (which, er ... controls volume). Confused as to which one to use?

Expression (controller 11) events should be the only type of events used to create crescendo and diminuendo effects. For instance, what could happen if you decided to ignore this advice and use volume events (controller 7) instead? If your song was subsequently played on a different device it's a good probability that the mix will sound wrong. If it's too loud you'll have to alter dozens, possibly hundreds of controller 7's to bring the volume back down. If you had used controller 11 instead you'd only have to alter a single controller event, the main volume (7) controller in the set up measure, to produce the same effect.

With the expression command effectively 'out of the picture' you're left to choose between using velocity and/or volume (7) events when mixing, but which actually sounds better?

Consider this:

1 A single word shouted as loud as humanly possible without using any electronic assistance.

2 The same word whispered through a good quality PA system

ensuring that the actual decibel level from our PA system exactly matches our larynx wrenching version.

Although our actual audio volumes may be identical the natural harmonics and overtones of these sounds makes it easy for us to distinguish between them. The type of waveform (tone) an instrument produces will depend on its velocity level and the threshold at which certain filters and noise gates open.

## Producing real time fade ins and fade outs

As we know, control code 11 (expression) is the ideal controller to use for fading instruments in and out. For absolute precision, drawing every event using a suitable editor would be best but this type of editing takes too much time. Wouldn't it be much quicker if we could devise a way of doing the same thing in real time?

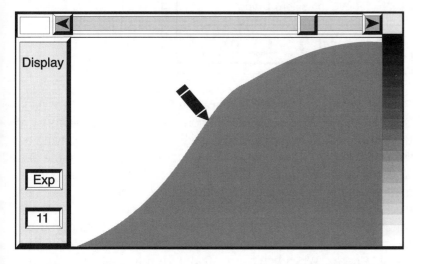

Figure 11.3 Drawing and modifying controller data on screen with a pencil or mouse.

### Avoiding MIDI choke by nudging the controller track

Using the mouse to create controller data can have its own drawbacks. Some sequencers will request a resolution to place these events and will space them accordingly, 32nds, 32nd triplets, 64ths etc. Drawing control events this way places them exactly on the beat and sub-beats. When this happens, you should nudge the entire controller track forwards and backwards in time by a few ticks.

If there are multiple tracks, all using some kind of controller data at the same time, make sure each track is nudged by a different amount. This nudging of tracks will prevent the module having to process all this information at the same time – one of the causes of MIDI choke.

**PROJECT**

*Select a brass patch and play a series of notes that all have a fairly low velocity value but use a high volume (controller 7) level. Listen carefully to the sound that's produced, and repeat the experiment with higher velocity values and lower volume. Notice the higher velocity version has more punch and vitality but the low velocity version sounds considerably weaker. Don't dismiss weak sounding timbres as useless, they can work very effectively as pad synths.*

## Remapping the mod wheel to produce other types of event

Some sequencers have the capability to convert incoming data and change it (in real time), to another type. If your sequencer has this facility you can re-map the modulation wheel (controller 1) to expression (controller 11). Now when the modulation wheel is moved to and fro you'll be creating expression events not modulation events.

Figure 11.4 Converting mod wheel movements to expression events

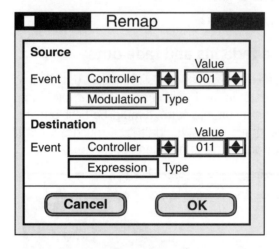

## Record expression events separately from the actual notes

Don't try and record note information *and* expression events all at the same time. Why wait you may ask? – Well, if you're playing big spread chords with both hands you've got no way to move the data wheel have you? The first thing to do is record all the note information on one track and give it a rough mix. Create and use a new track, set to the same MIDI channel as the notes, for recording controller data. If you make a mistake during recording you can delete whole sections without worrying about erasing any of your valuable notes. When you're satisfied with the results you can mix (merge) the two tracks together.

It's very important to roughly mix the notes before you start applying expression events because until you've balanced all the notes you don't know how your expression commands will work in context. You may put them all in and find, after mixing, the depth of fade you want doesn't quite happen like you'd hoped. If this happens you'd only have to go in and edit them all over again, and that's dumb!

When the modulation wheel has been re-mapped to produce expression events, pay particular attention to how the wheel is centred. Producing a fade is a simple matter of slowly turning the wheel down but notice, as indicated by the circle in Figure 11.5,

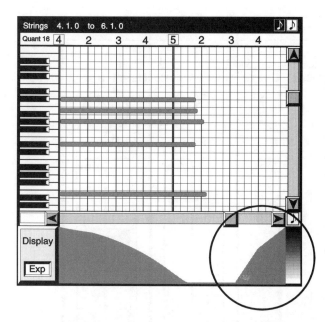

once the fade is complete (and all ambient noise has disappeared), when the wheel is centred it still produces expression events on the way up. If you use this re-mapping technique, edit each part and delete all unwanted events so that the values jump from your minimum value (0?) straight back to 127. That is unless the next time the instrument plays you require it to fade in.

This logic can be applied to new fade ins as there'll be many unnecessary expression events produced on the way down to the starting point. Lastly if the instrument in question fades in and out all the time it's acceptable practice to leave the expression level low until it's time to ramp back up on the new fade in. By paying attention and removing all extraneous expression events it'll reduce the size of the song file considerably and allow your sequencer to work more efficiently.

## Use the mixer page if you have one

There may be an alternative to re-mapping a hardware controller like the modulation or pitch wheel, and this requires using a mixer page (if one exists). Some sequencers have a special edit page which emulates a traditional mixing desk, except all the sliders and knobs are software icons. Unless there's a provision to modify these icons you'll probably find the volume events will be true MIDI volume events (controller 7). Once recorded these events will need transforming into expression events using a transform or logical editor of some kind.

### LIVE PLAYING

*If the song is used in a live situation (where disk space is at a premium or where available memory is critical), reducing continuous data will make the MIDI file more efficient (and a lot smaller).*

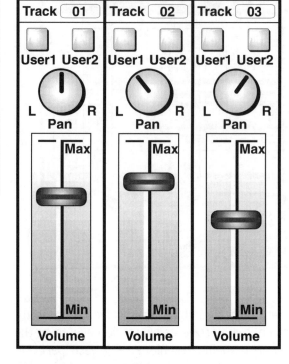

Figure 11.6 Mixer page

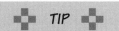
### ✚ TIP ✚

*If the thin continuous controllers command is used on pitch bend data, check manually to ensure that it has not removed any pitch wheel centring commands (0, 64).*

Figure 11.7 Reducing controller data

## Thin the controller data

Using real time controllers will create huge amounts of data, most of which is superfluous, and actually becomes more of a hindrance than a help (too much controller data reduces the effectiveness of the sequencer). You may find after mixing one track this way, you can barely perceive any difference in performance at all, but if you've done a complete production number on every track, the song may start to sound somewhat laboured.

There's nothing wrong in using real time controllers but after you've finished the mix, you ought to run the track and/or the whole song through a 'thin continuous controllers' process. This will remove a lot of unwanted data without degrading playback.

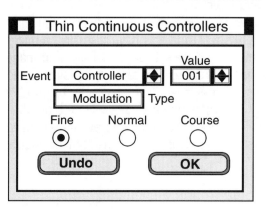

# Using multiple tracks with the same MIDI channel

Why would you want to use more than one track with the same MIDI channel? Here are a few good reasons that instantly spring to mind.

## Separate drum tracks

Each drum or cymbal could have its own track. Having separate tracks for kick drum, snare drum, closed hi-hat etc., can be handy when recording or mixing. Furthermore, if the song is going to be accompanied by an 'organic' drummer it would be useful to have the option to mute some drum track(s) and allow percussion tracks to play on.

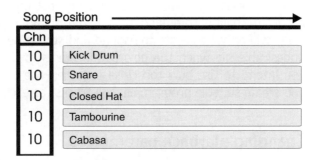

Figure 11.8 Multiple drum tracks give more flexibility

## Put different instruments on different tracks

If there are more than 16 instruments playing at different times during the song you'll soon run out of MIDI channels. When making song data ensure that every track contains data for only one instrument. Mixing different instruments on the same track can result in confusion at a later date if ever you need to re-edit or re-mix the song.

As Figure 11.9 shows, there are three different types of instrument on MIDI channel 5: strings, slow strings and a chime synth, but they are all on separate tracks.

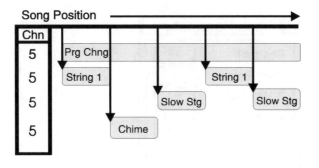

Figure 11.9 Using only one track per instrument avoids confusion

### Program change track

Notice the Prg Chng (program change) track which should contain only program change commands. Although each person has a different way of working, I've found that by keeping the program changes together on a separate track it makes access to them easier than embedding each of them into a data track.

Note: *Do not* send a program change command at exactly the same time as a new note, or midway through a held note. If you use a separate program change track (which should span the entire length of the song) you can move any program changes around slightly so they take effect a fraction of a second before your new instrument begins to play. A gap of about eight ticks should be ample time for the module to respond.

Take special care with slow decaying instruments as sending a program change command before the sound has finished dying away will either truncate the sound and stop it dead or produce an undesirable hic when the new sound starts to play. If the sounds you intend to use butt too close together, use two MIDI channels and create suitable program change tracks for each.

## Changing playback parameters

**INFORMATION**

*Entering a minus delay setting (-48) will in fact advance the track by that amount of ticks (after all two negatives make a positive don't they!)*

You can alter the playback of each track using the tracks parameter box. Using this method doesn't alter the raw data in each track but it's a quick and easy way of modifying all the existing data, in real time, to the values entered in each of the options.

Any values entered into the parameter box affect only the playback of the data. If you intend to keep these settings you should hard code (encrypt) them and change the raw data accordingly.

Don't forget that if a standard MIDI file is saved without making any changes to the raw data, the playback parameters are often ignored. The MIDI file may contain only the original (unmodified) data.

Figure 11.9 The track parameters box offers a quick way of editing track data

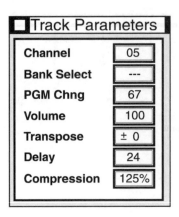

**Track Parameters**

| | |
|---|---|
| Channel | 05 |
| Bank Select | --- |
| PGM Chng | 67 |
| Volume | 100 |
| Transpose | ± 0 |
| Delay | 24 |
| Compression | 125% |

## Creating echoes

You can create the illusion of an echo by using two tracks. First duplicate the source track and give it a new (un-used) MIDI channel. You should delay the duplicated track until you obtain a pleasing effect. You can get the best from this technique if you ....

1 Pan the original and duplicate tracks to be on either side of the audio spectrum.
2 Lower the velocity of the duplicate track.
3 Increase the reverb level on the duplicate track.

Newer GS modules (SC-88 onwards) have included an extra controller designed to reproduce an echo effect. This delay parameter (sometimes called echo) is listed as a system effect controller (controller 93) and it can be applied to any of the tracks/MIDI channels. The availability of this extra effect means that you can save polyphony by simply assigning the delay effect to the required MIDI channels (range 0 – 127)

## Chorusing

As mentioned earlier, the General MIDI protocol doesn't support chorus but you can create an illusion of it by using duplicate tracks. First you must duplicate the source track and give it a new (un-used) MIDI channel. Insert a pitch bend command just before the first note is played and then decrease its value so that it starts to produce a slight phasing (chorusing) effect.

If the track you intend to chorus contains any pitch bend information there's a likelihood that the copy track will return to being perfectly in tune (as any self-respecting pitch bend should do!) effectively destroying the chorusing effect you've carefully created. Either use a logical type editor to modify any pitch bend centring commands or check them all manually and adjust them accordingly – only on the copy track of course.

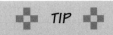

*TIP*

*If you decide to chorus a chord playing track (keyboard/guitar) remember the polyphony will be reduced dramatically.*

## Creating drum parts

Use the cycle feature to create drum parts. First enable the automatic quantise feature, just in case you're a little premature with your timing. Let's explain. Say you are running through the last measure of a two measure section (just before it cycles back) recording the snare drum part and you intend to play – say closed hi-hats – starting on the first beat of the new repeat. You need to

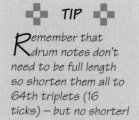

ensure the first closed hi-hat plays exactly on beat one of your new repeated section and not tick three hundred and seventy something of beat four of the previous cycle. When you've finished recording all the instruments, undo the forced quantise feature on the track to return the drums to their actual recorded (un-quantised) positions.

When using cycle mode it's easy to produce doubled notes. As you keep repeating the same section over and over, it's possible at some point to forget what you've already played, until it's too late of course and you've played the same part again. If this happens don't be overly concerned, wait until the take is over and then use the delete doubles function or use an edit page and remove them manually.

### Drum edit – defaults

When you first open the drum edit screen you'll probably find the drum instruments listed chromatically:

Acoustic kick drum – note 35/B0

Kick drum 1 – note 36/C1

Side stick – note 37/C#1

Acoustic snare – note 38/D1

etc.

You should re-arrange the drum order to reflect your preferred method of working and save this new configuration as part of the default song.

## Manufacturers' differences

It's well worth remembering that a song mixed on one device will sound very different on another even if it does bear the same GM logo and conforms to the GM specification. Two of the ways data can be affected on playback are:

1  The quality of the samples used and the way each sound is recreated electronically can affect the timbre or tone of an instrument. If the actual tone of an instrument is different from the one for which the song was mixed, it'll change the way the sounds inter-react with each other, and therefore affect the overall ambience and balance of the song.

2  Unfortunately there's no definitive rule relating to the volume of a sound. A velocity level of 90 might sound loud on one device but rather feeble on another.

## Velocity

If you look at the velocity peaks and troughs in Figure 11.11 you can see that some of them can be regarded as rather extreme. It may be you get so enthusiastic you start bashing out a rhythm really loud or try something a bit tricky, fumble, and produce wimpy and uneven notes.

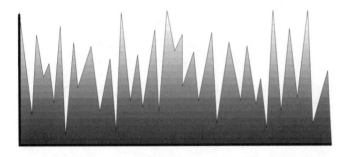

Figure 11.11 Velocity characteristics pre-edit (notice the large peaks and troughs)

Matters compound even more when you construct a song from smaller, and more manageable sections. These sections might vary from one measure to possibly dozens of measures, so it is virtually impossible to maintain an exact consistency throughout. When all the various sections have been pasted/mixed together, use either a global velocity command or a graphic editor to smooth out all the rough edges.

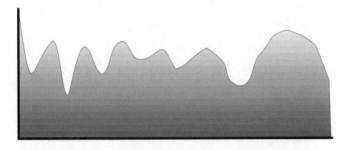

Figure 11.12 Velocity characteristics after smoothing.

Adjust the velocity range of the notes to fall somewhere between 85 to 110. Having a theoretical ceiling of 110 will allow you to peak up to 127 when it's really, and I mean really, necessary. Avoid getting into the habit of playing parts 'balls out' all the time, as this shows poor programming technique and restricts any musical manoeuverability.

When it comes to deciding the level to use for the main volume (controller 7), try setting it so it averages about 100 for each MIDI channel, not 127. Setting levels around 100 gives you the headroom you may need, and conversely if you feel the instrument in question is too loud (see section on volume vs velocity) you can decrease it to a more suitable level.

### Tempo considerations

If the song you've created is to be saved in standard MIDI file format, keep the tempo values between 30 to 240BPM. If tempos exceed these limits they might not be interpreted correctly by budget priced software. If the tempo must fall outside these recommendations try doubling or halving the resolution accordingly. e.g.

| | |
|---|---|
| 4/4 at 340BPM | change to 4/2 at 170BPM |
| 4/4 at 25BPM | change to 4/8 at 50BPM |

If you change the tempo resolution, the lengths of notes, when seen in a editor, will be doubled or halved accordingly. Quantisation values should also be changed to suit.

## Instruments and channels

What instrument goes where? We all have our own preferences for what instrument plays on what MIDI channel and there are no hard and fast rules. Whatever system is eventually adopted maintain the same format and save it as part of the default song.

Listed below is just one suggested layout.

| | |
|---|---|
| 1 | Leave empty for 'live' MIDI overdubs |
| 2 | Bass guitar or bass synth |
| 3 | Keyboard 1 (piano/organ/pad synth) |
| 4 | Keyboard 2 or guitar 1 |
| 5 | Guitar 2 |
| 6 | Important lead (brass/string) or synth figures |
| 7 | Secondary lead or synth figures |
| 8 | * Auxiliary 1 * |
| 9 | * Auxiliary 2 * |
| 10 | Drums and percussion |
| 11 | * Auxiliary 3 * (secondary rhythm part in GS/XG) |
| 12 | * Auxiliary 4 * |
| 13 | * Auxiliary 5 * |
| 14 | Choir or group vocal |
| 15 | Group vocal or secondary lead vocal – (FX unit 2) |
| 16 | Lead vocal (melody) – (FX unit 1) |

If the song is going to be performed in a live situation, MIDI channel 16 (and possibly 15) can be used to control outboard effects units – MIDIverb, lights etc.

## Step enter/step time

### Note lengths

If you've entered notes using a step entry method you'll need to modify note lengths and velocities to produce a more convincing performance. The problem with step entry is that when notes are entered this way, not only are notes placed on exact time points, but they also take on their exact (full) length.

In Figure 11.13 you can see three chords have been 'played' as whole notes, each of them has been given their full length of 1536 ticks, butting them perfectly against the notes in the forthcoming measure.

As previously discussed when a keyboard player changes chords, the hands are momentarily lifted from the keys so there is a measurable amount of space. Step input or length quantisation doesn't take account of this space and if there's not enough (or none at all) they'll sound wrong!

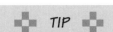

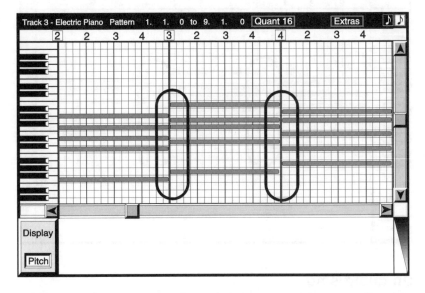

**TIP**

*If a note quantise or legato function is applied to a single (monophonic) part (which is currently emulating a 'blowing' instrument – like a saxophone or trumpet), make sure enough space is left at the end of phrases to indicate where the player would naturally breathe. And before you ask – no you can't breathe through there, so leave those gaps!*

Figure 11.13 Original data as entered using step time or after note length quantisation

The amount of space to leave between notes is proportional to the speed of the song. For average speed songs try leaving a gap somewhere between a sixteenth and an eighth note and decrease or increase this gap as necessary.

When changing note lengths avoid making them the same. Better results are obtained if the note off commands are slightly staggered. To stop every note in a chord at exactly the same time point sounds unrealistic and increases MIDI traffic.

Figure 11.14 Leave a gap between notes of between a sixteenth and an eighth note

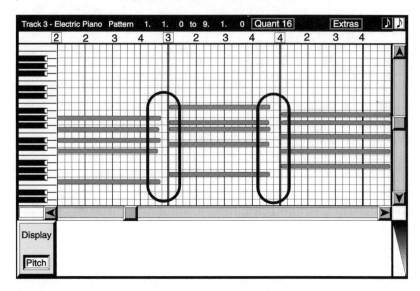

Figure 11.15 Same as Figure 11.13 after full unquantise editing (notice the start positions of each note and the staggered gaps at the ends of the notes)

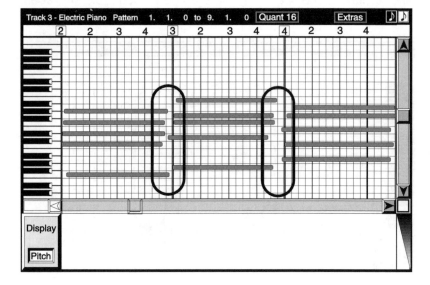

## Un-quantising

The final stage in creating realistic music is to *un-quantise* the notes and loosen up the velocities. There are a couple of ways to achieve this:

1  Change every note individually. This is definitely the worse case

scenario, so if your sequencer has no ability to help you out, you should seriously consider piano lessons or invest in more powerful software!

2 If one exists, use the humanise feature which randomly nudges every note a few ticks either positive or minus from its present (quantised) position.

3 Use a logical (transform) editor of some kind often found on the more expensive sequencers. You can use your logical editor to change notes, en masse within certain defined parameters.

The way you use this type of editor relies upon a logical approach to the problem. The first question to ask yourselves is how do you want the notes of the chord spread? Do you want the highest notes to play first or do you want the lower notes to play first? Let's assume you wanted the higher notes to sound after the others. You could draw up a series of instructions to perform this task, something like:

| | |
|---|---|
| Notes C0 to C1 | minus 2 ticks from their present position |
| Notes C1 to G1 | ignore (leave them alone) |
| Notes G1 to C2 | add 2 ticks from their present position |
| Notes C2 to C3 | add 3 ticks from their present position |
| Notes above C3 | add 4 ticks from their present position |

The number of discrete steps to employ is a matter of personal taste as is the number of ticks to add or subtract.

The same principle can be used for note lengths:

| | |
|---|---|
| Notes C0 to C1 | minus 6 ticks from overall length |
| Notes C1 to G1 | minus 18 from overall length |
| Notes G1 to C2 | minus 24 ticks from overall length |
| Notes C2 to C3 | minus 32 ticks from overall length |
| Notes above C3 | minus 48 ticks from overall length |

Instead of using note values as the focus for your calculations you could've used velocity values instead.

| Notes with velocity 35 to 45 | minus 6 ticks from overall length |
| Notes with velocity 46 to 68 | minus 6 ticks from overall length |
| Notes with velocity 69 to 87 | minus 6 ticks from overall length |
| | etc., |

I can't stress enough that this technique should only be used for step entered parts. It'll randomise the parts enough to give an illusion of a live performance and with a little attention it could sound quite realistic. No doubt there are a few pedantic musical snobs who would condemn this sweeping technique as musical sacrilege – well, whoopee do!

## MIDI traffic

Catchy little phrase you'll agree. MIDI traffic is a combination of note on commands (new notes), note off commands (end of old notes) any currently held notes and any continuous controller information, including system exclusive events. If you play a certain section of music you may hear MIDI choke (we can produce a similar effect by exceeding the available polyphony). MIDI choke is quite distinctive. You may experience notes dropping out, or hear sections of music that seem to falter and labour even though the actual data is positioned correctly and there's no deliberate tempo change.

If you count the amount of new notes being played it may only be 20 or so, but if you look very close and then add these 20 note on commands with the 5 note (ons) that are still sounding over from a previous measure, then add this running total to the 18 note off commands which are happening at the same time, and finally add to these events (now at 43) all the controller events, system exclusive commands and pitch wheel data, you could have an overall total count of 60+ events all being processed within a milli-second of each other or more. Be aware of the MIDI traffic problem – most 'traffic jams' can be avoided at the early programming stage (oh for a MIDI protocol that uses a parallel interface!).

## Measure repeat error

To the novice programmer measure repeat errors can seem like MIDI traffic problems. This problem occurs when a single measure or worse still, a section of music is repeated over before being edited. If you examine the data on every track at the beginning of a new phrase you'll often see the note on events often start a few ticks into the measure. A few ticks late on a single part is no big deal in itself but if every track starts a few ticks late the flow from verse to chorus (or whatever) can stall quite noticeably.

To overcome this problem ensure every part/section is given a quick look over before repeating it, especially true for rhythm section instruments (drums, bass, keyboards and guitar). Sometimes, when a small section is repeated – say a four measure chorus hook over and over, *ad nauseam*, I manually go in to each part and pull some of the notes nearer the first beat and sometimes even before it, this works particularly well with crash cymbals.

## Editor/librarian

Changing waveforms can produce new and refreshing variations of the original sound, but making these changes using the front panel of a module or keyboard can be torture. It often happens that layer upon layer of edit pages have to be accessed and modified – great fun! There are commercial and public domain editor programs available which are designed to access all these discrete variables from the relative ease of a computer screen.

Figure 11.16 represents a typical ADSR edit page on a synth editor. The mouse can be used to drag the nodes of each parameter around the screen in real time changing both amplitude, depth and duration. When you've created a new sound you can save it to disk for later use. Using this method complete libraries of sounds can be created and sent to your modules(s) as system exclusive messages.

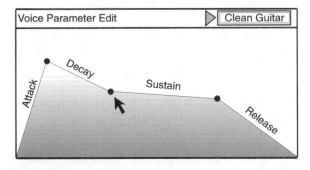

Voice Parameter Edit ▷ Clean Guitar

Attack Decay Sustain Release

Figure 11.16 Create your own sounds using an ADSR edit page

## Recording in sections

When you are recording parts, limit the number of measures to record in a single 'take' to a realistic amount. Good players may be able to play a complete 12 or 16 measure section without any problems but if your technique isn't too hot dissect the phrase into more manageable sections. Record parts of no more than four

## GHOST PARTS

When you repeat a phrase you may be prompted to create a 'real' part or just a ghost part. Ghost parts are very handy if memory is limited, but ensure any ghost parts are transformed back into real parts before saving it as a standard MIDI file.

measures at a time unless it's very straightforward and as soon as you've finished – SAVE! After you've saved examine the part and tidy up the data.

With popular music you may be able to repeat a four measure phrase to produce a complete eight measure section or perhaps repeat a two measure phrase three times to give the eight measures (2 + 6 = 8).

### Pattern repeat

Although pattern based sequencers seem to be losing their popularity slightly, they are very memory efficient. Drum and percussion measures are often repeated during the main song body so these could benefit considerably from pattern based sequencing. First of all study the song and determine how many different drum patterns and variations are used and record these first. List (in a similar way to the table below) the differences between every variation and assign each a unique pattern number.

| 1 | Introduction – 4 measures |
|---|---|
| 2 | Start of new phrase (A) – 1 measure (this may include a crash cymbal) |
| 3 | Basic drum pattern (A) – 1 measure (main song body – verse?) |
| 4 | Drum fill (A) – 1 measure |
| 5 | Drum fill (B) – 1 measure |
| 6 | Basic drum pattern (B) – 1 measure (main song body – chorus?) |
| 7 | Start of new phrase (B) – 1 measure |
| 8 | Drum variation (A) – 1 measure (this might be the inclusion of an open hi-hat or similar) |
| 9 | Drum fill (C) – 1 measure |
| | etc........ |

When all the different patterns have been recorded they are then listed (copied) in their playing order, i.e.

| Measure | *3 | 4 | 5 | 6 | 7 | 8 | 9 | 9 | 11 | 12 | 13 | 14 | 15 | 16 | 17 | 18 | 19 | 20 | 21 | 22 | 23 | 24 | 25 | 26 | 27 | |
|---|---|---|---|---|---|---|---|---|---|---|---|---|---|---|---|---|---|---|---|---|---|---|---|---|---|---|
| Pattern | 1 | 2 | 3 | 3 | 8 | 3 | 3 | 3 | 4 | 2 | 3 | 3 | 3 | 8 | 3 | 3 | 5 | 7 | 6 | 6 | 6 | 6 | 6 | 6 | 9 | (Etc.) |

*The song above starts from measure three. This takes into account a one measure set-up and a one measure count-in.

## Voice modifications

If you have an editor/librarian of some sort or intend to modify the voices on your device using NRPNs it's often a good idea to do this before you start recording. Not only will the change of timbre affect the velocity characteristics of the voice, it will also help create a better mix as you're mixing the actual sounds you intend to use.

You may find if you program first (using the standard voices available) and then modify the sound, such a drastic change to the waveform will necessitate a complete and sometime radical re-mixing of the song.

# Control codes and SysEx

## Introduction

As we'll be using computers and synthesisers it's often a good idea to occasionally remind ourselves that they're pretty stupid. 'What!?' I hear you ask. 'Aren't computers those really clever things that can perform wonders?' Well yes, but the real truth lies somewhere in the middle. On the one hand computers and synthesisers can process immense amounts of information with incredible speed and efficiency. On the other, they have to be instructed precisely how to perform the most simplest of tasks.

To just fire notes at a synth and hope that everything will respond correctly is a rather naive attitude. What if the previous song changed the waveforms of some of the sounds in the module. Do we know for sure that the pitch wheel has returned to zero and that the modulation is off?

In this chapter we'll examine many of the commonly used control codes and system exclusive commands that can be used to set-up and configure our equipment.

## GM v GS/XG

Do you recall in earlier chapters I mentioned there are quite a few differences between GM and GS/XG devices. These differences relate to the facilities they offer and the way they're controlled. GM has many codes it can recognise and implement, but GS and XG devices have considerably more. We'll start with some of the more general codes and then introduce specific GS and XG control codes (and how to use them) later on.

## Control codes

Any MIDI module or synthesiser can be set-up and manipulated using control codes. Control codes have a range from 0 to 127 and each controller number performs a different function. An interesting point to notice here is that most parameters have a range from 1 to 128, but control codes have values from 0 to 127.

## Hexadecimal

When we count numbers we use a decimal system, units become tens, tens become hundreds and hundreds become thousands. This numbering system is based around a unit of ten. If we were to count numbers aloud we would say 1,2,3,4,5,6,7,8,9 and then10. After 10 the whole process is repeated over starting with eleven. When computers count they do so using a number base of 16. This means there are 16 steps before we reach the number 10. The extra numbers are represented by the letters A, B, C, D, E and F, therefore if we count in hex, we would say 1, 2, 3, 4, 5, 6, 7, 8, 9, A, B, C, D, E, F and then comes 10.

A metric system of counting is now the standard throughout the world, although some non-decimal measurements still exist. Three hundred and sixty degrees still make a complete circle and sixty minutes make up one hour. With a small amount of application we should be able to understand the principle of hexadecimal numbering without too much difficulty.

With most technical manuals it's normal practice to present all numbers in hexadecimal format. Numbers in hex format normally have a capital H next to them, therefore 12H is a hex number and 12 is a decimal number. Look at the list below to see a direct comparison between decimal and hex values. This table only goes as up far as 13H but a complete decimal to hex conversion chart is listed in Appendix D.

| Dec | 0 | 1 | 2 | 3 | 4 | 5 | 6 | 7 | 8 | 9 | 10 | 11 | 12 | 13 | 14 | 15 | 16 | 17 | 18 | 19 |
|-----|---|---|---|---|---|---|---|---|---|---|----|----|----|----|----|----|----|----|----|----|
| Hex | 0 | 1 | 2 | 3 | 4 | 5 | 6 | 7 | 8 | 9 | A | B | C | D | E | F | 10 | 11 | 12 | 13 |

## Commonly used control codes

### Modulation (controller 1)
Modulation is an undulation effect that can produce an illusion of vibrato when applied to an instrument  (range 0 – 127).

### Volume (7)
Different volume levels can be applied to each MIDI channel, but these are not to be confused with the main (physical) volume knob

on the front panel of a synthesiser. Although 127 is the maximum value allowed, setting the volume to around 100 will provide ample space for us to increase or decrease it if required. (range 0 – 127)

### Pan (10)

The stereo positioning of any instrument (except the drums which are pre-defined in the audio spectrum by the manufacturer) can be set anywhere within 128 discrete steps. A value of 64 will place an instrument in the centre position. A value of 0 puts it at the extreme left and 127 extreme right (range 0 – 127).

### Expression (11)

Often confused with MIDI volume, expression should be used only for fading instruments in and out. The more expression commands we use, the smoother our fades will be (range 0 – 127).

### Damper pedal (64)

Often referred to as the sustain pedal, the damper pedal is used to help a pianist negotiate difficult passages. A pianist's hands can stretch an interval of about a ninth and there'll come a time when a chord has to continue to sound when fingers are moved to a new position which exceed these physical limitations.

When the damper pedal is held the fingers can be safely lifted from the keyboard without the chord cutting short. The damper pedal must be released a split second before the new chord begins (value 127 = on, value 0 = off).

### Reverb (91) and chorus (93)

Reverb and chorus can be applied to any part (instrument) and can have a range from 0 to 127. Chorus is not an officially recognised parameter of General MIDI although some manufacturers are now bowing to pressure and including it on their GM units.

### All sounds off (120)

All sounds off will silence any notes that may be droning.

### Reset controllers (121)

When this control code is sent the receiving module will respond on the designated MIDI channel by returning the module to its default values, I.e.

*Synth/module default values*

| Controller | Value |
|---|---|
| Pitch bend | 0 (centre/off position) |
| Polyphonic key pressure | 0 (off) |
| Channel pressure | 0 (off) |
| Modulation | 0 (off) |
| Expression | 127 (max.) |
| Hold 1 | 0 (off) |
| Portamento | 0 (off) |
| Sostenuto | 0 (off) |
| Soft | 0 (off) |

## Bank select

### 0  Bank select (MSB) and 32 Bank select (LSB)

Roland GS and Yamaha XG equipment use a different conventions, but both enable selection of a totally new variation of an instrument which is based loosely around its original waveform. If a non variation (normal) tone is used it could be thought of as a principal tone. Principal tones are identical to those of the GM tone map.

To select a variation tone a complete set of bank select messages (MSB and LSB) have to be sent. These codes have to be sent in the correct order and before the program change command. If we were to list them in order they would appear thus:

*Roland GS*

| Position | Val1 | Val2 | Channel | Status |
|---|---|---|---|---|
| 0001.02.008 | 0 | xx | 1 | Bank select MSB |
| 0001.02.012 | 32 | 0 | 1 | Bank select LSB |
| 0001.02.016 | yy |  | 1 | Program change |

*Yamaha XG*

| Position | Val1 | Val2 | Channel | Status |
|---|---|---|---|---|
| 0001.02.008 | 0 | 0 | 1 | Bank select MSB |
| 0001.02.012 | 32 | xx | 1 | Bank select LSB |
| 0001.02.016 | yy |  | 1 | Program change |

The unknown xx refers to the variation number we can use. Most GS and XG equipment use variation numbers that are multiples of 8, i.e. 8, 16, 32, etc.

yy is the program change number of the principal tone, i.e. piano, guitar, etc. Now let's substitute real numbers for xx and yy. With some GS devices (the SC88 for instance,) we can see that instrument 29 (muted guitar) has two variation tones, funk guitar and funk guitar 2, and these can be accessed by sending 8 and 16 respectively. We'll select funk guitar, (variation 8) for our example. Now if we substitute actual numbers in our listing it would change to this:

*Roland GS*

| Position | Val1 | Val2 | Channel | Status |
| --- | --- | --- | --- | --- |
| 0001.02.008 | 0 | 8 | 1 | Bank select MSB |
| 0001.02.012 | 32 | 0 | 1 | Bank select LSB |
| 0001.02.016 | 29 | | 1 | Program change |

*Yamaha XG*

| Position | Val1 | Val2 | Channel | Status |
| --- | --- | --- | --- | --- |
| 0001.02.008 | 0 | 0 | 1 | Bank select MSB |
| 0001.02.012 | 32 | 8 | 1 | Bank select LSB |
| 0001.02.016 | 29 | | 1 | Program change |

Note: Roland GS equipment uses the MSB to switch to and from the variation banks. This offers a theoretical limit of 128 (principal) x 128 (variation MSB) sounds. Yamaha XG uses the LSB to switch between variation banks. XG has an addressable limit of 128 (principal) x 128 (variation LSB) x 128 (variation MSB) tones – enough for most people I think!

## Registered parameter numbers

### Registered parameter LSB (100) and registered parameter MSB (101)

The most common use for registered parameter numbers is for setting up the pitch bend range although RPN's can also be used for setting the master fine and master coarse tunings. After a GM or GS/XG initialisation is received, the default range for pitch bend sensitivity is set to plus or minus 2 semitones. This means that if a note is played and the pitch wheel moved to its extreme limit, the effect of pitch bend affecting it would be limited to a maximum of two semitones. There are times when it would be advantageous for us to have a bigger range. This can be set using RPN's.

| Position | Val1 | Val2 | Channel | Status |
|---|---|---|---|---|
| 0001.02.052 | 101 | 0 | 1 | Registered Parameter No. MSB |
| 0001.02.056 | 100 | 0 | 1 | Registered Parameter No. LSB |
| 0001.02.060 | 6 | zz | 1 | Data Entry MSB (LSB not used) |
| 0001.02.064 | 101 | 127 | 1 | Registered Parameter No. MSB |
| 0001.02.068 | 100 | 127 | 1 | Registered Parameter No. LSB |

The most important code in this instance is the data entry 6. Value 2, (currently referred to as zz) which can have a range between 0 and 24 If zz were set to 12, a full throw of the pitch wheel would change the pitch of the note (up or down) by a full octave. When using any kind of RPN (registered parameter number, including non registered parameter numbers) disable the ability for any values to be changed by spurious outside influences such as knocking the data slider on a mother keyboard. The 'locking off' of parameter numbers can be performed by sending a value of 127 to both MSB (101) and LSB (100).

## Non registered parameter number

### Non registered parameter LSB (98) non registered parameter MSB (99)

Non registered parameter numbers can also be used to control Roland GS and Yamaha XG equipment. Non registered parameter numbers differ slightly from RPN's in the way they control a piece of equipment. NRPN's are used to control more of the subtle features of a device such as the ability to modify the waveform of a sound and/or create special effects such as portamento.

We'll now examine two different examples of NRPN messages. If you refer to your manufacturer's manual and turn to the pages that deal with MIDI implementation, find the section that deals with NRPN MSB/LSB.

Below is a typical example of how this technical information is laid out. This particular example explains how to change the pitch of any drum instrument using NRPN's:

*Changing the pitch of a drum*

| NRPN | | Data Entry | Description |
|---|---|---|---|
| MSB | LSB | MSB | |
| 18H | rrH | mmH | Pitch coarse of drum instrument |
| | | | relative change on specified drum instrument |
| | | | rr : key number of drum instrument |
| | | | mm : 00H – 40H – 73H (– 64 – 0 – = 63 semitone) |

(i) Let's first translate all that techno babble into something we have a vague chance of understanding, and then we'll create a set of instructions to increase the pitch of the castanets by nine semitones to produce a sound that closer resembles finger snaps.

*Increasing the pitch of an instrument*

| Val1 | Val2 | Status |
|---|---|---|
| 99 | 24 (18H) | Non registered parameter no. MSB |
| 98 | 85 (rrH) | Non registered parameter no. LSB |
| 6 | 73 (mmH) | Data entry MSB (LSB not used) |
| 99 | 127 | NRPN (MSB) locked off |
| 98 | 127 | NRPN (LSB) locked off |

Note 18H = 24 (decimal) is the value used to instruct the module that we intend to transpose a drum or percussion instrument.

rrH = 85 (decimal) is the note number for the instrument we intend to modify (castanets = note number 85)

mmH = 73 (decimal) which is the decimal value for transposing the instrument up nine semitones. Remember a value of 64 is the centre or off position.

(ii)    As another example of using NRPNs we'll now change the cut-off frequency of an instrument and lower it from its default setting of 64 down to 40. Reducing the cut-off frequency tempers the timbre of an instrument.

*Reducing the cut off frequency*

| Val1 | Val2 | Status |
|---|---|---|
| 99 | 01 (01H) | Non registered parameter no. MSB |
| 98 | 32* (rrH) | Non registered parameter no. LSB |
| 6 | 40 (mmH) | Data entry MSB (LSB not used) |
| 99 | 127 | NRPN (MSB) locked off |
| 98 | 127 | NRPN (LSB) locked off |

In this example rrH is set to a decimal value of 32. If the following values are substituted for value rrH they would affect these parameters.

Value 2 set to 32 = TVF cut-off frequency *

Value 2 set to 33 = TVF resonance

Value 2 set to 99 = env attack time

Value 2 set to 100 = env decay time

(iii)   The following examples concentrate on changing the various values that produce vibrato (modulation) effects.

*Changing the vibrato rate*

| Val1 | Val2 | Status |
|---|---|---|
| 99 | 01 (01H) | Non registered parameter number MSB |
| 98 | 08 (rrH) | Non registered parameter number LSB |
| 6 | 54 (mmH) | mm=14 to 114 (64 is the default). A value of 14 produces a minimum vibrato rate, 114 produces a maximum vibrato rate. |
| 99 | 127 | NRPN (MSB) locked off |
| 98 | 127 | NRPN (LSB) locked off |

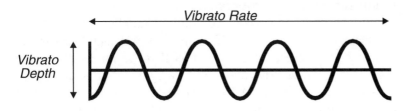

Figure 12.1 Vibrato rate and depth

**Changing the vibrato depth**

| Val1 | Val2 | Status |
|---|---|---|
| 99 | 01 (01H) | Non registered parameter number MSB |
| 98 | 09 (rrH) | Non registered parameter number LSB |
| 6 | 73 (mmH) | mm=14 to 114 (64 is the default). A value of 14 produces a minimum vibrato depth, 114 produces a maximum vibrato depth. |
| 99 | 127 | NRPN (MSB) locked off |
| 98 | 127 | NRPN (LSB) locked off |

Vibrato delay controls the delay from the of the start of the tone to full amplitude vibrato.

**Changing vibrato delay**

| Val1 | Val2 | Status |
|---|---|---|
| 99 | 01 (01H) | Non registered parameter number MSB |
| 98 | 101 (rrH) | Non registered parameter number LSB |
| 6 | 35 (mmH) | mm=14 to 114 (64 is the default). A value of 14 produces a minimum vibrato delay whereas 114 produces a maximum vibrato delay. |
| 99 | 127 | NRPN (MSB) locked off |
| 98 | 127 | NRPN (LSB) locked off |

# System exclusive commands

Every module, synth and keyboard has its own operating system of some kind. The use of system exclusive (SysEx) commands allows the device to be controlled from the front panel (by pushing buttons), or by special instructions transmitted down to the device via a MIDI cable.

### Manufacturers' ID numbers

Every manufacturer is allocated a unique number for this purpose. For instance, Roland has the ID number of 41H and Yamaha has an ID number of 43H. By sending this ID code immediately after a start of system exclusive message data byte, each manufacturer can access their own equipment exclusively. Some parameters can also be modified using standard control codes, but control codes would be implemented on every unit which could disrupt every module in a large array of synths.

## Manufacturer's IDs

| | | | |
|---|---|---|---|
| 07H | Kurzweil | 40H | Kawai |
| 08H | Fender | 41H | Roland |
| 0FH | Ensoniq | 42H | Korg |
| 10H | Oberheim | 43H | Yamaha |
| 18H | Emu | 44H | Casio |
| 24H | Hohner | 47H | Akai |
| 26H | Solton | 51H | Fostex |

When a string of SysEx instructions is sent the first byte of information is always F7H. This number says to all devices that a start of system exclusive message has been sent and they should expect the rest of the message to follow. When this byte is received all instruments will prick up their ears and wait for the next data byte which tells them which manufacturer's equipment is being addressed. If the second byte was a 41H for instance, all Roland equipment would continue to listen while other modules, Korg, Yamaha etc., would say to themselves 'Oh they want to talk with Roland gear, OK, I'm (whatever) so I'll ignore all these other instructions until I'm told this particular SysEx message is over'.

The Roland equipment is still listening, waiting for the next byte of information which tells it what device number it's calling. A device, or any number of devices can be set to respond to different ID numbers, therefore you could have three instruments that are identical in every way except the user sets the ID numbers for each to be 0FH, 10H and 11H.

When the ID byte is received (the normal default is 10H) modules 1, and 3 would return to monitoring. Module 2 is probably getting quite excited now because so far it has matched itself correctly to all the information sent. The next byte it receives is the Model ID. It's conceivable that in a large MIDI set up there could be two or three different Roland units which are all set to device ID 10H. The model ID refers to the model type, and informs all units that the information coming is for a specific model. If the model ID referred to a Sound Canvas device all other units, such as U and D series devices would return to monitoring.

A command ID is then sent which indicates the function of the exclusive message, and then the data is sent which starts with an address followed by the instructions. It might be said that with all these numbers flying around if one number is sent or interpreted incorrectly the whole message would be messed up, correct! Roland have devised a system that checks to see if the right information has been received. If so, the device will respond, and if not the error message 'checksum error' will be highlighted on the display and the unit will disregard the complete set of instructions. Before we explain how to calculate a checksum, let's take a look at a real SysEx message (note all values are in hexadecimal format).

This exclusive message is a Roland GS initialisation command designed to set all internal parameters back to their default (factory) settings of the GS format.

*Roland GS initialisation SysEx string*

| FO | 41 | 10 | 42 | 12 | 40 | 00 | 7F | 00 | 41 | F7 |
|----|----|----|----|----|----|----|----|----|----|----|
| I | I | I | I | I | I————————————I | I | I | I |
| I | I | I | I | I | I | | I | I | I |
| I | I | I | I | I | I | | I | I | I |
| I | I | I | I | I | I | | I | I | End of exclusive |
| I | I | I | I | I | I | | I | Checksum | |
| I | I | I | I | I | I | Data | | | |
| I | I | I | I | I | Address (MSB to LSB) | | | | |
| I | I | I | I | Command ID | | | | | |
| I | I | I | Model ID | | | | | | |
| I | I | Device ID | | | | | | | |
| I | Manufacturer's ID (41=Roland) | | | | | | | | |
| Start of exclusive | | | | | | | | | | |

## Roland checksums

A Roland checksum uses the address bytes and data bytes only, therefore everything else can effectively be ignored. In the example above the address bytes are 40,00,7F and the data byte (there's only one in this instance) is 00. If these were first converted into decimal the numbers become 64, 0, 127 and 0. Now add them all together = 191. Keep subtracting 128 from the result until we produce a negative number

$$
\begin{array}{r}
191 \\
-128 \\
\hline
63 \\
-128 \\
\hline
-65
\end{array}
$$

Disregard the negative sign and convert the new number (65) back into hexadecimal format, giving 41H. And that's it!

To recap:

1 Convert all the address bytes and data bytes into decimal format
2 Add together all address bytes and data bytes.
3 Keep subtracting 128 from the result until a negative number or zero is produced.
4 If it's zero, stop and convert to hex (zero decimal = zero hexadecimal). This is the checksum.
5 If it's negative, ignore the minus sign and convert the number back into hex. This is the checksum.

Finally, once all data have been sent, an end of exclusive message (F7) data byte is sent.

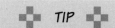

> **TIP**
>
> *S*ome later Roland models use an automatic checksum system (ACS). If your device does support ACS, all checksum calculations are unnecessary, but ensure the checksum byte is set to 00 to enable ACS to work.

## Yamaha XG initialisation SysEx string

F0,43,10,4C,00,00,7E,00,F7

Note: Users with MU50 and MU80 devices can display the SysEx string of a parameter by pressing the `ENTER` button twice in rapid succession.

## GM initialisation SysEx string

F0, 7E,7F,09,01,F7

This message will perform a GM initilisation to a device irrespective of the manufacturer. As I mentioned earlier, SysEx strings always have a manufacturer's ID as the second data byte but as all rules go, there are always exceptions aren't there? We can see the second and third data bytes are 7E and 7F. These are 'Universal' System Exclusive codes which are non-manufacturer specific. This means no matter who made the device (Yamaha, Korg, Casio, Roland etc.) this message will perform the correct function.

## Don't forget

You can see that by using system exclusive commands you can modify the parameters of every instrument in a whole rack of synths and modules remotely from our computer. There are a few pointers to remember when using system exclusive commands.

1 Never start a new SysEx command until the previous one has finished.
2 If the same result can be achieved using control codes, use these in preference. (System exclusive messages can grow quite large and can choke a busy system.)
3 It has been known for SysEx messages to fail for no apparent reason.
4 SysEx is non-channel specific. This means there is no need to wonder what MIDI channel to give it. This message changes the unit on a global type basis. MIDI channel settings are irrelevant.

5 SysEx takes precedence over every type of event. The playing of note data will be temporarily suspended if a SysEx message is being sent. Only when the entire SysEx string has been sent will the module process the note data held in its buffers.

## Pitch bend commands

There are a possible 16,384 different degrees of pitch bend, 8192 positive and 8192 negative. This figure may be considered by some to be a little unmanageable to use (I wonder why?), so some software sequencers prefer to display pitch bend data as a series of 128 degrees with each degree having another 128 discrete steps. This information is shown using two values, the first (value 1) is the micro tuning steps and the second (value 2) is the coarse tuning; i.e.

*Pitch bend values*

|  | Val1 | Val2 |
| --- | --- | --- |
| Example 1 | 105 | 90 |
| Example 2 | 58 | 37 |
| Example 3 | 0 | 64 |

The first example has the coarse tuning as 90 and the micro tuning as 105, the second has 37 for coarse tuning and 58 for micro tuning. The final example shows the coarse tuning as 64 and the micro tuning as 0. This is considered as being the centre position or off.

## Aftertouch

Aftertouch is a unique controller that's produced when extra weight is applied to a held note or chord. Aftertouch can be used to modify sounds or introduce special effects to any note(s) once they've been played. It may be that aftertouch produces modulation or perhaps changes the waveform. The function of aftertouch is determined by the programmer who in turn has to ensure that the module will respond to it in the correct way. If a module ignores aftertouch information but a keyboard produces it, either filter out these events at source or delete them afterwards.

# Set-up codes

To devise fool-proof set-up codes is very difficult if not impossible. Many instruments respond in different ways, but by following the codes set out below your sequenced song stands a very good chance of being played correctly no matter what condition the module was in.

| Position | Val1 | Val2 | Channel | Status |
|---|---|---|---|---|
| 0001.01.004 | F0, 7E, 7F, 09, 01, F7 | | | Universal Exclusive message 'turn General MIDI system on' |
| 0001.01.024 | | | | Any other exclusive commands |
| | | | | (SysEx messages take time to send. Leave enough space so that any previous messages have finished before a new one is |
| to | | | | sent. Some sequencers can display event timings in SMPTE format. If not average the space between short messages to be at least 12 ticks, 48 for larger ones. Be prepared to shuffle the start times. |
| 0001.01.380 | | | | |
| 0001.02.000 | 120 | 0 | 1 | All sounds off |
| 0001.02.004 | 121 | 0 | 1 | Reset controllers |
| 0001.02.008 | 0 | 0 | 1 | Bank select MSB * |
| 0001.02.012 | 32 | 0 | 1 | Bank select LSB * |
| 0001.02.016 | 1 | | 1 | Program change |
| 0001.02.020 | 1 | 0 | 1 | Modulation |
| 0001.02.024 | 0 | 64 | 1 | Pitch wheel |
| 0001.02.028 | 64 | 0 | 1 | Damper pedal |
| 0001.02.032 | 7 | 100 | 1 | Volume |
| 0001.02.036 | 11 | 127 | 1 | Expression |
| 0001.02.040 | 10 | 64 | 1 | Pan |
| 0001.02.044 | 91 | 50 | 1 | Reverb |
| 0001.02.048 | 93 | 50 | 1 | Chorus |
| 0001.02.052 | 101 | 0 | 1 | Registered parameter number MSB |
| 0001.02.056 | 100 | 0 | 1 | Registered parameter number LSB |
| 0001.02.060 | 6 | 12 | 1 | Data entry |
| 0001.02.064 | 101 | 127 | 1 | Registered parameter number MSB |
| 0001.02.068 | 100 | 127 | 1 | Registered parameter number LSB |
| 0001.02.072 | 120 | 0 | 2 | All sounds off |
| 0001.02.076 | 121 | 0 | 2 | Reset controllers |
| 0001.02.080 | 0 | 0 | 2 | Bank select MSB * |
| 0001.02.084 | 32 | 0 | 2 | Bank select LSB * |
| 0001.02.088 | 1 | | 2 | Program change |
| 0001.02.092 | 1 | 0 | 2 | Modulation |
| 0001.02.096 | 0 | 64 | 2 | Pitch wheel |
| 0001.02.100 | 64 | 0 | 2 | Damper pedal |
| 0001.02.104 | 7 | 100 | 2 | Volume |
| | | | | etc., etc. |

Always use the first measure to set-up the system, and while these codes are being transmitted don't send any note data. Not to be overlooked, ensure that the module or synthesiser is set to respond to system exclusive commands. Some may argue that the initial GM initialisation command should be sent at 0001.01.000 but I prefer to send it once the sequencer is up and running.

These codes are repeated and continue being spaced every four ticks apart, progressing through each MIDI channel in turn until all 16 MIDI channels have been reset.

The reason we space these codes four ticks apart is because it will help tremendously if we ever need to save our song in standard MIDI file format and import it into a different sequencer package. Some software runs at a different resolution than others and may have a different ticks per quarter note time base.

Most sequencers can write and save MIDI data at resolutions of 384 TPQN and in some cases higher. If this MIDI file was imported into an older sequencer, that was capable of processing data only at 192 TPQN, it would automatically divide every time point by two to get it to fit. When this happens the distance between our codes is still two ticks. Even if we load the same MIDI file into a sequencer with a resolution of only 96 TPQN (the lowest resolution I would ever recommend) the positions, even being a quarter of what they were before, are still placed one tick apart and so can still be sent sequentially.

### Non GM sound banks

Some keyboards and modules not only contain the General MIDI tone bank but may contain a set of proprietary sounds (non GM). This enables the user to use whichever sound they prefer. GM users should delete all occurrences of bank select messages (controller 0 and 32). When an instrument receives the system exclusive message to turn GM on, it obviously does so. If there are bank select codes sent after the initialisation message, it may switch the module out of GM mode and return it back to its own set of generic voices. Do we really want our Jazz guitar voice (program change 27) to sound like a Peruvian nose flute?

Once a sequenced song has finished, and after the natural reverb has died away, it's good practice to send another GM Initialisation command as this will restore all the internal parameters to factory presets and return sound envelopes to normal.

Inserting controller messages may just be a simple job of selecting the required controller from a palette (Figure 12.2) and placing it onto the correct time point, in the right track and on the appropriate MIDI channel. As soon as the code is in place it's just a simple matter of modifying the default values.

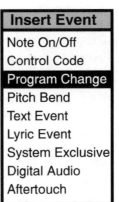

Figure 12.2 Inserting
controllers from a palette

## Reverb effect

When we recreate a part we may experience difficulty in reproducing that studio type reverb. What can we do, if after we crank up the reverb value to 127, find it's still not enough?

### Increase the amount of reverb applied globally

GS and XG initialisation commands set the global value for reverb to 64. Beware – increasing this value will increase the amount of reverb applied to every part (instrument), so unless we intend to wash the song with over the top amounts of reverb, the reverb levels of most instruments (parts) should be decreased accordingly.

Let's say we wanted to increase the value of reverb (and chorus) from 64 to 90 using system exclusive commands. Enter the following values:

*Roland GS*

| Reverb to 90 (remember to include the SysEx start and end bytes, F0 and F7) | |
| --- | --- |
| Hex | 41, 10, 42, 12, 40, 01, 33, 5A, 32 |
| Dec | 65, 16, 69, 18, 64, 01, 51, 90, 50 |

*Yamaha XG*

| Reverb to 90 (remember to include the SysEx start and end bytes, F0 and F7) | |
| --- | --- |
| Hex | 43, 10, 4C, 02, 01, 0C, 5A |
| Dec | 67, 16, 76, 02, 01, 12, 90 |

### Roland GS

Chorus to 90 (remember to include the SysEx start and end bytes, FO and F7)

| | |
|---|---|
| Hex | 41, 10, 42, 12, 40, 01, 3A, 5A, 2B |
| Dec | 65, 16, 69, 18, 64, 01, 58, 90, 43 |

### Yamaha XG

Chorus to 90 (remember to include the SysEx start and end bytes, FO and F7)

| | |
|---|---|
| Hex | 43, 10, 4C, 02, 01, 2C 5A |
| Dec | 67, 16, 76, 02, 01, 44, 90 |

Note. General MIDI (level 1) doesn't acknowledge chorus as a valid parameter.

## Changing the global type of reverb

GS default is Hall 2 and XG default is Hall1. These can be changed by a tiny amount of SysEx. Try these

### Roland GS

Hall 1 (remember to include the SysEx start and end bytes, FO and F7)

| | |
|---|---|
| Hex | 41, 10, 42, 12, 40, 01, 30, 03, 0C |
| Dec | 65, 16, 69, 18, 64, 01, 48, 03, 12 |

Pan delay (remember to include the SysEx start and end bytes, FO and F7)

| | |
|---|---|
| Hex | 41, 10, 42, 12, 40, 01, 30, 07, 08 |
| Dec | 65, 16, 69, 18, 64, 01, 48, 07, 08 |

### Yamaha XG

Hall 2 (remember to include the SysEx start and end bytes, FO and F7)

| | |
|---|---|
| Hex | 43, 10, 4C, 02, 01, 00, 01, 01 |
| Dec | 67, 16, 76, 02, 01, 00, 01, 01 |

Tunnel (remember to include the SysEx start and end bytes, FO and F7)

| | |
|---|---|
| Hex | 43, 10, 4C, 02, 01, 00, 11, 00 |
| Dec | 67, 16, 76, 02, 01, 00, 11, 00 |

# MIDI implementation chart

Understanding a MIDI implementation chart can be of tremendous help in understanding what a device is capable of transmitting and receiving. Figure 12.3 is the chart for a hypothetical sound module, although it is based closely around currently available technology.

Date: Jan 1, 2000

Model: Sound Module     **MIDI Implementation Chart**

Version: 1.00

Figure 12.3 Standard MIDI implementation chart

| FUNCTION | | TRANSMITTED | RECOGNIZED | | REMARKS |
|---|---|---|---|---|---|
| **Basic Channel** | Default | 1~ 16 | 1~ 16 | | Memorised |
| | Changed | 1~ 16 | 1~ 16 | | |
| **Mode** | Default | | Mode 3 | | |
| | Messages | X | X | | |
| | Altered | **************** | | | |
| **Note Number** | | 0 ~ 127 | 0 ~ 127 | | |
| | : True Voice | X | 0 ~ 127 | | |
| **Velocity** | Note ON | X | O | | |
| | Note OFF | X | O | | |
| **After Touch** | Key's | X | O | | |
| | Ch's | X | O | | |
| **Pitch Bender** | | X | O | | |
| | 0,32 | X | O | *1 | Bank Select (MSB, LSB) |
| | 1 | X | O | *1 | Modulation |
| | 5 | X | O | *1 | Portamento time |
| | 6,38 | X | O | *1 | Data Entry (MSB, LSB) |
| | 7 | X | O | *1 | Volume |
| **Control** | 10 | X | O | *1 | Panpot |
| | 11 | X | O | *1 | Expression |
| | 64 | X | O | *1 | Hold 1 |
| | 65 | X | O | *1 | Portamento |
| **Change** | 66 | X | O | *1 | Sostenuto |
| | 67 | X | O | *1 | Soft |
| | 84 | X | O | *1 | Portamento Control |
| | 91 | X | O | *1 | Effect 1 Depth (Reverb) |
| | 93 | X | O | *1 | Effect 3 Depth (Chorus) |
| | 98,99 | X | O | *1 | NRPN (LSB, MSB) |
| | 100,101 | X | O | *1 | RPN (LSB, MSB) |
| | 120 | X | O | *1 | All Sounds Off |
| | 121 | X | O | *1 | Reset All Controllers |
| **Program Change** | : True # | X | O | *1 | |
| | | | 0 ~ 127 | | |
| **System Exclusive** | | O | O | | |
| **System Common** | : Song Pos | X | X | | |
| | : Song Sel | X | X | | |
| | : Tune | X | X | | |
| **System Real Time** | : Clock | X | X | | |
| | : Commands | X | X | | |
| **Aux Messages** | : Local ON/OFF | X | X | | |
| | : All Notes OFF | X | O (123 ~ 125) | | |
| | : Active Sense | X | O | | |
| | : Reset | X | O | | |

| Notes | *1    O/X is selectable | | O : Yes |
|---|---|---|---|
| **Mode 1** : OMNI ON, POLY | **Mode 2** : OMNI ON, MONO | | |
| **Mode 3** : OMNI OFF, POLY | **Mode 4** : OMNI OFF, MONO | | X : No |

The *function* column refers to what MIDI equipment, in general, can respond to. The *transmitted* column indicates if this particular device can send these types of messages and the *recognised* column tells us if it can receive them. The *remarks* column is used for notes relating to certain functions.

The most important symbols are O (yes) and X (no). If we look down the transmitted and recognised columns we can see at a glance what this device can do. That may be fine but if we don't really understand the question the answers are useless, so let's have a closer look at the functions column shall we?

## Basic channel

Basic channel has two options (default and change). Remember we have just a sound module so we know it can't transmit any information relating to MIDI channels, but we can see, by looking in the recognised column, that it can respond to them. The default refers to the MIDI channel the module will default to on power-up. If the remarks column says 'memorised' we know the device has a battery backup facility so our settings will be remembered when the device is switched off. The changed option refers to the MIDI channels the device is capable of receiving, in our case it can respond to any one of 16.

## Mode

The mode feature refers to the four available modes of operation available to any MIDI device.

Taking a closer look we can see that omni can be either on or off and that the device can be in mono or poly mode. Omni refers to the way the device listens for incoming information. If it's set to 'on' the device will respond to all notes irrespective of their MIDI channel and play them on all its available MIDI channels at once. Changing the omni setting to 'off' instructs the device to be more selective in what it hears. Every MIDI channel would then respond only to incoming information on its own MIDI channel and ignore any data transmitted on any other MIDI channel.

The difference between poly and mono is that poly (polyphonic) enables multiple notes to be transmitted and received at once, mono (monophonic) can support only one note being sent or received at any one time.

*Mode 1*

A pretty unrealistic situation (every note played on every MIDI channel all at once) but who knows?

### MIDI MODES

1   Omni on, poly
2   Omni on, mono
3   Omni off, poly
4   Omni off, mono

*Mode 2*

This mode is slightly different to mode 1 because our device (still responding to all channels) can play only one note at a time – still a pretty unrealistic situation and hardy ever used.

*Mode 3*

This is the default mode for most of today's devices and one which allows multiple note ons (poly) to be sent and received discretely on their own MIDI channels (omni off).

*Mode 4*

This mode is favoured by MIDI guitarists who send just one note per string (mono) but every string can have its own MIDI channel (omni off).

**Note number**

Note number is the note range that the device can recognise. This will have a range of 0 to 127. The true voice function refers to what would happen if the device ever received a note out of this range – say note number 453! True voice overcomes this potential problem by 'rolling over' at each end of the extremes of note range and automatically transposes notes up or down accordingly, so that they'll now fall within our defined parameters.

**Velocity**

The velocity function tells us if our device is velocity sensitive and whether it will respond to differences in key pressure.

**Aftertouch**

Aftertouch is produced when additional weight is applied to an already held note or chord. Two types of aftertouch exist. One is called key pressure, which sends information about the pressure of every key that is currently being played. As you can imagine this type of aftertouch will produce reams and reams of information. Realising the potential problem another type of aftertouch was devised and adopted as the default. Channel aftertouch combines all the key pressure values and then produces an average after-touch for the complete MIDI channel.

**Pitch bender**

Pitch bender displays the transmit and receive attributes for pitch bend events. Sometimes the remarks column may contain further details on the maximum amount of bend range the device can be configured to. In some instances we may find there is a remark relating to the resolution of the pitch bend data the device can support. This may be written as '9 bit resolution'.

### Control change

This is probably the area of most interest to us. The numbers rolling down the function column are the control change numbers we'd have to send or receive to perform the functions listed in the remarks column. The transmitted and recognised column indicates which of these codes are available for us to use.

### Program change

It's quite common to see an asterisk next to a number in the recognised column (*1) From the key below the table we see that this option can be enabled or disabled by the user. Turning this to X (no) will cause the unit to ignore any and all incoming program change commands. Situated just below and in the same section is the function True #. This works in a similar way to true voice as described above, but this time it modifies only incoming program change commands.

### System exclusive

System exclusive commands are used to control and change the parameters on a manufacturer's device in milliseconds rather than having to spend hours of painful button pushing. Another use for system exclusive commands is to send and receive sounds and sound parameters – although this can take up a lot of disk space. We'll often see a O (yes) symbol even on a sound module. This gives us the opportunity to send bulk dumps of our systems settings to an external device like a computer for editing or archiving.

### System common

System common refers to the control of any external devices attached to our MIDI set-up ensuring (we hope) that every device will respond in a similar (common) way. If for example, an external drum machine was used to replace the drums in the box, we would want it to be able to keep in sync with the sequencer if we jumped to a point further up the song. If song position flag, is set to X this means that the drum machine would always start to play from the beginning of the song.

Many drum machines can store their own data as separate songs in their own memory or save them to tape or disk. A song select feature would enable us to switch between the different songs currently held in the drum machines memory. The tune function allows us to send tuning information to a device – say transposing them or ensuring every unit is tuned to concert pitch (A = 440).

## System real time

Clock refers to a small and invisible pulse which is sent every 96th note which enables two machines to remain locked together. The command feature is a secondary set of commands which indicates if the device will also respond to start, stop and continue messages.

## Auxiliary messages

Local on/off is a way a disabling the internal sound generators of a device. This is useful if a keyboard is used to play the sounds on another external unit. All notes off is self explanatory, and if this command is enabled, it will turn off any notes within a specified range, often displayed in the recognised column.

Active sensing could be thought of as the device knowing what to do if it detects a hardware problem, such as a broken MIDI lead or the MIDI cable being pulled out of the socket while it's in use. Active sensing uses a kind of ping-pong system and if doesn't get a response (after about 400 – 500ms) it will interpret it as an error. When an error of this kind is detected, the unit often sends an all notes off command to silence any droning notes.

This brief insight into the MIDI implementation chart should enable you to examine the features of any device you may encounter and judge whether it is suitable for your needs.

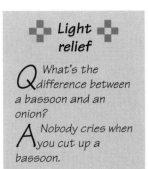

**Light relief**

Q What's the difference between a bassoon and an onion?

A Nobody cries when you cut up a bassoon.

# 13

## Getting that syncing feeling

### Down the line

If it's vital to exchange data between systems that don't support the standard MIDI file protocol, the only way is to send all the data down the MIDI cable from one device to the other, in a similar way to the method we use for recording onto tape. This requires the destination (slave) machine to be put into record mode while the source (master) machine plays its data down the MIDI cable. Once the transfer is complete the destination machine is stopped and the song saved.

### MIDI clock

Wouldn't it be much better if we could lock these machines together in such as way that every measure is identical on both machines? We can if we use MIDI clock. MIDI clock is a special electronic pulse which can be transmitted along with all the other MIDI information. Our slave sequencer can listen to these pulses and every time one is heard the slave sequencer advances by 1/96th note.

To transfer songs down the line follow this procedure:

1  Connect a MIDI lead from the MIDI OUT socket on the master machine to the MIDI IN socket on the slave machine.
2  Connect a MIDI lead from MIDI OUT socket on the slave machine to the MIDI IN socket on the master machine.
3  Load the sequencer package and song into the master machine
4  Load the sequencer into the slave machine and select the new song function.
5  On slave machine only:
   (i)  Disable the MIDI click (metronome). This click (often C#1 – stick across) may get recorded and mixed into the incoming data stream, even if it doesn't the constant clicking could drive you crazy!
   (ii)  Disable all pre-counts so that when the recording starts it will capture all incoming data. In most circumstances there is a

one or two measure count-in before the machine starts to record. If you forget to disable the pre-count you could miss the set-up measure and possibly the count-in as well.

(iii) Select/highlight a track to record onto.

(iv) Set the synchronisation mode to be external clock (this feature may be called something slightly different).

(v) Press record (nothing should happen yet!)

6 On master machine only:

(i) Disable the MIDI click (or else that'll be recorded as well)

(ii) Disable the tempo track if possible.

(iii) Set the playback speed for the song quite low (under 65 BPM).

(iv) Activate/send clock command.

(v) Press play.

At this point the destination machine should start recording. When the song has finally finished playing (make sure it's played right through to the end and captured the very last note off command) stop the master machine. The raw data now sits on your slave machine. The conversion process is nearly over but you just need just a few more tweaks to enable you to present the data in a more user friendly form.

7 Immediately save the new song to disk.

8 Disable the slave to external sync option and return the slave machine to its own internal timing.

9 Use the remix command to automatically make new tracks and separate all the data back onto its own MIDI channels.

10 Check the tempo changes and time changes on the original file and re-enter these manually into your new song (MIDI tempo commands are not transmitted down the line).

11 Rename each track to reflect the instrument allocated to it.

12 Re-save the final tweaked version of the song.

13 Reset the master machine back to normal.

Instruction 6 (iii) tells you to set the playback tempo below 65 BPM. If you intend to edit your new version and perhaps copy chunks of it to different places in the song, it's pretty important to have your (new) data as close to your existing time points as possible. The more accurate the timing the less chance there is of grabbing extraneous data which could've spilled into your capture area.

At a speed of about 65 BPM the data drift should be about 1 to 3 ticks, at a tempo of 200+ the drift could increase to well over 5 or 6. If you can afford to spend the time waiting for the song to transfer over, select the slowest tempo common to both machines before starting.

Note: If there are tracks on the master sequence that share the same MIDI channel and you wish to retain their independence on the slave sequence, you must either record the song twice (if you don't, this process will merge the data together during the transfer process), or copy the track that contains both instruments (after re-mixing) and delete the irrelevant data from each.

**Points to remember when recording down the line**
- If the destination sequencer does not have the ability to re-mix the data back onto separate tracks, every track will have to be recorded individually.
- If there is a track designated purely for SysEx messages record this track separately.
- Don't record from the THRU of a module or via a MIDI merge box. Only use machine to machine connections.
- To improve timing use the shortest MIDI leads available.
- Never re-quantise the destination sequence.

## Syncing to multitrack tape

To achieve maximum benefit from a multitrack tape recorder the understanding of synchronisation is vital. There are two main methods of synchronising to tape. One method uses a process called frequency shift keying (FSK) and the other uses SMPTE.

Figure 13.1 Computer – multitrack connections

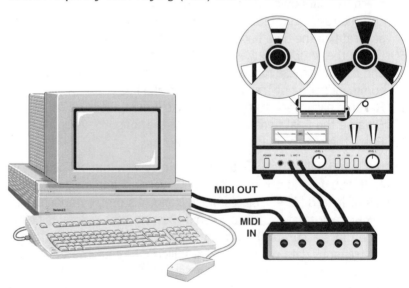

MIDI OUT

MIDI IN

## FSK

Both of these systems often require additional hardware to encrypt and decipher the timing information striped (recorded) onto one of the (empty) tracks on the tape. Striping a tape is a pretty straight-forward process. You must first select a track that you intend to use as the control track.

When the sync box is activated a signal is produced. Adjust the levels on the multitrack to indicate a healthy signal, so it peaks between – 10 to – 6 dB VU on multitrack machines, and about – 3 to 0 dB VU on cassette machines (ensure that any noise reduction is disabled), and put the tape into record mode. After several seconds press play on the sequencer and play the song right through to its end.

When the song has finished, stop the tape, rewind it to the beginning and set the sequencer to receive external synchronisation. Put the sequencer in play mode and start the tape. When the sequencer hears the timing codes it will start to play. Hopefully you've remembered to select record on another track.

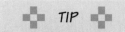

**TIP**

*Using an outside track (normally the highest one available) reduces the chances of material recorded on adjacent tracks breaking through and corrupting the timing signal. When you decide on the (tape) tracks you intend to record onto leave the adjacent track free. If you do need to use it, avoid percussive or harsh bass heavy sounds.*

## Smart FSK

The drawback of using ordinary FSK is that the song has to be played from the start every time in order to send the correct start command to the sequencer, even though the desired instrument you wish to record may only appear in the last measure. To over-come this potential mind numbing and boring process, Smart FSK was introduced which can recognise song position pointers so you can leap to the last few measures and drop-in.

## SMPTE

A more versatile form of synchronisation was designed by the Society of Motion Picture and Television Engineers and was given the really catchy acronym SMPTE – pronounced simp-tee (psst! to avoid terminal damage to your credibility *never* call it SMPTE !). Like FSK, a designated control track has to be striped before it can be used. Always stripe more code than required – most engineers stripe the whole tape in one go.

When the machines are locked together they use a different type of code from the normal measures, beats and ticks. SMPTE/EBU uses hours, minutes, seconds, frames and bits. Firstly there are four different frame rates. 35mm film uses 24 frames a second, European video PAL uses 25 frames, American NTSC uses 30 frames per second and American colour video uses 29.97. Unless you really need to change these settings, you should set your frame rate at 25 fps and leave it there. There are 80 bits for each frame (1 bit is about half a millisecond).

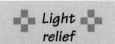
When the song has been successfully recorded and mixed, it's common protocol to archive a tape tails out. This requires the tape to be reversed so that it reduces the likelihood of tape break-through. The tape should also include at least a 20 second test tone (sine wave) at the start (write this level on the tape box) which can be used to re-configure the tape machine to the recording levels on the tape.

# 14 ❖

# Copyright and copywrong

This chapter concentrates on the use of MIDI files in a commercial environment. Their commercial use has raised many issues, and probably the biggest relates to copyright. For the vast majority of users, knowing the legalities of musical copyright is not really necessary, but this potted guide will clarify some of the hitherto grey areas.

There are different types of copyrights attached to different types of product, and most music publishers assign their licensing rights to the different associations and societies that specialise in copyright administration. A musical work can be reproduced in quite a few different ways, each of which has its own copyright aspect. This stuff could be important if we're fortunate enough to get that elusive top-ten number one with our song 'Forget the musicianship gimmie the dosh!' – me cynical? Anyway, let's think for a moment how we could hear our music:

1  Live performance by the original artists.
2  Commercial radio broadcast of the song by the original artists.
3  Television/satellite/cable broadcast of the song by the original artists.
4  Chart video or album video by the original artists.
5  Film rights if our song is used for incidental music or as a main title soundtrack.
6  CDs, cassette, DAT, Vinyl records - original artists
7  CDs, cassette, DAT, Vinyl records - soundalikes.
8  Karaoke and backing tapes.
9  Printed sheet music.
10  MIDI files.
11  Sampled and used as part of a new work.
12  Instrumental musak versions (lift music, shopping malls etc.)
13  Paper pianola rolls (own up, who remembers them!)
14  Fairground organs (I think we're getting rather silly now)

**Commercial MIDI files**

*By their nature, commercial MIDI files reproduce existing copyrighted works. For instance Crazy Little Thing Called Love is the copyright of Queen Music Ltd., and any person or company who wishes to manufacture this particular song as a MIDI file would have to pay a royalty to the writer of the song. Note that the royalty is not paid to the artist (although in some circumstances they will be one and the same). If we produced a MIDI file of Hound Dog for instance the royalty from our MIDI file would be paid to Leiber and Stoller (the writers) and not to Elvis's estate.*

## MIDI data

Each of these types of product enjoys some kind of copyright. It may be a pure mechanical right (audio backing tapes) or a pure print right (sheet music). MIDI files, by their versatility, can encapsulate quite a few different rights all at the same time. It's now been agreed (in principle) that a MIDI file includes the following:

- Mechanical rights – well the disk is a piece of spinning plastic isn't it?
- Arrangement rights – MIDI files are created by individuals and companies who try to arrange the song so that it can play within the GM sound and its polyphonic limitations.
- Adaptation rights – taking the original song (from CD, vinyl or tape) and adapting it to another (different) medium (to disk in our case)
- Synchronisation rights – Using SMPTE, FSK or any other form of time code it's possible to synchronise a MIDI file to film or video.
- Print rights – some sequence packages include the facility to display and print out the MIDI file in traditional musical notation.
- Lyric rights – lyrics can be encrypted into a MIDI file and therefore reproduced on a VDU or printed out onto hard copy.

## Moral rights

For all the working musos reading this, you'll probably have already heard that some artists refuse absolutely to give their permission for their works to be recreated as a MIDI file. All songs writers have complete control over their work by invoking, what is called, their moral rights. This right prevents a song being used in such a way that it could compromise the integrity or morals of the writer. For instance a writer might allow their work to be used within the video medium but they would probably take great exception if the same song was used as a backing track to a porn movie!

Publishers, MIDI file producers and the public must respect the wishes of the writers and not produce material that would impinge upon these rights.

## Binary data

There's another copyright attached to MIDI files and that's in regard to all those cute little 1s and 0s that make up the actual file. If a programmer sits and slaves over a hot keyboard for hours on end producing MIDI files is there any legal protection available? Fortunately the law accepts that a copyright exists in the binary data as well as the original sound recording, and therefore the work of a MIDI file programmer is now recognised.

When a MIDI file is supplied to an end user (the public) the MIDI file company often imposes certain conditions on its use. Common restrictions include:

1 A user is considered by the MIDI file company to be a person or group of people that use the MIDI file for rehearsal purposes, live performances or as source material for the manufacture of its own promotional material (i.e. demo tapes/CDs).
2 Any organisation or company which intends to use MIDI files in a commercial environment (backing tapes, karaoke etc.) must obtain permission from the original MIDI file producer to use its data. A special licence may be required.
3 The production of printed sheet music from the MIDI file is strictly prohibited.
4 To protect against media (disk) failure, the user is permitted to make a duplicate copy of the original disk for archiving purposes.
5 If the software is sold on to a third person all copies (including back-ups) must be passed over to the new owner or destroyed.

## Public domain MIDI files?

One of the biggest concerns of copyright owners is the growing misconception that MIDI files are public domain (free) and that anyone who buys them has the absolute freedom to (ab)use them however they like. Common abuses of MIDI files include the manufacturing of multimedia CD ROMS which are often made without the prior knowledge and permission of either music publisher or MIDI file producer.

Another frequent offender is the Internet/World Wide Web. By connecting a modem to a computer, and with the correct software, it's possible to trawl the Web looking for MIDI files and associated material. Experience has shown that many of the sites, including stand alone BBS's, offer this service as a hobby and these sites are acting in ignorance of the legal repercussions that could befall them. These sites are now being contacted and closed down by the music publishers.

The third common misconception relates to the ownership of a MIDI file. This often happens when a user suggests that by changing the data slightly the data is not exactly the same as the original so they (the user) have created their own, completely new copyright work. The law in this matter states simply that if a substantial part of the new work is based around an existing copyrighted work the copyright remains with the original owner. Phew!

This means that if a person considers that by changing the order of tracks, remixing the velocities, changing the key, substituting different instruments and even changing the notes and note lengths slightly constitutes a significant change, they'd be greatly disappointed and probably sued into the bargain.

Any UK person or company that deals in copyright material must be aware of the relevant law that relates to such material. The relevant law of copyright in the UK falls under section 107 of The Copyright and Patents Act of 1988, Section 107 (similar laws exist in other countries).

Listed below, is the act and as can be seen it's very specific about what is, and what isn't legal.

### Copyright and Patents Act 1988 Section 107

(1) A person commits an offence who, without the licence of the copyright owner:

    (a)    makes for sale or hire

    (b)    imports into the United Kingdom otherwise than for his private and domestic use.

    (c)    possesses in the course of a business with a view to committing any act infringing the copyright, or

    (d)    in the course of business

    (i)    sells or lets for hire, or

    (ii)    offers or exposes for sale or hire, or

    (iii)    exhibits in public, or

    (iv)    distributes, or

    (e)    distributes otherwise than in the course of a business to such an extent as to affect prejudicially the owner of the copyright.

## Sampling

Some sequencers have the ability to incorporate sample data into the data stream of a MIDI file. This ability allows us to play a James Brown 'Oww!' along with the MIDI file. If done correctly this combination of sample and MIDI data can produce stunning results. The same can be said for looping drum samples (the good 'ole funky drummer loop instantly springs to mind) that can be used as a basis of a new song.

From a copyright standpoint both of these would infringe. If we need that 'extra' hit (and I believe this is a natural evolution for the standard MIDI file – only time will tell), we should record our own samples and use them. As testament to this a good friend of mine released a commercial recording (it made the charts) and created his unique snare sound by using a sample of a cat sneeze which he pitch shifted and tweaked.

## Printed music

If a MIDI file is loaded into a dedicated print package there lies an ability to produce a full score or individual parts from it. For original material this poses no problem but if the work is within copyright, the rule of thumb to adopt is quite simple:
*Unless you have written permission from the copyright owner, don't!*

It's common practice to publish a musical work in many forms. The first type is often the traditional piano/vocal lead sheet which has changed little (unfortunately in my opinion) from those published during the early part of this century.

Well known personalities often promote their own particular versions of songs (i.e., Dave Clackett and his famous B*b* kazoo play Meatloaf's greatest hits!). And dare we forget those easy to play watered down adaptations that roll off the production line at the 'crotchet factory' to be consumed by the insatiable public.

The infrastructure required to produce all these different variations on a theme (what a pun!) is sometimes too involved for even the biggest of publishers. Most publishers therefore assign their print rights to third parties whose specific job is to produce all the variations of print required for each work. It's fair to say that the print rights to a considerable number of popular works have been assigned to either of these two companies.

1    **International Music Publications Ltd**
Woodford Trading Estate
Southend Road
Woodford Green
Essex IG8 8HN
Tel : 0181 551 6131, Fax : 0181 551 3919

2    **Music Sales Ltd**
8/9 Frith Street
London W1V 5TZ
Tel : 0171 434 0066, Fax : 0171 439 2848

Both IMP and Music Sales are part of:

The Music Publishers' Association Ltd
7th Floor
Kingsway House
103 Kingsway
London WC2B 6QX
Tel : 0171 831 7591
Fax : 0171 242 0612

Example selection of catalogues and agencies represented:

Chappell Music Ltd
Jobete Music (UK) Ltd
Queen Music Ltd
Virgin Music (Publishers) Ltd
Warner Bros Music Ltd
ATV Music
Chrysalis Music Ltd
Northern Songs
Rondor Music (London) Ltd
Walt Disney Productions

If your desire to produce printed music or lyrics which are currently in copyright is overwhelming (a work becomes public domain 70
years after the death of the composer not when it was first
released), I strongly suggest contacting the above companies before
proceeding any further.

## The performing rights

Once we've bought our MIDI file and practised it to perfection (we
hope) it's time to introduce it into our set at the next gig, but do
we need another licence to perform it? As far the MIDI file producers are concerned it's not their responsibility (or in their power) to
grant one. If a pub or club intends to have music on its premises it
has to register with the Performing Right Society (PRS). A fee is
paid to PRS every year which is divided between its members. This
licence enables us to perform any material quite legally but if we're
in any doubt about whether a venue has a licence, examine the
plaque (normally displayed over the door at the entrance or behind
the bar). For absolute confirmation ask the landlord.

Listed below are the contact details for a few copyright societies.

**United Kingdom**
Mechanical Copyright Protection Society (MCPS)
Elgar House
41 Streatham High Road
London SW16 1ER
Tel +44 0181 769 4400
Fax +44 0181 769 8792

**Australia**
AMCOS
PO Box 2135
North Sydney
New South Wales
2059
Australia
Tel +61 2 954 3655
Fax +61 2 954 3664

**Germany**
GEMA
Postfach 80 07 67
D 81607
Munchen
Germany
Tel +49 89 4800300
Fax +49 89 4800 3414

**United States of America**
Harry Fox Agency
711 Third Avenue
8th Floor
New York
NY 10017
USA
Tel +1 212 370 5330
Fax +1 212 953 2384

# 15

# Transcribing from record

## Introduction

It would be impossible for any one book to cover in depth every conceivable type of music and style that everyone would ever want to program, so I've limited our analysis to generalisations. When it comes to the actual hands on programming, you will soon settle down and adopt a style you feel most comfortable with.

## Classical repertoire

There's a great feeling of achievement in sequencing classical works but there are a few drawbacks. A lot of the larger classical works are meant to be played by a full size symphony orchestra, and this would far exceed our humble 28 voice polyphony. On the positive side however, most classical works are free from any copyright restrictions and, better still, many of the larger public lending libraries have music departments which contain the complete miniature short scores of many of the major works – great for sequencing, terrible on the eyesight!

Remember that many of the instruments in these scores have already been transposed into the correct key for the instrumentalist to play (violas are nearly always written in alto clef – trombones and cellos frequently use tenor clef).

## Arranging vs. transcribing

For many years there have been artists who have re-arranged old classic songs and given them their own interpretation. It can be said some of these covers are enhanced versions of the original and some might say they're not.

Some examples are:

| | | |
|---|---|---|
| *Locomotion* | Kylie Minogue | orig. Little Eva |
| *Love is all around* | Wet Wet Wet | orig. The Troggs |
| *Run to you* | Rage | orig. Bryan Adams |

There's a great deal of satisfaction in improving upon a classic, per-haps for gigging purposes, but there'll be people who don't like anyone tampering with original works. Be prepared to accept the inevitable criticisms.

Transcribing a song from tape or CD is probably the hardest dis-cipline to master as there's no latitude for error or interpretation. You've no opportunity to introduce any of your own ideas, and deviation from the original is unacceptable. To be fair to yourself, to produce a perfect transcription of a band comprising of Steve Gadd, Stanley Clarke, Chick Corea with Michael and Randy Brecker heading up the brass section, playing the Quincy Jones version of *Birdland* could start to get a bit tricky – well no one said it was easy!

## First, set up a work station

Without turning yourself into a hermit, try and set aside a dedicat-ed area for working, away from continual interruption and normal family chaos. Try and position the keyboard/synthesiser close to the stereo and computer system, and if at all possible merge the audio streams from the synth and tape so that they're mixed together on playback. Merging and balancing the sounds this way will be helpful in selecting the correct voices to use plus it helps us recapture the mix of the original.

If you intend to take down by ear, record the source material onto a good quality cassette tape or use a CD player to play the reference material. If tape is chosen record the song without using any type of Dolby noise reduction. Dolby is a very good system for eliminating unwanted background noise and tape hiss but unfortu-nately it also suppresses a lot of the upper harmonic frequencies.

When working, disable the loudspeakers and use a pair of good quality headphones for the actual transcribing process. Taking down will require immense amounts of concentration and you'll have to listen to the same section of music over and over again. Using 'cans' produces a much clearer audio picture than listening through conventional speakers – even good ones. Disabling the external speakers will also reduce the risk of driving everybody within earshot totally mad!

 *TIP*

*Best results can be achieved if you employ the services of a graphic equaliser. A graphic can be a life saver when it's used to boost certain frequencies and lift 'hidden' instruments from an otherwise mediocre mix.*

## Ear training

If you're going to take a song down by ear you'll be relying on what your ears are telling you so if you can improve your aural skills you'll automatically become more efficient in your work. Interval recognition is one facet you can improve with training. There'll come a time when you'll hear intervals and immediately know what they are. Until that happens you have to start slowly and practice.

Start interval training by listening to the pitches of two notes and associate that interval with a easily remembered tune. For example if you play an octave (C2 to C3) this is the interval used for the first two notes of *Somewhere over the Rainbow*. Here are a few more:

| | |
|---|---|
| C up to A (major sixth) | *My bonnie lies over the ocean* |
| C up to G (perfect fifth) | *Chariots of fire* |
| C up to F (perfect fourth) | *Amazing grace* |

## Metronome substitute

When we're recording a passage of music, the metronome sets the tempo by continually playing a click on each beat of every measure. If the song you're working on is a slow ballad and the part you're recording is quite complex there's a good chance your timing will go awry because there'll be too much time elapsing between each click. Record a simple drum part using sixteenth notes on the closed hi-hat and in a style not too far away from the original. Repeat this reference 60 or 70 times and use it in conjunction with the metronome click. Indeed any type of music would benefit from having a real drum track to lock into instead of a bland and boring click. Don't worry if your cobbled together drum part is not exactly, or even remotely, like the original, you'll be replacing it later on with the real one.

One of the many questions often asked of me is the amount of time it takes me to sequence a song. It is difficult to answer this exactly as the time varies from song to song depending upon it's complexity. I normally set aside about 20 – 25 hrs to produce a polished product. For newcomers to sequencing don't become too disillusioned if it takes considerably (up to 3 or 4 times) longer.

After each section of music has been recorded, take the time and edit the data before moving on. As soon as you've ironed out all the kinks from a part you can feel safe to copy this part over and use it elsewhere in the song.

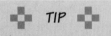

**TIP**

*As mentioned earlier, each person will develop their own methodology for transcribing/ arranging songs from tape or CD. The following just happens to be the way I (and some of my colleagues) prefer to work, but don't think this is the only way, if you devise a system that works for you – use it.*

## The *I've had enough* syndrome

I have heard many MIDI song files that start out really well and then falter and fade as the song progresses. More often than not the programmer starts off with good intentions but rushes to get to the end for whatever reasons (difficulty – boredom). This seems to happen more with people who program in sections, by that I mean those people who like to program every instrument in the introduction of a song before moving on to every instrument in the verse. By the time the third chorus comes around it's very tempting to say 'Oh it's just another chorus', and then copy and use old chorus data instead of listening for anything new or different. Likewise programming solos from the record. Taking down solos is one of the very hardest things to do properly, so if you intend to create an off the record MIDI file then do the hardest bits first.

## Ready? Let's go!

The example below is based on Tina Turner's *The Best*, see Chapter 16 for the full MIDI score.

### 1 Jot down the structure

Listen to the song over a few times and jot down a structure - something like this:

| | |
|---|---|
| Tempo | About 110 |
| Time signature | 4/4 |
| | |
| 3* – 7 | Introduction |
| 7 – 19 | Verse |
| 19 – 31 | Verse |
| 31 – 39 | Chorus |
| 39 – 47 | Verse |
| 47 – 59 | Verse |
| 59 – 67 | Chorus |
| 67 – 75 | Verse |
| 75 – 83 | Bridge |
| 83 – 91 | Sax solo – key change |
| 91 – 99 | Chorus |
| 99 – 107 | Chorus |
| 107 – 117 | Middle |
| 117 – 125 | Chorus |
| 125 – 133 | Verse |
| 133 – 141 | Verse |
| 141 – 144 | Ending – (sustained pause) |

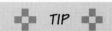

*TIP*

*Don't try and program for hours on end. It is a proven fact that if the brain is worked hard it starts to lose its edge after about 45 minutes of continual use. So after each 45 minute period stop and take a rest, get something to drink, walk around, kiss the dog and kick the wife (oops – wrong way round) and give yourself a break away from the music for about 10 to 15 minutes. When you return to working it'll take a few minutes to get back into the flow but this technique will enable you to work for longer periods without burning out the brain cells. Above all – Ignore all those people who boast about sequencing a complete song in a couple of hours – I've heard a lot of them and they sound awful!*

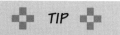 **TIP**

*The structure listing must start after the set-up measure. By starting at measure three it will enable us to insert a count off in measure two – this could be four closed hi-hats or perhaps four side-sticks.*

## 2 Choose your instruments

Listen to the instruments that the song uses and select corresponding instruments and allocate MIDI channels and program changes for them. Remember that you're limited to a maximum of 16 different instruments playing at any one time – one per MIDI channel.

| Channel | Name | Comments | GM program change # |
|---|---|---|---|
| 10 | Drums | Power kit 17 | |
| 2 | Bass guitar | | 34 |
| 3 | Bass synth | | 40 |
| 4 | Guitar 1 | | 31 |
| 5 | Guitar 2 | | 30 |
| 6 | Synth 1 | Warm pad | 96 |
| 7 | Synth 2 | Stringy pad | 51 |
| 8 | Chime synth | | 89 |
| 9 | Bottle blow | | 77 |
| 11 | Sax solo | | 67 |
| 15 | Group vocals | | 54 |
| 16 | Lead vocals | | 88 |

**TIP**

*When programming, stick to recording small(ish) phrases. The maximum amount to record in any one take should be about eight measures at normal speed, 16 if double tempo.*

## 3 Sketch out the chord sequence

Play along with the song to determine the key and roughly sketch an idea of the chord sequence – I prefer to use Acoustic Piano for this purpose.

Key(s) Bar 1 = F Major, Bar 83 = G Major

Some recordings are tuned slightly off key. We don't notice this ordinarily, but when you play your module (tuned perfectly to 440) alongside the original, the beat frequencies (two notes slightly out of tune producing a pulsating effect) will render transcribing impossible. Tune the module accordingly.

If the original recording falls between F and F#, are you going to tune up, or down? All masochists reading this, please tune to F#, the rest of us will wimp out and play in F. Interestingly, a lot of guitar based music is written in sharp keys (try asking a guitarist to play simple rock and roll in Ab and see what happens). If you decide your recording really is in F# then proceed as normal (in F) and when the song is finished, transpose all of it – except the drums – up a semi-tone (cheating, of course!).

*Verse chords*

| Measure | Beats 1 | 2 | 3 | 4 |
|---------|---------|---|-----|---|
| 7 | F | / | / | / |
| 8 | F | / | / | / |
| 9 | F | / | F? | / |
| 10 | F? | / | F | / |
| 11 | F | / | / | / |
| 12 | F | / | / | / |
| 13 | F | / | F? | / |
| 14 | F? | / | F | / |
| 15 | Dm | / | / | / |
| 16 | Dm | / | / | / |
| 17 | Bb | / | / | / |
| 18 | Bb | / | / | / |

*Chorus chords*

| Measure | Beats 1 | 2 | 3 | 4 |
|---------|---------|---|---|---|
| 31 | F | / | / | / |
| 32 | F | / | / | / |
| 33 | F | / | / | / |
| 34 | F | / | / | / |
| 35 | Dm | / | / | / |
| 36 | Dm | / | / | / |
| 37 | C | / | / | / |
| 38 | C | / | / | / |
| etc | | | | |

Note that I've not worried overly about working out the exact make-up of the chords but I've kept to just majors and minors. If there are a few chords that seem a bit 'funny' I use a ? symbol to remind me to check these chords more closely. When I've done my preliminary run through I go over the song again and fill in the blanks (marked *).

### 4 Fill in the blanks

*Verse*

| Measure | Beats 1 | 2 | 3 | 4 |
|:---:|:---:|:---:|:---:|:---:|
| 7 | F | / | / | / |
| 8 | F | / | / | / |
| 9 | F | / | F6* | / |
| 10 | Fmaj7* / | F | | / |
| 11 | F | / | / | / |
| 12 | F | / | / | / |
| 13 | F | / | F6* | / |
| 14 | Fmaj7* / | F | | / |
| 15 | Dm | / | / | / |
| 16 | Dm | / | / | / |
| 17 | Bb | / | / | / |
| 18 | Bb | / | / | / |

### 5 Program the bass

When it comes to choosing the first 'real' instrument to start programming, I normally prefer to start with the bass. Why? – Well, the bass is normally playing constantly throughout the song, and when you get this instrument down it'll give you a good idea of what the complete chord structure of the song will be.

True, you may encounter a few chords along the way that use substitute bass notes (Bb/C etc.), but as this doesn't happen very often, you could possibly generalise and say that the first note of each measure will probably be the root of the chord. I prefer to work out everything an instrument is playing from start to finish before changing. I find that by constantly listening to just one instrument my ears become finely tuned to it and I can distinguish its sound above all the others.

### 6 Play the main chords

Next comes the main chord playing instrument. This might be piano, organ or perhaps a pad synth of some kind. There may be a couple of chord playing instruments to choose from, so do yourself a favour and choose the easiest first. If the song you're working on contains only fast guitar strumming it helps to create a simple guide chord part which provides a basis to work from. After the guitar parts are eventually recorded you can go back and delete your chord guide part. Always bear in mind the polyphony issue so don't use large numbers of notes to build up each chord.

## 7 Record the real drum part

Now it's time to replace the dummy drum track with the real one. Use a different track for each instrument because it'll make mixing the drums a lot easier. I usually start by recording the kick drum first. The kick drum often works in conjunction with the bass guitar/synth, stressing key points within each measure.

There have been times when the sounds used for the kick drum and bass have been so similar it's been really hard to tell them apart. I find that by boosting all the bass frequencies on the amplifier and graphic and cutting all the top frequencies the separation between the kick drum and bass guitar starts to appear. Even with a mushy mix the kick drum will have a slightly sharper attack to each note than the bass, and it's this attack I listen for.

The cymbals are the next instruments to be programmed and it'll help if you completely reverse all your previous EQ settings and boost all the upper frequencies. Closed hi-hats should present no major problem for you, but listen out for the odd rhythmic variation and obligatory open hi-hat that sneaks in from time to time.

Pay particular attention to any cymbals that have sustaining characteristics and ring on (top cymbals, crash cymbals and the like). All that constant ringing coupled with all those overtones can confuse you into spotting exactly what's happening underneath it all. Sure, it's pretty easy to spot the isolated crash at the beginning of a phrase, but if you're working on a hard rock number which is subjecting you to a constant barrage of cymbals, you could find it difficult to spot the odd sixteenth note in with all the others.

Now you can start to lay down the snare and tom tracks. I suggest the first pass should concentrate on the main snare beats, normally those on beats 2 and 4. Repeat the section over for any fills, flams or rolls. If the snare part is recorded at a slower tempo, be careful with the number of notes used for rolls. Increase the speed so the song is playing in true tempo before editing them.

Having just successfully recorded all the drums it's now time to record any percussion parts. I like to use separate tracks for all my percussion instruments so that if I (or my customers) have to use the sequence in a live situation with an 'organic' drummer, the drum track can be muted leaving the percussion track to play on.

## 8 Record the guitars

Guitar programming is one of, if not the hardest instruments to recreate authentically. Listen carefully to the song and try and pick out the guitars used. Use the GM guitar bank as a reference point (nylon, steel, jazz, clean, muted, overdrive or distortion). Although you may only be able to hear one type of guitar, say a clean guitar, listen closely to see if it's been overdubbed or double tracked. To create an authentic effect you may have to cheat (what again!?) and program a couple of guitar tracks. For more details about programming guitar refer back to Chapter 5.

### 9  Start on the melody line
It's about now that I play in the melody line. I often choose an expressive instrument such as a saxophone or harmonica to carry the tune, and I try to use plenty of bends and vibrato to produce a realistic performance. Playing the melody at this stage can make it easier when over-dubbing any auxiliary synth parts.

### 10  Add all the other instruments
Play in all remaining instruments. This could be synth effects, group vocal parts or perhaps a solo.

### 11  Join all the parts together
Join (glue) all parts together to form single instrument track. Check note data for smooth and even playing as well as tempering any sporadic extremes of velocity. Lastly check for doubled notes and note overhangs. Verify the correct values and placement of any controller data and/or pitch bend events.

### 12  Check all the codes
Check the set-up codes, tempo, SysEx and program changes.

### 13  Do the first mix
Once you've created all your individual parts and tweaked the odd bit of data here and there, it's time to polish the overall performance with the first mix. On the first time through the song I mix it totally dry (without any reverb or chorus applied to any parts). Mixing this way may seem very strange at first but it soon becomes second nature.

Many songs could've sounded so much better if the programmer had taken the time to mix the track dry first instead of trying to hide a bad mix and bad playing by making it too wet. Once a good balance between the instruments has been obtained dry, the sprinkling of any fairy dust will enhance the overall sound.

When it comes to mixing a song, start with the drum tracks and concentrate on balancing the kick, snare and closed hi-hats. Now balance all the other drum and percussion instruments.

- Add the bass and other rhythm section parts
- Mix sustained parts (often strings or other pads)
- Add auxiliary synths and other instruments
- Introduce vocal tracks.

This first mix will immediately knock the track into rough shape but there's still a long way to go. At this point you have to make a decision. What type of mix are you after? Is it a gigging mix or do you want an off the record mix?

With a gigging mix the drums, especially the kick and snare are very upfront. The bass guitar is often cranked up a shade and brass parts are often played 'in your face'. A home mix is a lot more subtle. Try and remember how difficult it was to hear certain instruments when the data was first recorded. It may have been quite difficult to distinguish the kick drum and pad synth parts from all the other instruments.

## General guidelines on mixing

1 Whatever instrument the programmer plays for real is often too proud in the mix. This sparked the infamous, and oh so true saying of 'Never let the guitarist do the mix'.
2 Some parts too loud? Ask yourself how loud should that instrument really be against everything else? If you had to strain your ears to hear a part in the original recording it should be the same in your MIDI version.
3 Owing to the fact that we, as musicians, have programmed the song, we're likely to believe that anything that was technically very difficult to play or a part that was severely edited but sounds stunning must be heard above everything else – *wrong*! Sometimes the really difficult and tricky parts are more effective when they are allowed to sit down in the mix.
4 As more instruments are introduced, their tonal weight will start to increase the overall volume.
5 Don't mix the song using 'cans', always use loudspeakers.
6 Record the finished mix onto cassette tape and play it on as many systems as possible. A car stereo is one of the best places to audition a new work because it's so unforgiving.

## 14 Edit each track in turn

Edit every track in turn. Refer back to any chapters on specific instruments and remix again. Check that all pitch bend data, when appropriate, are correct. This is when I concentrate on fine tuning and record expression commands (controller 11).

Be sure to pay lots of attention to the velocity characteristics of the instrument being edited. Merge all the separate drum and percussion parts onto two tracks.

### 15 Check MIDI data

Check and correct data for MIDI lumps caused by:

1 Excessive MIDI traffic
2 Excessive polyphony
3 Excessive use of controller information gunging up the plumbing
4 Repeated part error

### 16 Add effects

Start applying small amounts of reverb (and chorus) to finished parts until the desired result is obtained.

### 17 Massage the tempos and velocities

As explained in the drum programming chapter, it's often a good idea to slightly increase the tempo and note velocities of a song in the chorus section and reduce them for the middle eight. So check verse/chorus velocity and tempo balance.

The difference in velocity levels between a verse and a chorus should be quite small. An increase of just five for each chorus will produce good results. Remember to decrease by five for the verses. Middle eights and bridge passages are often quieter. Try and match the tempo ebb and flow with a corresponding tempo track.

### 18 Add the final polish

This is the time when you can introduce your non registered parameter numbers if you want to (GS and XG users only). You must first ask yourself if you think any changes to the sound of an instrument will help. Is it worth changing the pitch of a single drum (often the snare) to re-create the sound of the original? Do you want to change the reverb type via SysEx or perform any other commands which will affect the playback of the song?

If you've used any clever tricks somewhere in the song it's a good time to give them a once over just to make sure everything is all right.

Note: If the sound of an instrument is so different from the principal tone I have available I often change the waveform before recording.

### 19 Done!

Save, archive and go to the pub.

# Original compositions

To compose any type of original music there must be a spark of inspiration somewhere to get you going. Whatever your 'hook' happens to be, make sure it's the first thing you record. Don't worry about a few fluffs along the way as you can correct them later.

### Tip 1

Put the sequencer into record mode and set it to stop at measure 999. As the sequencer is recording everything you'll be playing (crap et al) there may be certain sections somewhere in the take that you can cut out and file away. These blocks can be used later for a basis of a new work. Just to make sure you don't lose any data, as soon as the sequencer stops, save! After saving, carefully delete all waste data and save a second version.

### Tip 2

Try and copy the style of a favourite artist. When you use this technique the first version can often sound really quite puerile but by the time you tweak the odd bit here and odd bit there, the song will have changed into something completely unique – we hope!

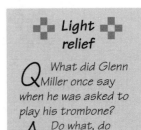

**Light relief**

Q What did Glenn Miller once say when he was asked to play his trombone?

A Do what, do what?

# 16

# 'The Best' – MIDI score

Before launching into a programming frenzy, take time to read these special observations regarding the way the score to 'The Best' is written and refer back to any specific chapters if necessary.

**General**

All numbers in square brackets [3] refer to sequencer measure numbers. I have started from measure three so that a series of set-up codes and a count off can be inserted at measures one and two respectively. For multiple repeated sections, measure numbers are given for each repetition, i.e. [117/125/133].

The global crescendo ('cresc ...) marking should start about the third beat of measure 114 and should build in intensity until it reaches forte (loud) at beat one of measure 117. For instruments that are re-playing notes, use a gradual increase in velocity level, and for sustaining instruments (synth 1 and guitar 2) reduce the expression level first, play the notes quite hard and ramp the intens ity level back up.

SAVE after every take and good luck!!

**Guitars**

The guitar (and basses) are transposing instruments, and recording bass parts can be problem with five octave keyboards. Transpose the range of the keyboard (either on the keyboard itself or from the sequencer) so that you'll be able to play the lower extremes of range and play the parts in the range they are written (guitar 1, guitar 2, bass synth and bass guitar). When all the parts are pasted together transpose the relevant tracks down an octave and reset the keyboard.

Guitar 1 starts with written eighth notes but be aware of the instruction to play them 'detached'. This prevents the part being played legato as this would destroy the character of the piece. At measure 15 there is the instruction to 'let ring'. This particular figure should be played with the length of the notes extending (over-lapping) underneath the following notes.

## Basses
In measure two (bass synth and bass guitar) there is a repeat mea-sure sign and the instruction '(sim)'. This should be quite obvious to mean that not only should the notes from measure one be repea ted but their accented style should also be duplicated in a similar way.

## Drums
The second time through the repeated section [59/67], the drums should play, at measure 62, an open hat at 62/2/192 and back to closed hat on 62/3/000.

## Synths
The slur markings for chime cynth and bottleblow synth (measure 55) should be played as notes *not* as pitch bends.

## Saxophone
The B*b* tenor sax is a transposing instrument. For the sake of clari-ty I've left it in concert pitch but this part should be transposed in a similar way to the guitar and bass parts we've previously men-tioned. The bend markings indicate where pitch bends should be used.

# The Best

*Tina Turner*

Comp: Knight/Chapman

need.

Give me a life time of prom-i-ses an' a world full of dreams

Aah

Speak a lang - uage of love____ like____ you know what it means,____

Ooh____

strong___ a - gain_____ you're simp - ly the best,_____ bet- ter than___
I hang on ev - ry

Aah_____

arms I could be in no bet-ter place._____ You're simp-ly the best_____

Ooh_____

Ah!

los- ing con - trol    you're  walk- in'  a - way___ with my heart___  and my soul._____ I  can feel you  ev - en

when I'm a-lone._____ Oh,_____ ba-by don't let go_____

Oh you're simp - ly the best,_____

Oh you're simp - ly the best, _____ you're bet - ter than all the rest,

You're bet - ter than all the rest

# 17

## Using MIDI files live

Using MIDI files for live work can be a great benefit to the working band as it allows you to compete against the plastic spinning parasites out there in gig-land (I refer of course to the disco – am I being too kind?) Take time to examine the material used for each 'normal' gig and a pattern will soon emerge of songs that are normally played in the first set, songs played in the second set, and so on. Copy these onto separate 'set' disks and label each one clearly.

There'll be times when a party-goer will ask for a special request so carry a set of disks labelled alphabetically. Disk A would contain all songs starting with A, disk B contains songs starting with B, and repeat the process for each letter of the alphabet.

If the song title is slightly ambiguous, like the example in this book – is it called *The Best*?, *Simply the Best*? or *Best (the)*? For the sake of a little bit of disk space I would copy the same song onto disks T, S and B renaming them to suit. This belt and braces approach could prevent a major screw up.

## Playback

There're two ways a MIDI file can be played. The first loads the MIDI file into the memory of the playback device. When it's loaded the song can be played. Other devices read directly from the disk so playback is instantaneous. Each method has its advantages and disadvantages. Those devices that load the entire song before playing it can take quite some time, especially if the file is large. In reality it may take less than 20 seconds, but this seems like an eternity with a floor full of people waiting for the next song.

With the 'load first' system we do know that if the song has loaded it will play. Not so with direct from disk systems, it's possible for disk surface errors to upset the playback half way through a song. If I had to choose between them however I would still opt for the play from disk method – but I would use very good quality disks.

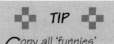

**TIP**

*W*aiting for a set-up measure of a new song to finish running through can seem like an eternity with a floor full of people. Ballads and slow tempo numbers are the worst offenders so get the set-up codes out of the way quickly by setting the tempo of the first measure to 225+ BPM. Make sure to insert a second (slower) tempo command at measure

**TIP**

*C*opy all 'funnies' onto their own disk. By funnies I mean all those little throw away numbers: Happy Birthday, Auld Lang Syne, National Anthem, etc.

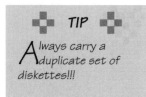

**TIP**

*Always carry a
duplicate set of
diskettes!!!*

You could take your computer to the gig of course but this would be a bit risky. No matter what any manufacturer might claim, no software is 100% bug free and the best place to find them is when you're using the software 'live'.

Secondly it seems that the sight of a VDU on stage is a cue for the biggest asshole in the hall to make a point of coming out with side splitting comments about you watching telly instead of playing the gig – bless 'em! I'm not against the principle of taking a computer on stage, but I would limit my choice to machines that are subtle and could be visually lost in the general electric spaghetti. I would use either an old Mac SE or a 386 PC laptop (mainly because these machine are cheap!). Both of these computers will have integral hard drives so although the files will still need to be loaded before they're played, the access time is just a second or two.

Commercial MIDI file players prefer to use type 0 MIDI files. To recap (refer to Chapter 2), a type 0 file contains all the information for all 16 channels on a single track. This type of file is more efficient than type 1s (multiple track) because the software engine only needs to concentrate on one track at a time and doesn't have to scan multiple tracks of data to get its information. Another benefit of type 0s is that they're smaller than type 1s so more songs can be stored per disk.

There's a slight anomaly with some playback devices which state they can read type 1s and type 0s. In reality the type 1 MIDI files they can read must be limited to just 16 data tracks and one tempo track. Anything bigger and the unit will fail. Unless there's strong reason to gig with type 1s save all songs as type 0s.

## Additional devices

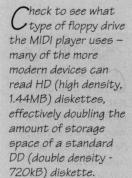

**TIP**

*Check to see what
type of floppy drive
the MIDI player uses –
many of the more
modern devices can
read HD (high density,
1.44MB) diskettes,
effectively doubling the
amount of storage
space of a standard
DD (double density –
720kB) diskette.*

A MIDI file can be used to drive other external hardware effects. It's possible to switch a reverb unit in and out and select different settings midway through a song. It's also relatively easy to switch the reverb effect off at the end of a song and turn it on again when a new song begins. The addition of a MIDI controlled lighting unit can enhance the overall appearance of a band, just as some form of vocal enhancer will improve the sound. Guitarists can benefit greatly from MIDI files as they can be used, in a similar way to the reverb unit, to make changes to their effects units.

If external devices are used in a live environment always make sure the same MIDI channels are used for the same piece of equipment. If you need to, switch MIDI channels around at the programming stage so that everything is consistent. If you're fortunate to have a multi port playback system (32 MIDI channels or above), use the higher set of MIDI channels on your second bank of 16 (11B – 16B) for all external units.

The most compact way of playing MIDI song files is by using a disk player and sound module combined into one integral unit. Figure 17.1 uses a separate disk player and sound module connected by a single MIDI cable. The data is read from the disk and pumped (OUT) down the cable INto the module – no worries, no fussy wiring, and regrettably limited versatility!

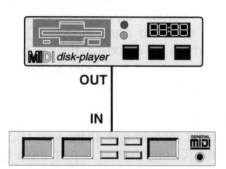

Figure 17. 1 Basic MIDI set-up

The MIDI set-up in Figure 17.2 is considerably more complex and offers greater expansion possibilities. With this particular system we have a total of five different devices all being driven simultaneously from a 32 MIDI channel computer based system.

Figure 17. 2 A more sophisticated arrangement

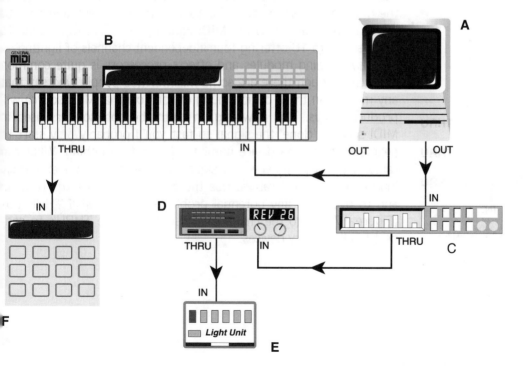

A     32 MIDI channel playback device (Apple Macintosh)
B     GM (GS/XG) keyboard
C     Non GM sound module – (8 part multi-timbral)
D     MIDI controlled reverb unit
E     MIDI controlled Lighting system
F     dedicated drum machine

If we look closely we can see that one bank of 16 channels is rout-ed to our GM keyboard (B). As we intend to use the samples from our dedicated drum module (F) we have to disable the internal drums in the keyboard (this can be performed from the front panel or by sending a suitable SysEx message). The INcoming data is echoed out from the THRU socket to the MIDI IN on the drum module.

The second set of 16 MIDI channels is first sent to a non-GM sound module (yes there *was* MIDI before GM!). This particular unit (C) only has an 8 part multi-timbral capability but it can be used to complement or replace certain sounds from the keyboard and/or expand our amount of available polyphony. The data is retransmitted INto the reverb unit (D) courtesy of the THRU socket on (C) and in turn the reverb unit passes the data onto the MIDI lighting unit (E). To correctly implement this system no two devices should be set to receive on the same channel therefore we could set the module to respond to channels 1 to 8, the reverb unit to 9 to 12 (4 modes) and lastly the MIDI lighting unit is set to respond to channels 13 to 16 offering four independent channels of lighting.

Daisy-chaining modules and effects processors is quite common practice although there are some misinformed people who say that any more than three devices hung off one original MIDI source will produce delays. This is wrong, in truth the optoisolators used in MIDI sockets 'clone' the signal so fast you'll probably only start to hear a slight lag on device number 300 and something. What can cause a problem however is signal degeneration from extremely long or cheap MIDI cables. Use the shortest quality leads you can and to overcome any potential problems insert a MIDI THRU box (Figure 17.3) into the chain, then use its multiple THRU's to con-nect to all ancillary devices.

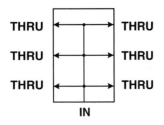

Figure 17.3 MIDI THRU box

# 18 ♥♦♣♠

## Help!

### Introduction

I hope that by the time most of you reach this chapter you'll know enough about MIDI to troubleshoot your own problems. But just in case we've missed a few pointers along the way, here's a selection of the most frequently asked questions (FAQs). Notice some questions can have more than one answer.

### When I play my MIDI file, my module doesn't produce any sounds

• Er.... Check that it's switched on, plugged in to a sound system, and the volume knobs on the amplifier and module are turned up (well you never know!)
• Check that the sequencer is actually sending data by checking the MIDI send/receive indicator on the sequencer and module. If the data is being sent from the computer but is not being received, consider:

1  Checking the integrity of the MIDI cables. Try swapping them around or even replacing them.
2  Checking and confirming the MIDI routing is correct. If the module is hung off a secondary port (on multiple MIDI channel systems), make sure the data is being routed properly and it's not being sent to another port - or anywhere else for that matter.

• Switch off and re-initialise the module – WARNING! – This may delete any user defined presets/edits, so if possible save everything to the sequencer first using a complete system exclusive bulk dump.
• Check the sequencer settings to make sure the tracks are not muted.
• Check the data to see if a volume command (controller 7) or expression command (controller 11) has been sent. If they have,

they could be set so low that the module gives the appearance of not working. Find them and increase their values accordingly. (expression at 127, volume about 100)

### I have a hardware MIDI file player and my MIDI files refuse to play

• Most hardware MIDI file players prefer to use type 0 files (single track) MIDI files or type 1 files with a maximum of 16 tracks. For greatest compatibly re-save your MIDI file as a type 0 and ensure your disk is formatted to 720k DOS.

• Also check to see that the song name you've used conforms to DOS protocol – eight characters for the name with a three character suffix. This is a common problem with users who are using Windows 95 or Macintosh operating systems. These systems allow file names to exceed 8.3. The suffix for most MIDI files is .MID but some hardware players, such as Yamaha devices, can opt to have a suffix .X01 – X99 instead. Using this method songs can be selected to play in any order, based on their numerical suffix not the alphabetical name.

• Thirdly, ensure the only thing on the disk are MIDI files. Most hardware MIDI file players will not play files that are located in sub-directories. Be aware that some devices try to play absolutely anything and everything they find on the root level of the disk – including text files!

### When I sync my two machines together and record 'down the line', all my tempo changes and time signature changes are not included on my new version

• Tempo and time signature changes are not transmittable MIDI events. When MIDI data is transferred down the line these events are omitted from the data stream. The receiving device will have no idea what type of music it's receiving so it'll default to a predetermined time and key signature – say 100BPM in 4/4 time. If you need the music to be edited or imported into a typesetting program you'll have to re-insert the tempo/time signatures manually in the new version. If you don't need that kind of precision, disable the slave to sync option on the slave machine and just record 'a la' tape to tape. This will work fine for ordinary live playback.

### Every time I try to save a MIDI file I can't seem to do it properly and get a memory error message

• A computer often builds a standard MIDI file in an empty part of its memory (RAM) before it saves it (that's why some sequencers allow you to play a song while it's saving) If there is not enough memory available it simply can't do it. This is a common problem with Atari ST's that only have 1 Megabyte of RAM. If this happens try thinning out the data, starting with controller information and delete all extraneous events (aftertouch and channel pressure). If this fails to cure the problem your only recourse is to add more RAM or use a software program which produces the illusion of doubling available RAM.

### I've sent some SysEx messages to my module and it's not working!
• Check the receive channel of the module – a common problem with Roland device numbers.
• Check the MIDI routing of your system, especially important if a merge/splitter box is used.
• Ensure the module isn't set to ignore all incoming SysEx information.
• Make sure any SysEx messages you send contain a valid checksum (if required). If it doesn't get the right one the receiving device will ignore the complete SysEx string and display an error message

### I understand my sequencer has resolution of 96 PPQN. Can I load and save MIDI files so that I can share them with my friends knowing that their software loads and saves at a much higher resolution?
• Yes. When a MIDI file is imported into another make of sequencer it will automatically round event positions and note lengths either up or down. This will ensure that imported events fall onto the nearest acceptable time points on the new sequencer.

### After I've edited my song file I can't seem to re-save it
• Check that the disk is not write protected or full.
• Also check the file path. If you loaded a MIDI file from floppy (I.e. A:\SONGFILE\MY_SONG.MID), then wanted to save it after editing, if you select SAVE from the file menu the program will automatically try to save it back to exactly the same place as it loaded it from (A:\SONGFILE\MY_SONG.MID). If in the meantime you've changed disks the computer won't be able to find the right area (as it probably doesn't exist on the new disk) and flag a disk error.

### When I stop my sequencer half way through some notes continue to drone
• Avoid using program change commands while a note is playing. If you do the sequencer will send the note on command to one instrument but when it effects the program change it will send its note off command to a different instrument. This could result in

the first instrument never receiving a note off command and a drone will be produced.

• Make sure there are no identical notes that overlap. When this happens some sequencers get confused. They send a note on command as normal, then they send another note on command, albeit for the same note. After a time the sequencer would send a note off command. What often happens is the sequencer forgets to send a second note off command – hence the drone. This shouldn't really be considered a bug, after all it shouldn't be possible to play two notes of the same pitch at the same should it? Spotting doubled notes can be quite easy if you look at the gate times in the edit pages. You'll find the second note has either a very short duration or a very long duration – sometimes tens of thousand of ticks. This problem is most noticeable with strings and other instruments that have a long sustain.

• MIDI can understand and process about 32,000 bits of information per second. The computer can easily create MIDI events 20 times that amount. If all this data is sent down the MIDI lead at once the buffer on the receiving device might get overloaded. If this happens it may just dump all unprocessed data in an effort to keep up! If one of the events it just happens to dump is a note off command – hello drone!

### When I play my song, some notes stop playing for no apparent reason

• You've exceeded the polyphony limitations of your module. Remember that GM has a polyphony of only 28 voices, not notes.

• Check to see if the note overhang problem has truncated some notes – see above.

• If the song contains any system exclusive data it will take priority over everything else, including notes. Any notes that should be playing at the same are temporarily suspended until the sending of any SysEx messages has been completed. When the notes are finally sent they often rush out, seemingly all at once – it sounds awful! If you need to send SysEx messages, take the time to send the minimum amount of information to perform the function you need. Avoid complete bulk dumps.

### I've edited my song and although it's in the right key for me, it sounds pretty awful

• When a song is originally recorded the arrangement is tailored to suit the instruments used (obviously). If you transpose the data the timbre (tones) of the instruments will change. The more extreme the transposition the worse the results will be. If you transpose down too far you'll produce bass parts that flap about and sound really silly, and if you transpose up to far you'll produce brass parts that are so high only dogs could truly appreciate them. Some tracks therefore may have to be transposed a second time (by an octave) to produce a realistic effect. For any errant notes select a note range, (i.e. any notes below EO – the lowest note on a standard bass guitar) and transpose them back into a playable range.

### As a Mac/PC user when I double click on a commercial MIDI file I can't load it as I do with my other files

• Mac users are used to launching programs by clicking on their files. This association between file and program is embedded into the file when the Mac saves it. A file is saved with two attributes. One is the 'creator', which tells the file the name of the program that it was created from and the second is the 'file type' which tells us what type of file it is. With commercial files there is no way the MIDI file producer can personalise every file for every customer so the file type and creator are deliberately omitted. To overcome this problem, load the sequencer program first and then use the 'Import' facility to initially load the MIDI file. Once loaded, re-save the file so that the creator and file type can be embedded in the new version. Now, whenever the file is double clicked from the desktop, the correct program will be launched and the file loaded.
• PC users must first load Windows, select a MIDI file and then use the 'Associate' option (situated under the file command – Win 3.11) in file manager. Once selected, a file with a .MID suffix can have any program associated to it.

### When I save my work as a MIDI file I lose some tracks

• If there is insufficient memory to correctly perform an export, some tracks may be automatically removed to free up more memory.
• Some tracks are muted when the song is saved, the sequencer may automatically remove them thinking (as they are deliberately muted) they're not required.

### I've used the track parameters box to alter the playback characteristics of my data but when I save my song as a MIDI file it loses it all and I'm back to the original version

• Using a track parameter box to audition and mix data is a handy facility to have but most sequencers ignore these settings and save just the original (un-modified) data. Hard code your modifications into each track before saving. Alternatively check to see if your sequencer has a feature that can perform this function automatically.

• If you've used the above technique and your software does create these events you'll often see them positioned at 1/1/000. Most commercial files use the complete measure for setting up the song. It could be that your settings are being implemented but along comes the commercial set-up a millisecond later and overwrites everything.

**My song has 'forgotten' all it's program changes, why?**
• See above ...

**When I play a new song the instruments sound kinda funny**
• Make sure the 'new' song has reset the module correctly. If the previous song altered the waveforms of the instruments in some way they'll need to be reset back to their factory defaults. This can be performed quite easily by sending the correct GM, GS or XG initialisation message.

**When I play one song, the subtle pitch bend information I've carefully programmed, works very well and at other times it sounds really naff**
• By using controllers 100 and 101 (registered parameter numbers) you can set the amount of range that the pitch wheel will respond to. If you haven't embedded your own unique parameters into the file, the song will use the settings of the previously played song. Remember if a SysEx initialisation command is used, the range of the pitch wheel will be preset to plus or minus 2 semitones.

**Some of my sounds flange**
• Flanging sounds are often produced when two notes, of the same pitch (double notes) are played simultaneously. Check your data.
• Reset the sounds that you intend to use and confirm that the flanging effect is not produced by modifications to a voice's parameters carried over from a previous song.

**When I use MIDI song files live I have to hang around on stage waiting for ages for the song to load. Is there a quick way to speed things up?**
• Some keyboards take longer to load songs than others. Use a direct from disk playback device – see Chapter 17.
• Increase the tempo, say 225 – 240 BPM, for the first (set-up) measure. Insert a tempo change at measure 2 to lower the tempo for the song 'proper'. This is extremely effective if the song is a ballad as it gets that first measure out of the way as fast as it can.

**I've purchased some commercial MIDI files and I need to convert them from a single track into multiple tracks for editing**

• Check to see if your sequence package has a 'Remix' facility. Remixing the data will explode the data into separate tracks, each containing one MIDI channel. The new tracks will have track names relating to MIDI channels so they should be renamed to reflect the instruments used.

• Copy the source track and delete any events that are not of the desired channel. This may mean performing the task numerous times. For instance if you wanted to keep MIDI channel 1 only you would need to delete channel 2, then 3 then 4 and so on until channel 16 is deleted. Only at this stage can you be sure that your track only contains data for MIDI channel 1.

**I have a separate drum module and I want to use this for my drums and ignore the drums in my GM box. How do I do it?**

• If you are using a different device for your drums and percussion you can send a SysEx command to turn off a part, but the data will still be re-transmitted from the MIDI THRU socket to your dedicated module.

• With multiple MIDI OUTs select a different port for the drum and percussion information.

**I have a real drummer and I want to send him a click on his headphones so that he can play in time with the sequencer without sending the click back to the main PA system**

• Unfortunately there only seems to be a compromise solution. As most GM, GS and XG devices use just a stereo left and right output the best solution would be to pan every instrument to one extreme and pan the drums to the other extreme – this may mean using SysEx commands. The instrument channel can be routed to the PA and sent to the front of house while the drum part (using another input on the desk) is sent back to the drummer on cans. The biggest drawback with this method is that the front of house mix will be in mono not stereo.

• To make things really difficult you may want to send the percussion track front of house but send the drum click as above. Your only recourse is to split the percussion and click onto two different MIDI channels. By using SysEx commands it's possible to transform an instrument channel into a secondary drum part (GS and XG only). Use an unused MIDI channel (MIDI 11?) for the live click and pan the tracks accordingly.

### When I've been jumping around my song editing and mixing I experience some funny pitched notes and different instruments sometimes play

• When moving around a sequencer it's easy to stop the sequencer at such a point that it's only part way through a particular function. This could be a pitch bend command on a note for instance. When the song is re-wound and played again the instrument playing will play its notes with the midway pitch bend setting making it sound dreadfully out of tune.

• Some sequencers have a chase or remember facility. If numerous program changes are used in a MIDI channel it's easy to scroll past a few and then start playing the song. This will result in the notes on the selected MIDI channel being played by the currently selected instrument – which is not necessarily the right one! Chasing events is a function that makes the sequencer read back past the present (new) position to see if there should be any special events it should process before playing. In this case it would send the last program change command.

• With chase mode enabled all the time it can cause a few problems as well. It's very easy to record a series of pitch wheel events – say bending off a note, and forget to include a centring command (0,64). When the sequencer stops (after the take) it will often reset the device automatically by sending note off, damper off and pitch centring commands. If you continued to play from that point you may think that everything is fine only to find when all the parts are glued together and run contiguously your missing pitch centring commands will make themselves known all too soon.

# *19*

# *Glossary*

*Aftertouch* Is a special type of controller that is produced when extra weight is applied to held notes. Aftertouch, when implemented, can be used to affect subtle playback parameters in real time such as introducing vibrato to notes or perhaps opening a filter which changes its waveform slightly.

*Attack* The first part of a sound's overall characteristic. The attack of a sound is the time taken for it to reach its maximum volume when struck. See *decay* and *release*.

*Bank select* With GS and XG devices additional (variation) sounds can be accessed using bank select commands (controller 0 and controller 32). Bank select messages include both the most significant bit (MSB) and least significant bit (LSB).

*Bulk dump* All the parameters of a device can be transmitted as a system exclusive message. This message can be captured on a sequencer and re-transmitted back to the same device at a later date.

*Channel (MIDI)* MIDI can be sent and transmitted over banks of 16 channels. Most GM, GS and XG devices access just one bank of 16 channels, although it's quite common for professional studios to use multiple bank systems. For instance a four bank configuration would offer the ability to play back (and record) 64 different channels of MIDI data.

*Controller* Controller events are used to control the operating parameters of a device. There are 128 different types of control messages available, each performing a unique function.

*Crescendo* Getting louder in volume.

*Cutoff frequency* Filter in which frequencies of a given value can be removed. The lower the cutoff values the deeper and more rounded the tone of the sound will be. Inversely, the higher the cutoff point, the thinner and brighter the tone becomes.

*Decay* Is the amount of time it takes for a held note to die away. See *attack* and *release*.

*Diminuendo* Getting quieter in volume.

*Directories* See *folders*.

*Disk* Sometimes called disk, disc or diskette, a disk (including a hard disk) is a type of magnetic medium used for storing and loading computer data. The amount of data it can store is determined by its size. e.g. 720K (DD), 1.44M (HD) and 450Mb (hard disk)

*Element* Yamaha term for the number of voices used to produce a note. See *voice*.

*Envelope generator (EG)* Envelope generators are used to shape the way the sound is produced.

*Folders* Data can be stored on the computer disk in folders (sometimes called directories). The name of the folder often reflects the type of information we might expect to find there. A typical folder/file path might be A:\MIDI\MY_SONGS\ROCK_ME.MID. Here the A:\ means the file is located on a floppy disk.

*FSK* Frequency shift keying. Although not as versatile as SMPTE (but often cheaper), FSK can be used to synchronise and lock a sequencer to multi-track tape.

*GM (General MIDI – Level 1)* Is the adopted standard for the way GM compatible MIDI keyboards and modules will respond to incoming MIDI information. GM dictates that the polyphony will be 28 voices, and the number of MIDI channels it can play simultaneously will be 16. The drum and percussion instruments will comply to a preset note to drum allocation table, further all drum and percussion instruments will use only MIDI channel 10. Voice allocations (program change messages) have also been standardised so a program change number used on one GM device is guaranteed to call up the same type of instrument on another GM device even if they originated from different instrument manufacturers.

*GS (sometimes referred to as General Standard)* GS is proprietary to Roland. Roland's GS may be regarded as a development of GM. GS allows the user to access some of the more interesting effects and parameters the device is capable of producing. Such effects include portamento and waveform editing.

*Local on/off* Some keyboards are only ever used to send digital MIDI information to a sequencer or external device, relying upon these units to producing the 'noise'. As the only sounds we will ever hear are those that come from the external devices the internal sounds of the keyboard are effectively redundant. If the voices in the mother keyboard were allowed to sound they could possibly interfere with those being produced externally. One function of local on/off is to enable or disable the sounds in the mother keyboard.

*LFO* Low frequency ocillator.

*LSB* Least significant bit. See *MSB*.

*MIDI choke* MIDI choke is caused when too much information is sent to a device in a very short space of time. This overloading of the system (even temporarily) will affect the smooth processing of data. MIDI choke produces a rather laboured and lurching feel to the music, especially around the first beat of each measure. See *MIDI traffic* and *note stealing*.

*MIDI clock* MIDI clock is an invisible pulse which can be sent along with the normal MIDI data stream. As this pulse can be detected by other MIDI devices it allows them to lock together so their sounds are played (synchronised) together.

*MIDI traffic* MIDI traffic is a combination of every type of MIDI event. This includes note on, note off, pitch bend, system exclusive and controller information. If too much information is sent to a device within a very short space of time it can produce MIDI choke.

*MSB* Most significant bit. When a complete set of controller information is sent it uses two bits of information, the most significant bit (MSB) and the least significant bit (LSB). Most modern devices only require the sending of the MSB to implement a change of some kind, the obvious exceptions being the sending of bank select messages and setting the pitch bend throw rate.

*NRPN* Non registered parameter number. NRPN is a special name given to controllers 99 (MSB) and 98 (LSB). NRPN's can be used to modify certain parameters of a device including the resonance, attack and decay times of a sound as well as allowing the pitch of any drum to be altered. NRPN's are commonly implemented in GS and XG equipment.

*Note stealing* Note stealing is caused when the maximum available polyphony of the device has been exceeded. Notes that are already sounding may be prematurely truncated in an effort to keep up with new (incoming) notes. See *MIDI choke* and *MIDI traffic*.

*Pan* Position of an instrument within the audio spectrum.

*Partial* Roland term for the number of voices required to produce one note. See voice.

*Pitch bend* Special events that can be used to change the pitch of a note. By moving a wheel or level to and fro the pitch of a held note will be increased or decreased. The default setting on GM devices is set to two semitones although this limit can be increased using RPN's.

*Polyphony* Polyphony is the number of voices available to the user which can played simultaneously. See *voice*.

*Portamento* Portamento is a sliding effect produced when an interval is played. When changing notes, portamento will gradually change its pitch (in a similar effect to the effect produced by the pitch bend lever) until it matches the pitch of the new note. The speed of the swoop can be changed using controller information (GS and XG only).

*Program changes* Sometimes called patch changes. Any instrument can be assigned to a MIDI channel by using program change commands. Instrument locations (in GM) are grouped by voice type (keyboards, tuned percussion etc.). Consult Appendix A for an example General MIDI tone map.

*Quantising* Quantising is a feature (found on every sequence package) that automatically moves notes onto a user defined musical value.

*RAM (random access memory)* Volatile area of memory where the computer loads programs and data from diskette or hard drive. RAM does not permanently store any information so if the computer is switched off before saving all data will be lost.

Release Determines the amount of time taken for a note to completely die away after a note is released. See *attack* and *decay*.

*ROM (read only memory)* Type of memory used when data needs to be permanently etched onto a computer chip or CD (hence CD-ROM). This type of memory can never be altered by the user. The way the default sample data is held for the voices on our module is a classic example of a ROM chip.

*Sequencer* Software program that allows MIDI data to be recorded, edited and saved. The facilities available can vary dramatically between manufacturer and version.

*Smart FSK* Similar to ordinary FSK except smart FSK can interpret song position pointers.

*RPN* Registered parameter number (controller 101 – MSB and 100 – LSB ). RPN's are frequently used to alter the amount of pitch bend available to a specific MIDI channel.

*SMPTE (Society of Motion Picture and Television Engineers)* SMPTE is a system that writes an electronic code into a special track on film, video or multi-track tape. Once written this code can be read by computers enabling them to synchronise together with pinpoint accuracy.

*Standard MIDI file (SMF)* Is a universal file type that allows MIDI data to be saved in such a way that it can be transported between different sequencer packages. There are two types of MIDI files generally supported – multiple track (type 1) and single track (type 0). Virtually all commercial sequencers can load and save type 1 MIDI files.

*Step time* A method that allows notes to be entered into the sequencer without having to play them directly in from a MIDI device.

*System exclusive messages (SysEx)* Unique to every manufacturer, SysEx can be used to activate and modify the parameters of a receiving device which may be inaccessible from the main panel. SysEx can also be used to send or receive factory or user defined voices.

*THRU* Socket on the rear of most devices which re-transmits the data received from the MIDI IN socket.

*Thru box* Multiple output device similar to the THRU found on the rear of a keyboard or module.

*Velocity* The weight or loudness of notes we play can be recorded using velocity values. Every note will have a corresponding velocity value between 1 to 128, A value of 1 would produce a very quiet note and 128 would produce a very loud note.

*Virus* Frequently destructive program that can infect computers often destroying any data it comes into contact with.

*Voice* There is some slight confusion in the industry regarding the interpretation of the word 'voice'. GM protocol has stated that any GM device must have a minimum polyphony of 28 voices. Some manufacturers use layered voices to create lush sounds. If it took four voices to produce one type of sound the polyphony of the GM device would be just seven notes. Thankfully most manufacturers mainly use one voice per sound although thicker sounds on GS and XG units sometimes use more.

*XG (Extended General MIDI)* Developed by Yamaha, XG works in a similar way to Roland's GS system, allowing the user to access certain extra parameters not available on GM devices.

# Appendix A

**GM tone map**

*Pianos*

| | |
|---|---|
| 1 | Acoustic grand piano |
| 2 | Bright acoustic grand piano |
| 3 | Electric grand piano |
| 4 | Honky-tonk piano |
| 5 | Electric piano 1 |
| 6 | Electric piano 2 |
| 7 | Harpsichord |
| 8 | Clav |

*Chromatic percussion*

| | |
|---|---|
| 9 | Celeste |
| 10 | Glockenspiel |
| 11 | Music box |
| 12 | Vibraphone |
| 13 | Marimba |
| 14 | Xylophone |
| 15 | Tubular bells |
| 16 | Santur |

*Organ*

| | |
|---|---|
| 17 | Full organ |
| 18 | Percussive organ |
| 19 | Rock organ |
| 20 | Church organ |
| 21 | Reed organ |
| 22 | Accordion (Francias) |
| 23 | Harmonica |
| 24 | Bandoneon |

*Guitar*

| | |
|---|---|
| 25 | Nylon string guitar |
| 26 | Steel string guitar |
| 27 | Jazz guitar |
| 28 | Clean guitar |
| 29 | Muted/damped guitar |
| 30 | Overdrive guitar |
| 31 | Distortion guitar |
| 32 | Guitar harmonics |

*Bass*

| | |
|---|---|
| 33 | Acoustic/wood bass |
| 34 | Fingered electric bass |
| 35 | Picked electric bass |
| 36 | Fretless bass |
| 37 | Slap bass 1 |
| 38 | Slap bass 2 |
| 39 | Synth bass 1 |
| 40 | Synth bass 2 |

*Strings and orchestral*

| | |
|---|---|
| 41 | Violin |
| 42 | Viola |
| 43 | Cello |
| 44 | Contrabass |
| 45 | Tremolo strings |
| 46 | Pizzicato strings |
| 47 | Harp |
| 48 | Timpani |

*Ensemble*

| | |
|---|---|
| 49 | Ensemble strings |
| 50 | Slow attack strings |
| 51 | Synth strings 1 |
| 52 | Synth strings 2 |
| 53 | Choir – aahs |
| 54 | Choir – oohs |
| 55 | Synth vox |

| | |
|---|---|
| 56 | Orchestra hit |

*Brass*

| | |
|---|---|
| 57 | Trumpet |
| 58 | Trombone |
| 59 | Tuba |
| 60 | Muted trumpet |
| 61 | French horn |
| 62 | Brass |
| 63 | Synth brass 1 |
| 64 | Synth brass 2 |

*Reed*

| | |
|---|---|
| 65 | Soprano sax |
| 66 | Alto sax |
| 67 | Tenor sax |
| 68 | Baritone sax |
| 69 | Oboe |
| 70 | English horn |
| 71 | Bassoon |
| 72 | Clarinet |

*Pipe*

| | |
|---|---|
| 73 | Piccolo |
| 74 | Flute |
| 75 | Recorder |
| 76 | Pan flute |
| 77 | Bottle blow |
| 78 | Shakuhachi |
| 79 | Whistle |
| 80 | Ocarina |

*Synth lead*

| | |
|---|---|
| 81 | Square wave (lead 1) |
| 82 | Saw wave (lead 2) |
| 83 | Synth calliope (lead 3) |
| 84 | Chiffer lead (lead 4) |
| 85 | Charang (lead 5) |
| 86 | Solo vox (lead 6) |
| 87 | Fifth saw wave (lead 7) |
| 88 | Bass and lead (lead 8) |

*Synth pad*

| | |
|---|---|
| 89 | Fantasia (pad 1) |
| 90 | Warm pad (pad 2) |
| 91 | Polysynth (pad 3) |
| 92 | Space voice (pad 4) |
| 93 | Bowed glass (pad 5) |
| 94 | Metal pad (pad 6) |
| 95 | Halo pad (pad 7) |
| 96 | Sweep pad (pad 8) |

*Synth sound effects*

| | |
|---|---|
| 97 | Ice rain (FX 1) |
| 98 | Soundtrack (FX 2) |
| 99 | Crystal (FX 3) |
| 100 | Atmosphere (FX 4) |
| 101 | Brightness (FX 5) |
| 102 | Goblin (FX 6) |
| 103 | Echo drops (FX 7) |
| 104 | Star theme (FX 8) |

*Ethnic*

| | |
|---|---|
| 105 | Sitar |
| 106 | Banjo |
| 107 | Shamisen |
| 108 | Koto |
| 109 | Kalimba |
| 110 | Bagpipes |
| 111 | Fiddle |
| 112 | Shanai |

*Percussive*

| | |
|---|---|
| 113 | Tinkle bell |
| 114 | Agogo |
| 115 | Steel drums |
| 116 | Woodblock |
| 117 | Taiko |
| 118 | Melodic tom tom |
| 119 | Synth drum |
| 120 | Reverse cymbal |

*Sound effects*

| | |
|---|---|
| 121 | Guitar fret noise |
| 122 | Breath noise |
| 123 | Seashore |
| 124 | Bird |
| 125 | Telephone |
| 126 | Helicopter |
| 127 | Applause |
| 128 | Gunshot |

# Appendix B

### GM drum map

| Key No | Note Name | Instrument |
|---|---|---|
| 35 | B | Acoustic kick drum |
| 36 | C | Electric kick drum |
| 37 | C# | Side stick / stick across |
| 38 | D | Acoustic snare drum |
| 39 | D# | Hand clap |
| 40 | E | Electric snare drum |
| 41 | F | Low floor tom |
| 42 | F# | Closed hi-hat |
| 43 | G1 | High floor tom |
| 44 | G# | Pedal hi-hat |
| 45 | A | Low tom |
| 46 | A# | Open hi-hat |
| 47 | B | Low mid tom |
| 48 | C | High mid tom |
| 49 | C# | Crash cymbal 1 |
| 50 | D | High tom |
| 51 | D# | Ride cymbal 1 |
| 52 | E | China cymbal |
| 53 | F | Ride bell |
| 54 | F# | Tambourine |
| 55 | G | Splash cymbal |
| 56 | G# | Cowbell |
| 57 | A | Crash cymbal 2 |
| 58 | A# | Vibraslap |

| Key No | Note Name | Instrument |
|---|---|---|
| 59 | B | Ride cymbal 2 |
| 60 | C | Hi bongo |
| 61 | C# | Low bongo |
| 62 | D | Mute hi conga |
| 63 | D# | Open hi conga |
| 64 | E | Low conga |
| 65 | F | High timbale |
| 66 | F# | Low timbale |
| 67 | G | High agogo |
| 68 | G# | Low agogo |
| 69 | A | Cabasa |
| 70 | A# | Maracas |
| 71 | B | Short whistle |
| 72 | C | Long whistle |
| 73 | C# | Short guiro |
| 74 | D | Long guiro |
| 75 | D# | Claves |
| 76 | E | High wood block |
| 77 | F | Low wood block |
| 78 | F# | Mute cuica |
| 79 | G | Open cuica |
| 80 | G# | Muted triangle |
| 81 | A | Open triangle |

# Appendix C

## Control change table

| Control No | Name | Control No | Name |
|---|---|---|---|
| 0 | Bank select | 75 | Undefined / reverb |
| 1 | Modulation wheel | 76 | Undefined / delay |
| 2 | Breath controller | 77 | Undefined / pitch transposer |
| 3 | Undefined | | |
| 4 | Foot controller | 78 | Undefined / flange or chor. |
| 5 | Portamento time | 79 | Undefined / special effects |
| 6 | Data entry | 80–83 | General purpose 5-8 |
| 7 | Main volume | 84 | Portamento control |
| 8 | Balance | 85–90 | Undefined |
| 9 | Undefined | 91 | Effects depth (effect 1) |
| 10 | Pan | 92 | Tremolo depth (effect 2) |
| 11 | Expression | 93 | Chorus depth (effect 3) |
| 12 | Effect control 1 | 94 | Celeste depth (effect 4) |
| 13 | Effect control 2 | 95 | Phaser depth (effect 5) |
| 14–15 | Undefined | 96 | Data increment |
| 16–19 | General purpose 1–4 | 97 | Data decrement |
| 20–31 | Undefined | 98 | Non-reg param. no. LSB |
| 32–63 | LSB for ctrl changes 0–31 | 99 | Non-reg param. no. MSB |
| 64 | Damper/sustain pedal | 100 | Reg parameter no. LSB |
| 65 | Portamento | 101 | Reg parameter no. MSB |
| 66 | Sostenuto | 102–119 | Undefined |
| 67 | Soft pedal | 120 | All sound off |
| 68 | Legato footswitch | 121 | Reset all controllers |
| 69 | Hold 2 | 122 | Local control |
| 70 | Sound variation / exciter | 123 | All notes off |
| 71 | Harm content / compressor | 124 | Omni mode off |
| 72 | Release time / distortion | 125 | Omni mode on |
| 73 | Attack rime / equaliser | 126 | Mono mode on |
| 74 | Brightness / expander or noise gate | 127 | Poly mode on |

# Appendix D

*Decimal – hexadecimal conversion chart*

| Dec | Hex | Dec | Hex | Dec | Hex | Dec | Hex |
|-----|-----|-----|-----|-----|-----|-----|-----|
| 00 | 00 | 32 | 20 | 64 | 40 | 96 | 60 |
| 01 | 01 | 33 | 21 | 65 | 41 | 97 | 61 |
| 02 | 02 | 34 | 22 | 66 | 42 | 98 | 62 |
| 03 | 03 | 35 | 23 | 67 | 43 | 99 | 63 |
| 04 | 04 | 36 | 24 | 68 | 44 | 100 | 64 |
| 05 | 05 | 37 | 25 | 69 | 45 | 101 | 65 |
| 06 | 06 | 38 | 26 | 70 | 46 | 102 | 66 |
| 07 | 07 | 39 | 27 | 71 | 47 | 103 | 67 |
| 08 | 08 | 40 | 28 | 72 | 48 | 104 | 68 |
| 09 | 09 | 41 | 29 | 73 | 49 | 105 | 69 |
| 10 | 0A | 42 | 2A | 74 | 4A | 106 | 6A |
| 11 | 0B | 43 | 2B | 75 | 4B | 107 | 6B |
| 12 | 0C | 44 | 2C | 76 | 4C | 108 | 6C |
| 13 | 0D | 45 | 2D | 77 | 4D | 109 | 6D |
| 14 | 0E | 46 | 2E | 78 | 4E | 110 | 6E |
| 15 | 0F | 47 | 2F | 79 | 4F | 111 | 6F |
| 16 | 10 | 48 | 30 | 80 | 50 | 112 | 70 |
| 17 | 11 | 49 | 31 | 81 | 51 | 113 | 71 |
| 18 | 12 | 50 | 32 | 82 | 52 | 114 | 72 |
| 19 | 13 | 51 | 33 | 83 | 53 | 115 | 73 |
| 20 | 14 | 52 | 34 | 84 | 54 | 116 | 74 |
| 21 | 15 | 53 | 35 | 85 | 55 | 117 | 75 |
| 22 | 16 | 54 | 36 | 86 | 56 | 118 | 76 |
| 23 | 17 | 55 | 37 | 87 | 57 | 119 | 77 |
| 24 | 18 | 56 | 38 | 88 | 58 | 120 | 78 |
| 25 | 19 | 57 | 39 | 89 | 59 | 121 | 79 |
| 26 | 1A | 58 | 3A | 90 | 5A | 122 | 7A |
| 27 | 1B | 59 | 3B | 91 | 5B | 123 | 7B |
| 28 | 1C | 60 | 3C | 92 | 5C | 124 | 7C |
| 29 | 1D | 61 | 3D | 93 | 5D | 125 | 7D |
| 30 | 1E | 62 | 3E | 94 | 5E | 126 | 7E |
| 31 | 1F | 63 | 3F | 95 | 5F | 127 | 7F |

# Appendix E

Pitch bend to note ratio for pitch bend range of 12 semi-tones

| Val 1 | Val 2 | Bias |
|---|---|---|
| 0 | 64 | 0 |
| 58 | 69 | +1 |
| 104 | 74 | +2 |
| 18 | 80 | +3 |
| 60 | 85 | +4 |
| 105 | 90 | +5 |
| 18 | 96 | +6 |
| 58 | 101 | +7 |
| 105 | 106 | +8 |
| 15 | 112 | +9 |
| 60 | 117 | +10 |
| 110 | 122 | +11 |
| 127 | 127 | +12 |

| Val 1 | Val 2 | Bias |
|---|---|---|
| 0 | 64 | 0 |
| 98 | 58 | −1 |
| 50 | 53 | −2 |
| 15 | 48 | −3 |
| 93 | 42 | −4 |
| 58 | 37 | −5 |
| 14 | 32 | −6 |
| 100 | 26 | −7 |
| 54 | 21 | −8 |
| 10 | 16 | −9 |
| 95 | 10 | −10 |
| 54 | 5 | −11 |
| 0 | 0 | −12 |

# Index